Doheny Family Stories

for the Descendants of
William Doheny and Anne Scully
of County Tipperary, Ireland

by Catherine Doheny Dente

Cover was created by the author.

The decorative font used throughout the book is called Imprint MT Shadow.
The body text is Times New Roman.

ISBN: 9781793943699
Imprint: Independently published

© Copyright 2020 Catherine Doheny Dente
7333 Scotland Way Unit 2202
Sarasota FL 34238
greenbeyer@gmail.com

Printed in the United States of America by Kindle Direct Publishing,
a Print-on-demand affiliate of Amazon.com, Inc.

Acknowledgements and Dedication

My heartfelt thanks go to the many people who helped me during the process of creating this family history, especially V. Rev. John J. O'Rourke of Gortnahoe, Co. Tipperary, Ireland who so generously searched the parish records for me. Thank you to Father Richard Doheny of Gortnahoe and of Fair Oaks, California, who put me in touch with Father O'Rourke.

Thank you to Anne Murphy Heidel and her sister Kathleen Murphy McBride, who knew several of our immigrant family members, and who kindly shared many personal remembrances with me.

Thank you to Karen Heidel Uresti who sent me a childhood photo of her grandmother.

Through the wonders of the internet, I located some of Timothy Doheny's great-grandchildren. One of them, Tom Doheny, inherited Margaret Doheny Shepherd's photo album. I'm looking forward to enjoying those photos with him someday.

AncestryDNA matched me with a distant cousin, Sandra Spillane from Thurles, County Tipperary, Ireland. We have enjoyed frequent and delightful correspondence via email. Sandra sent me links to important Irish websites to enhance my research. Sandra and I are 4th to 6th cousins. We hope to determine our actual relationship someday and trace our lines back to our common ancestor. Sandra is multi-talented, and graciously edited several chapters of this work.

Thank you to Michael McKenna who shared some of his Farrell family research with me. We have proven our relationship as 3rd cousins; our common great-great-grandparents were John Farrell and Mary Kane of Ardagh, County Longford, Ireland.

Thank you to Regina Negrycz of the Genealogical Society of Sarasota for her research tips.

Thank you to Sharyn Van Epps for her kind and helpful editing suggestions.

Thank you to my husband, Tom Dente, and my sisters, Anne, Elizabeth, and Margo, for reading sections of the manuscript and offering their familial insights.

This book is dedicated *to my sisters and their children and grandchildren and to all the living Dohenys and their offspring. I hope the next generations of our extended Doheny-Green-Farrell-Kane family will feel more connected to their Irish roots because of this book.*

Catherine Doheny Dente

THE STORY TELLERS

The following words are found online in many forms and adaptations. They speak to why I have spent years researching our ancestors and writing our family history. The message's origins are explained at https://past-presence.com/2018/03/24/origin-of-the-genealogy-poem-the-storytellers/

We are the story tellers of the tribe. All tribes have one.

We feel called to find the ancestors – to put flesh on their bones and make them live again, to tell the family story and to feel that, somehow, they know and approve.

Doing genealogy is not a cold gathering of facts but, instead, it is a breathing of life into all who have gone before.

We have been called by our genes. Those who have gone before cry out to us: tell our story. So, we do. In finding them, we somehow find ourselves. How many times have I told the ancestors: *"You have a wonderful family; you would be proud of us."*

Our project goes beyond just documenting facts. It goes to pride in what our ancestors were able to accomplish. How they contributed to who and what we are today. It goes to respecting their hardships and losses, their never giving in or giving up, their resoluteness to go on and build a life for their family.

It goes to a deep and immense understanding that they were doing it for us. That we might remember them. So, we do remember them, and with love and caring and scribing each fact of their existence, because we are them and they are us. So, as a scribe is called, I tell the story of my family. It is up to the one called in the next generation to answer the call and take their place in the long line of family storytellers.

I became fascinated by family history when I was quite young. A cousin of my mother, Harold Helliesen, invited us to add our names to a family tree that he had hand-drawn. From that moment on, I dreamed about creating my own family tree, and I was determined to research my family history when I had the time. Genealogy became my favorite hobby in retirement.

So, who were our Doheny and Greene ancestors? For the curious, the answer is in this book. I have tried to make them real for you so as to keep their memory alive. Most ancestors mentioned here will have the usual genealogical facts, that is, dates of birth, marriage, and death, but you will also read about the circumstances of their immigration, occupations, homes and apartments, their religion, and stories that survived to the present.

Nothing on these pages is fiction. I've made a tremendous effort to document every fact in the book. When I have made a reasonable deduction, I have indicated this to the reader. You may certainly ignore the footnotes and simply enjoy the narrative, but the sources are there for anyone who is interested in them.

Catherine Doheny Dente

Table of Contents

Section I   The Stories and Family Trees

Section II   Doheny Family Genealogical Summary

Section III   Appendix

Table of Photos and Illustrations

Section I

The Stories and Family Trees

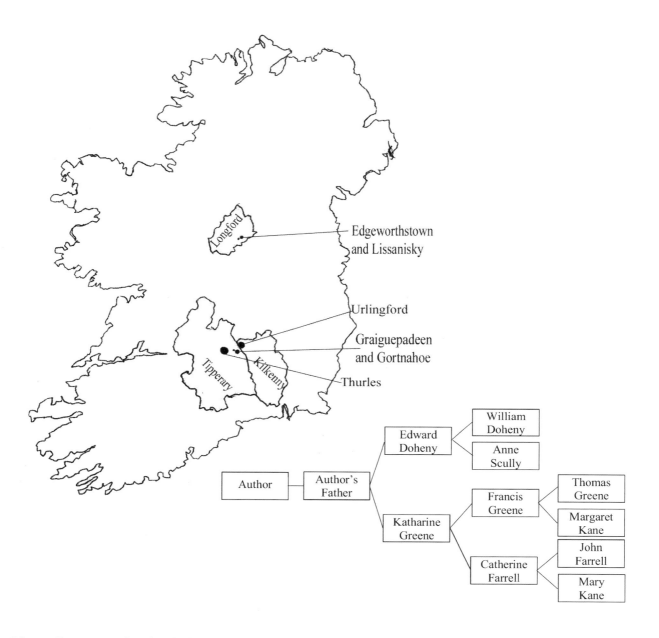

This outline map of Ireland shows the towns and counties associated with the author's ancestors.

William Doheny's family was from the village of Graigue, County Tipperary. Their baptisms, marriages and deaths were recorded in the Catholic parish records of Gortnahoe, County Tipperary, and some births and deaths were recorded in the civil records of Urlingford, Coounty Kilkenny, just across the county border.

The Greene Family was from Edgeworthstown. Baptisms were recorded in the Catholic parish of Mostrim. The Farrells were from Lissanisky. Their baptisms were recorded in the Catholic parish of Ardagh and Moydow.

Chapter One

Some Irish Background

My Irish Doheny ancestors were the tailors in their village.[1] Some of their descendants like to think the needle arts are in our genes, judging from all the handmade clothing and accessories some of us have created, and still enjoy making.

William and Anne Scully Doheny and their 10 children were from North Tipperary where it bordered on County Kilkenny, in a townland called Graigue or Graigue Paudeen near the village of Gortnahoe. When our Doheny ancestors left Ireland, the village was left without its tailors. The 1901 Irish Census in the National Archives of Ireland lists no tailors in Graigue or Gortnahoe [2]

What's in a Name?

Doheny is an Irish surname. We could be called the Little Black Doves, or the Black's Little Doves, because the name Doheny is a "reduced Anglicized form of the Irish Ó Dubhchonna 'descendant of Dubhchonna,' a personal name based on dubh 'black' + Conna, a pet form of Colmán, meaning 'little dove.' " [3]

Greater detail comes from this website: http://www.araltas.com/features/doheny/

> Doheny is the usual anglicized form of the Irish surname Ó Dubhchonna, the base word being "dubh" meaning black or dark and possibly "con" meaning a hound or dog. The sept of Ó Dubhchonna was of the tribe known as Corca Laoighdhe, the race of Lughaidh Laidhe, grandfather of Lughaidh MacCon, monarch of Ireland in the third century. This was a great clan in the south-west of County Cork, and of which the O'Driscolls and O'Learys were the chief families.

There are many variant spellings of our name. Among them are Doheny, Doheney, Dohony, Dohoney, Daughney, and Doughney. Dawney and Downey are anglicized variants. The heaviest concentration of Dohenys in Ireland today, and for the past 150 years, is in Tipperary and Kilkenny.

In many cases, the spelling of a name depended on the person recording it, rather than the preference of the person to whom it belonged. A parish priest, the town registrar, an immigration official, or the

---

[1] Phone conversation between the author and Father Richard Doheny of Fair Oaks, California in 2000. Father Doheny told me that "your Doheny boys" were the town tailors, and he said his family bought our family's property after our family emigrated to the USA.
[2] http://www.census.nationalarchives.ie/
[3] Dictionary of American Family Names, Oxford University Press, 2013

census taker, all may have spelled a name differently. In my search for family records, all possible spelling variations needed to be considered. I found that, where vital records do survive, they date to only about 1830 or so.

Famous People with the Name Doheny

There was a man by the name of Michael Doheny who was born in 1805 in the same county as ours, but not in the same town. This Michael Doheny became connected with the Irish nationalist movement in the 1840s and wrote influential prose and poetry. He took part in the Young Irelander Rebellion of 1848. After eluding capture and arrest and being hunted by the police for some time, he escaped to New York. He settled in the United States and became a lawyer and a soldier with the Fenian Brotherhood. He died in New York on 1 April 1863 and was buried in Calvary Cemetery in Queens. Most of our own immigrant Dohenys were also buried in Calvary Cemetery.

You may have heard of the infamous Edward Laurence Doheny (1856-1935), an American oil tycoon who drilled the first successful oil well in the Los Angeles City Oil Field, and who was involved in the Teapot Dome scandal of President Warren Harding's administration in the early 1920s. We are probably related to his ancestors in Ireland, but, so far, no documented connection has been established. Edward's second wife, Carrie Estelle Doheny, founded the Doheny Eye Institute in 1947, which is among the top five ophthalmology institutes in the United States.[4]

Some other famous Dohenys are:

- Ned Doheny (b.1948), born Patrick Anson Doheny, an American singer, songwriter and guitarist.

- Edwin Richard "Ed" Doheny (1874-1916), a Major League Baseball pitcher who played from 1895 to 1903. Apparently, he violently attacked several people, was declared insane and was then committed to an asylum, where he died.

- John Steven "Pip" Doheny (b. 1953), an American jazz tenor saxophonist and band leader. He also plays flute, clarinet and alto saxophone. He was originally from Seattle, Washington.

- Jer Doheny (1874-1929), Irish sportsman and hurler (1893-1905) for the Kilkenny senior team. Hurling was extremely popular in this part of Ireland, as it remains today.

There were many families of Dohenys in Gortnahoe, all of whom were related, but this book won't tell you how. Perhaps the book will spark further research and push time back to when the first Dohenys came to Gortnahoe. The rest of this book will describe the 19th and 20th century lives of one family of Dohenys headed by William and Anne Scully Doheny.

The final chapter will be about some Greene and Farrell in-laws, since they are related to the author's line of Dohenys. The Greene and Farrell families were from Edgeworthstown in Co. Longford, a more populous area than Gortnahoe. Edgeworthstown now has a population of about 1,000 people compared with Graigue's 300 people, according to the 2006 Irish census.

---

[4] https://www.houseofnames.com/doheny-family-crest

Daily Life of Our Ancestors in the 1800s

Our Dohenys shared the difficult lifestyle of the rural poor. They were the town tailors, but not among those with any wealth at all.

CHURCH: The Doheny's church was in the Roman Catholic parish of Gortnahoe and Glengoole in the Diocese of Cashel and Emly. All their baptisms, marriages and some deaths were recorded in the parish register. Their civil records were recorded in nearby Urlingford, Co. Kilkenny. They probably visited the very old Cistercian Kilcooley Abbey, dating from 1184, which is very close to Gortnahoe, and is actually on the private Kilcooley estate with public access. It is a treasure trove of wonderful stone carvings. The internet has many images of Kilcooley Abbey and its stone carvings.

EDUCATION: For 500 years, Ireland was known all over Europe as The Island of Saints and Scholars. Even though poor, Irish parents generally wanted their children to receive at least a basic primary education. From 1695 to 1782, Penal Laws were imposed upon Roman Catholics.[5] Among these were, for example:
- No Catholic could become a teacher (from 1790 onwards).
- It was illegal to send Catholic children to school.

To get around the Penal Laws, the Catholics in Ireland set up "hedge schools" that were illegally held in each other's cottages, barns or even outdoors, and taught by Catholic teachers who had varying amounts of education themselves. [6] The children were taught reading, writing, arithmetic, and sometimes Greek and Latin. After the penal laws ended, the hedge schools were no longer illegal, and they moved into larger buildings.

After 1830, schools provided a formal, standardized education. The schools tended to be under the control of the Roman Catholic Church, so Catholicism was taught in the schools. In 1837, about 250 children were educated in three schools in the general area around Fennor that includes Graigue.[7] There is evidence in the 1940 US Census that our ancestors all graduated from 8th grade during their youth in Ireland. Maria, Edward, and Annie all affirmed that they completed an 8th grade education.

WATER: Before the development of the water mains system, people in Graigue drew water from community wells. They walked to the nearest pump and hauled water back to their modest homes for cooking and cleaning. Some families had access to a nearby stream or had their own well, but I don't think ours did. These wells and pumps have not been operational for many, many years in Ireland, but you might still find them scattered around the towns and villages.

I consulted many online sources for stories about 19th century access to potable water in Ireland. My favorite was a Facebook site called "Ireland: Genealogy & Heritage," where people answered my queries about 19th century life in rural Ireland.

---

[5] https://www.libraryireland.com/articles/Eighteenth-Century-Ireland/Irish-Penal-Laws.php
[6] https://en.wikipedia.org/wiki/Hedge_school
[7] *A Topographical Dictionary of Ireland*, 1837, available online at www.libraryireland.com

Bernie Courtney said, "Rainwater was saved in a big barrel at the side of the house and used for washing, as it was very soft. We got drinking water from a well. There were many local wells at places where springs brought water to the surface naturally. The well was kept neat and clean by those who used it to prevent silting, and lime was used in summer to keep it clean. The water was therefore a little harder than the rainwater and more difficult to lather when washing."

Pearl Nesbitt said, "I now live in Australia but spent most of my life in Northern Ireland. My father's farm had two streams running through it, one of which ran down the back of the house, so getting water was never the problem that it is here in Australia. Our waste was put into the midden where the animal manure was kept until it was spread on the fields in the spring as fertilizer. My mother had a big bath tub which was put in front of the fire for us to bathe in, and she had another smaller one which she used to wash the clothes. She had a bar of soap and a scrubbing board to get clothes clean, then used a mangle to wring the water out of them. I remember her telling me that sheets should be dried flat on grass as it bleached them white. The water was heated in a boiler attached to the stove, the top of which was used as a griddle for baking and for heating the iron. We didn't get electricity until the late 1950's. It was a hard life for my parents but a marvelous childhood for me."

Not everyone had a convenient water source, though. Tracey Ann said, "We used to go to a well in the center of the village, and when that dried up, we had to walk a few miles to another."

Sarah Smith said, "My relatives lived in central west Ireland in County Roscommon, in a very small rural community. Wells were pretty common there. I guess those close to rivers were lucky. The original well is still on my family's land, around 200/300m from their home. My g-grandfather planted trees next to his house which are now a small forest; they were planted for shelter and for going to the loo. In winter they had a bucket in one of the outhouses/stables.

WASTE: Whatever waste was produced from household activities was thrown into a midden outside the dwelling. Some of it became compost for the vegetable garden or slop for the pigs, if the household had pigs.

SANITATION: Many homes had an outhouse, or shared an outhouse with a neighbor. Some families had one outhouse for the males, and one for the females. (I hope our Dohenys had this arrangement.)

ODORS: Poor households had very strong odors. The strongest one would probably be from the animals (a sheep or pig or cow) that a family often bedded inside their home at night. The open hearth inside the home was usually fueled by a peat fire, which had a very strong and distinct odor. Some smoke invariable escaped from the hearth into the common room where most cooking, eating, washing, reading, and socializing took place.

BATHING: Poor people didn't bathe every day. Imagine ten or more family members living in a cottage about 10 feet by 25 feet, each person contributing their own body odors. Most of the rural poor had spent hours in sweaty field labor and were happy to just wash their face and hands and maybe feet when they got home. Though our ancestors were the town tailors, they, too, did not bathe often.

CHILDBIRTH: Rural women did not go to a hospital to give birth. They were usually attended by midwives. The midwife was a very important person to rural people all over the world. She became quite experienced with all the vicissitudes of childbirth and was able to prevent many a disaster, and even then, infant mortality was high before relatively modern times.

FOOD: Every good cookbook has a recipe for Irish Soda Bread and for Irish Stew, the national dish. Irish Stew usually consists of boiled mutton or stewing beef or lamb, onions, cubed potatoes, half stock and half stout, parsley, rosemary, salt and pepper, and, curiously, no carrots. It is cooked for about two hours.

This was not the most common dish found in a rural Irish home in the 19th century, though. Yes, the Irish ate potatoes, lots of them. The potato is actually a rich subsistence food, a good source of fiber, iron, vitamin C and B6, and contains more potassium than a banana. The Irish also grew cabbage and often cooked that with the potatoes. A Dublin traditional recipe called Colcannon is made of boiled mashed potatoes, cooked chopped cabbage, butter, milk, scallions, and all heated in a skillet. Frequently, potatoes would be baked early in the morning and put hot into one's pockets to keep hands warm on cold days. A few hours later, they would be eaten for lunch.

Some Irish History Relevant to our Family's Story

THE GREAT FAMINE: No discussion of Irish food can be without details of the Irish Potato Famine which began in 1845 and lasted for six years, when the potato crop failed. The Irish had been growing just one variety of potato at the time. It was easy to grow and quite nutritious. But monocultures often fall victim to disease eventually. The entire crop was attacked in a few consecutive years by something called a blight, a hitherto unknown fungus that made the plant and its underground tubers turn black, mushy and inedible. There was no known antidote to the fungus.

Maybe you wonder why the rural Irish ate a diet so dependent on potatoes. It was because there was no other food to eat! A page on Ancestry.com says, "It is not that the Irish were somehow dumb, and only grew potatoes." It was that they were required to farm the good land for their absentee English landlords. A great variety of food (cattle, wheat, oats, and barley) was actually grown on the good land and exported to England while the Irish died in the Famine.

The tenant farmers had been forced into ever smaller units and ever less fertile land, and fortunately even on less fertile land, potatoes seemed to grow. The tenant farmers grew a lot of potatoes for their families, and they became totally dependent on them. When the potato blight struck, there was no other food to fall back on. During the Famine, if they became ill, they could be evicted, and often were. About a million people died in the Famine, and the population declined by about 20-25%. In the decades after the Famine, the population continued to decline from 8.5 million in 1845, to 6.6 million in 1851, to 4.4 million in 1911 due to death or emigration.

The English government passed the Poor Law Act in 1838 and raised money from every able person in Ireland for workhouses for the most desperate and destitute people. By the time of the Famine, there were 800 people in some workhouses. The nearest one to Graigue was in Thurles, Co.

Tipperary, about eight miles west-southwest of Graigue. The people in the workhouses were provided with imported corn. But this was not the sweet variety we associate with corn-on-the-cob. This was feed corn, which needed extensive processing to be humanly edible. Many people in the workhouses became malnourished when they ate this kind of corn, succumbed to infections and disease, and died anyway.[8]

County Tipperary was badly affected by the Famine. Some statistics: almost 70,000 people died in the county between 1845 and 1850, particularly in the years 1849 and 1850. The county population fell from 435,000 in 1841, to 331,000 in 1851 and to 249,000 in 1861. The rural population declined by two-thirds in that period and the town population by nearly one-half.[9]

THE IRISH REBELLION OF 1798: Though there were no recorded battles in Graigue during the 1798 Irish Rebellion against England, every person in Ireland was affected in some way or other by the struggle to hold on to family farms and the desire for self-government. Comparing the French Revolution with the Irish Revolution, a far higher percentage of Irish rebels lost their lives in the fight for independence than Frenchmen were lost during the French Revolution.

After the Irish Rebellion of 1798 was violently suppressed, London abolished the Irish parliament and passed the Act of Union, creating the United Kingdom of Great Britain and Ireland. Ireland became completely under English rule. Ireland was part of the Union until 1921. It was in the early days of the oppression in the Union that potatoes became one of the only crops cultivated for food by the rural poor. There was a crop failure in 1816-1817 leading to widespread famine, presaging the Great Famine that was to come in mid-century.

---

[8] https://brilliantmaps.com/potato-famine/
[9] http://www.inweb.ch/delaneyscorner/county_tipperary.php

Graigue and the Organization of Irish Geographical Regions

Our Doheny family lived in a cluster of homes in Co. Tipperary called Graigue or Graigue Paudeen, or in Irish, Gráig Pháidín.

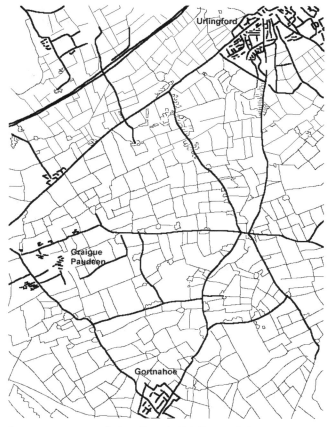

This is my sketched copy of a modern map showing the locations of Gortnahoe, Urlingford and Graigue and the myriad small farms in the region. The nearest major town is Thurles, a few miles to the west.

Graigue is technically a townland in the civil parish of Fennor. Fennor has an area of about 12.4 square miles, and Graigue comprises about 1.75 square miles of that.[10] Besides farming, sheep grazing is popular in Fennor.

Gortnahoe-Glengoole is the name of the Doheny's Catholic parish. Gortnahoe is also the name of the town nearest to Graigue. Gortnahoe had a population of 286 in the 2016 Irish census. Gortnahoe is the largest town in the civil parish of Fennor. Civil parishes and Catholic parishes often overlap, and their boundaries vary.[11]

Graigue is in a barony called Slievardagh in the northeastern part of the South Riding of County Tipperary. Baronies were old taxing divisions and are not in use now.

In the 19th century, civil records for Graigue were recorded in Urlingford, which was across the boundary of Tipperary into Kilkenny.

---

[10] https://www.townlands.ie/tipperary/fennor2/
[11] FindMyPast.com offers the best explanation I found of how Ireland is organized geographically and civilly.

Chapter Two

William DOHENY (ca.1837 – 1877)
Anne SCULLY (ca.1838 – 1893)

The Dohenys were a family of tailors who lived in a cluster of homes in the civil parish of Fennor, County Tipperary, Ireland. This cluster of mostly farm houses was called Graigue, or Graigue Paudeen. To get a sense of how small Graigue was, it was tiny in comparison with the nearest village, Gortnahoe, which itself had fewer than 300 residents in 1850[1].

William Doheny and Anne Scully married on 11 Feb 1858 in the town of Gortnahoe.[2] William was about 21 and Anne was about 20. Their witnesses were William Purcell and Judith Doheny. Here is the entry for their marriage in the parish record book.[3]

Perhaps Judith is William's sister and will lead us someday to their parents.

There were several Williams born in Graigue in the early 1800s, but no conclusive evidence has been found to determine which of them was our ancestor. The V. Rev. John J. O'Rourke's letter suggests that a William born to a William Doheny and Judy Conway of Graigue may be our ancestor. Future research will hopefully prove or disprove this. As more and more parish records are transcribed and put online, future researchers may be able to determine our family's earlier ancestors.

Our William Doheny and Anne Scully would have ten children between 1858 and 1877, most of whom would emigrate to the USA.

---

[1] Online, there are population estimates of Gortnahoe, County Tipperary, in the 19th Century. Always modest numbers.
[2] Letter from V. Rev. John J. O'Rourke P.P. to the author, dated 10 Aug 2000.
[3] Catholic Parish Registers, the National Library of Ireland, Microfilm No. 02493/05, available on Ancestry.com.

The home this Doheny family lived in was quite small by today's standards, especially as the family grew. Their cottage was probably about 10 feet wide and maybe 23 feet long. The narrowness of the cottage was determined by the length of logs that were used to support the roof.

Here is a description from www.irish-genealogy-toolkit.com of what their home was probably like.

"The population census of 1841 showed that almost one half of the families in Ireland in 1841 lived in one-room cabins sized at about 3m wide by 3m to 7m long. The smaller ones consisted of just one room while others would have separate kitchens. Only occasionally would they have a foundation of stone, and the floor was natural earth and sunken by a couple of feet below the level of the ground outside. The roof was made of sods of earth piled on rafters or straw for thatch." [4]

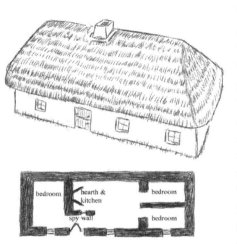

The inside of most homes in Tipperary had configurations similar to this. It is called the "Lobby Entry Cottage." There was a lobby entry in front of a "spy wall" to give the inhabitants some privacy, and a window in the spy wall allowed in light and allowed the inhabitants to see who was at the door. The spy wall also protected the hearth fire from drafts. Most cottages had split doors; the upper half could be opened while the lower half remained closed, maybe to keep the livestock out and keep the children in. The material for the walls was usually tempered clay with stones, and whitewashed. The roof style was most often an overhanging thatched roof, hipped on both sides. If a family couldn't afford glass windows, they put up boards to close the opening. [5]

Perhaps the Doheny cottage had a clay floor. The interior would have been smoky due to having an open hearth for cooking and heating, though there was probably a hood to direct most of the smoke up the chimney. The air would have had the distinctive smell of a peat fire, something very different from the smell of a wood fire. There definitely was no running water or interior toilet in the cottage. A nighttime chamber pot had to be emptied outside every morning. Water had to be hauled from either a well or a stream for cooking and for clothes washing. Outside, there likely was a "midden," a compost heap, that could provide fertilizer for a kitchen garden. Sometimes a pig or a cow or a couple of chickens would even share a family's living space.

Here is my sketch of a restored cottage found along a road in present day Gortnahoe. (I took a virtual trip there via Google Maps and saw many examples of new cottages "in the vernacular," but without the traditional thatched roofs.)

[4] https://www.irish-genealogy-toolkit.com/irish-census-fragments.html
[5] This is my own copy of a sketch found at http://DrMarionMcGarry.weebly.com

My first cousin Richard Doheny (son of Edward II, son of Edward I, son of William) visited Graigue in 2001 and took some photos of the actual homestead of William and Anne. William's cottage no longer exists, but Richard found a few remnants of the walls along the outline of the cottage. The next-door neighbor's cottage was still partially standing in 2001.

Richard took this photo of the front of the neighbor's cottage; the roof was gone after all these years. Our family's cottage was probably much the size of this one. Standing in front is John Doheny, the brother of Father Richard Doheny of Graigue, Tipperary and Fair Oaks, CA. John and Father Richard's family bought our property when all of William and Anne's children left home.[6]

Cathleen Murphy McBride sent me this message:

> When I was in Ireland on my way home from the Philippines with my parents, we visited a farm in Urlingford belonging to Dohenys. There was a man doing the farming and caring for his aging parents alone. He was probably in his 30s in 1967. His brother part-owned the Doheny-Nesbitt pub in Dublin. The old man was my grandfather's age and could have been a cousin.
>
> We are related to a Father Richard Doheny, who is an old man himself now, having celebrated his golden anniversary of ordination a year or so ago.[7]

Tailoring

Besides sending his children to school,[8] William taught his boys the family trade, which was tailoring. This work consisted of fashioning trousers, vests, jackets, and overcoats for the residents of Graigue, and maybe for clients in nearby Gortnahoe and even the larger towns of Thurles and Urlingford, which were just a few miles away. They also repaired clothes for clients and made new garments from old ones, if there was enough good cloth to salvage. Unlike today, there were very few ready-to-wear clothes. Most of the cost of clothing in the 19th century was for the material, not the labor. Today, it is the opposite. Labor is expensive compared with cloth. For today's ready-to-wear market, companies reduce their labor costs by sending cloth to sweat shops in third world countries where labor is cheap. There, skilled employees cut, sew and finish the clothing, and then send the finished goods back to the US where companies can sell the products at artificially low prices.

Here is what it might have looked like when William was teaching his sons the tailoring trade. The most surprising thing I learned during my research, was that groups of tailors commonly sat on low

---

[6] Conversation in 2000 between the author and Fr. Richard Doheny (b. 30 Oct 1923 – d. 4 Mar 2006).

[7] Excerpt of email to the author from Cathleen Murphy McBride on 11 July 2000.

[8] In the 1940 census, Maria, Edward and Anne all said they completed 8th grade; that would have been in Ireland.

tables while they were sewing their garments. This was true even up to the 1940s in the US!   It illustrates a story that Uncle Larry told my sister Betty, that when he was young, his father made his clothes while he sat cross-legged atop a table. [9]

A book about British tailoring in the 19th century says that journeyman tailors worked from six in the morning till eight at night, and their income was not very good after they bought all the materials for a new garment.[10]

Several of the Doheny boys, Timothy, Richard, and Edward, were listed as tailors on the ships that took them to the USA. The eldest, Timothy, was employed as a tailor in the USA, too. He seems to have found a job as a tailor right away in Bridgeport, CT, because he is listed as a tailor in Bridgeport city directories from 1890 to 1899.

Great Research Help from the V. Rev. John J. O'Rourke of Ireland and Father Richard Doheny of CA

When I first began to collect information about my grandfather Edward's family in Ireland, Anne Murphy Heidel told me, "We have a cousin, Father Richard, who is a priest from the Doheny clan. He spent some time with us when he came to this country. He is out in CA. Celebrated 50 years in the priesthood. He might be able to help you." [11]

I located his parish and phone number online and enjoyed a pleasant half-hour phone conversation with him. He gave me the name of the V. Rev. John J. O'Rourke, the parish priest in Fennor, and suggested I write to him for birth, baptism, marriage and death dates of my Irish ancestors. Fr. O'Rourke wrote a delightful letter back after he thoroughly searched his parish records. He gave me William and Anne's date of marriage, plus all their children's birth or baptismal dates. He said that all the Dohenys of Graigue were buried in Fennor Cemetery, Thurles.

---

[9] The sketch is my copy of "The Tailor's Shop, the Anniversary of the Little Boys Home at Farningham and Swanley, 19th Century" available online at www.alamy.com

[10] http://www.archive.org/stream/selectdocumentsi00galtiala#page/32/mode/2up

[11] Excerpt from a letter to the author from Anne Murphy Heidel dated 10 Jan 1999.

William and Anne had ten children in 18 years.

Timothy,	born Dec 1858,	emigrated in 1888 or 1889,	died Dec 1899 in Bridgeport, CT.
John,	born Sept 1860,	emigrated about 1893,	died May 1911 in Manhattan, NY.
James,	born July 1862,	not known if he emigrated,	died date and place unknown.
Maria,	born Sept 1863,	emigrated about 1890,	died March 1945 in Bronx, NY.
Patrick,	born Jan 1865,	emigrated about 1891,	died Feb 1906 in Yonkers, NY.
Richard,	born July 1866,	emigrated in 1895,	died Aug 1920 in Manhattan, NY.
William,	born Oct 1867,	*lived only about 4 months,*	died Feb 1868 in Graigue, Ireland.
Michael,	born Jan 1871,	*lived only 10 days,*	died Jan 1871 in Graigue, Ireland.
Edward,	born Aug 1874,	emigrated in 1895,	died April 1953 in Manhattan, NY.
Anne,	born Sept 1877,	emigrated in 1895,	died June 1952 in Manhattan, NY.

Many Irish families used the following conventions when they chose names for their children.[12] They were never hard and fast rules, but they do provide clues for future research:

Male children

The first son was named after the father's father…………………	Was William's father named Timothy?
The second son was named after the mother's father………….	Was Anne Scully's father John?
The third son was named after the father………………………	Then James should have been named William.
The fourth son was named after the father's eldest brother……	Was William's eldest brother named Patrick?
The fifth son was named after the mother's eldest brother or one of the father's other brothers………………………………	Was Anne Scully's eldest brother named Richard? Or was Richard the name of another of William's brothers?

Female children:

The first daughter was named after the mother's mother………	So, was Anne Scully's mother's name Maria?
The second daughter was named after the father's mother…….	Anne, perhaps?
The third daughter was named after the mother………………	Was Anne really the third daughter; or had the second daughter died, and we just don't know about her?

The fourth daughter was named after the mother's eldest sister.
The fifth daughter was named after the father's eldest sister or one of the mother's other sisters.

---

[12] https://www.familysearch.org/wiki/en/Ireland_Names_Personal
  and https://www.irishcentral.com/roots/genealogy/traditional-irish-naming-pattern-help-trace-family

Gortnahoe,
Thurles,
Co. Tipperary.
10th August '00.

Dear Catherine,
Sincerest thanks for your letter, information and gift recently received. I can see that you have done a good deal of research on your family at Graigue. I hope what I am now providing is of some help to you. Unfortunately all question cannot be answered with present information.

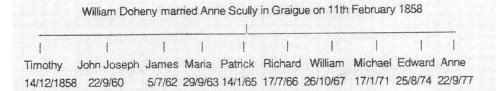

William Doheny married Anne Scully in Graigue on 11th February 1858

Timothy	John	Joseph	James	Maria	Patrick	Richard	William	Michael	Edward	Anne
14/12/1858	22/9/60		5/7/62	29/9/63	14/1/65	17/7/66	26/10/67	17/1/71	25/8/74	22/9/77

That is the information from our marriage and baptismal books. Further back I find that a William Doheny the son of William and Judy Conway was born in Graigue in July 1832. A Wlliam Doheny the son of Michael and Mary Lahert was born in Graigue on 1/1/1833. One or other probably married Anne Scully. I say probably as Doheny was a very common name in Graigue. In the Primary Valuation of Tenements (The Griffith Valuations) in 1850 the tenants of eight homes in Graigue were Dohenys, three of whom bore the Christian name William.
We have no record of the baptism of Anne Scully. She must have been living in the parish in 1858 as the marriage took place in this parish.
Our records do not contain dates of death. I have been speaking to Fr. Richard Doheny from California today. He told me that the property of William Doheny was bought by his father. In a Collection Book I find that at the oldest entry, Easter 1894, Widow Doheney (Annie) paid a collection on property to the value of £2 - 0 - 0. The entry also has the name Richard. The only other contribution was at Christmas 1894. This may indicate that William was already dead and that the family left Ireland early in 1895, probably after the death of Anne.
All the Dohenys are buried in Fennor cemetery, which was the cemetery visited by your niece. Not all families had headstones with inscriptions over their graves and records of burials going back to that time were not kept by the parish. There are a number of inscribed headstones to the Doheney families, but I could see no record of William and Anne.
I have no record of Catherine Greene in our parish records. Urlingford is the parish next to me and the Parish Priest is Canon Laurence Dunphy. His address is Urlingford, Thurles
The parish of Gortnahoe is in the diocese of Cashel, but Urlingford is in the diocese of Ossory.
All the Baptismal and Marriage records of our diocese are kept at Tipperary Heritage Unit at Marian Hall, St. Michael's Street, Tipperary. Their E. Mail Address is thu@iol.ie.
I hope this information may lead you some distance further in your quest.
With God's Blessing,

V. Rev. John J. O'Rourke P.P.

William and Anne both died rather young. William died on 20 May 1877 at the age of 40,[13] when Anne was pregnant with their last child. So, William never saw his little daughter, named Annie. My grandfather Edward had just turned two, and I can imagine his confusion, not knowing where his father was, or when, or if, he would return.

Anne Scully Doheny died on September 8, 1893, in Graigue, Tipperary, Ireland, at the age of 55.[14] Early in 1893 she had become gravely ill and suffered for eight months before she died.

The family had celebrated baptisms and marriages, nursed each other and their children through illnesses, and passed down their knowledge and Irish folklore they had learned from their own parents. They suffered in the Great Famine in the mid-19th century, and by the end of the century, the children joined the mass migration of people out of Ireland.

Emigration

Even before both parents died, the Doheny children began to emigrate from Ireland. Timothy seems to have been the first to leave. That was about 1888 or 1889. He was followed by Maria around 1890, Patrick about 1891, John around 1893, and Richard, Anne, and Edward in 1895.

i. Timothy, son of William and Anne Scully

Timothy A. Doheny was born in Graigue just a little more than nine months after his parents, William and Anne were married. He was baptized on December 14, 1858. His sponsors were Cornelius Doheny and Ellen Purcell.

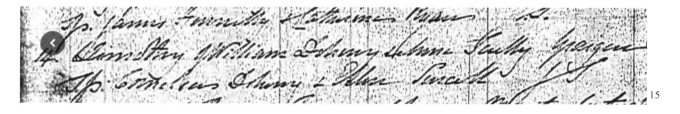[15]

He learned his father's trade as a tailor and was one of their only children to have found employment as a tailor in the USA. He seems to have been the first of his siblings to emigrate to the US.

Read more about Timothy and his family in Chapter Three.

---

[13] Kilkenny South Eastern Health Board, "William Dohony died 20 May 1877, tailor, age 40, married to Anne. Cause paralysis 1 month. Certified (means a doctor was present)."
[14] Kilkenny South Eastern Health Board, "Anne Dahoney died at age 55 on 8 Sep 1893 at Graiguepadeen, widow of tailor. Ill for 8 months. Son Richard present at death."
[15] Catholic Parish Registers, the National Library of Ireland, Microfilm No. 02493/04, available on Ancestry.com. Since Timothy was baptized on 14 Dec, he was probably born in Dec.

ii. John, son of William Doheny and Anne Scully

John Joseph Doheny was the second son of William and Anne. He was baptized on 22 Sept 1860.[16] It is difficult to decipher his godparents' names, perhaps they are James Morris and Joanna Morris.

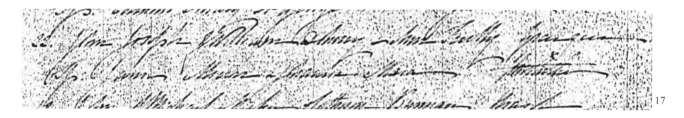

[17]

He emigrated to the US in 1893 when he was about 22, according to his death certificate[18] and according to the 1900 US Census.[19] So, along with Timothy, there is evidence that Maria, Patrick, and John left home before their mother died. Richard, Edward and Anne left home after their mother died.

In 1900, the census says John was living with his brother Patrick and Patrick's new wife, Bridget Corcoran. Their residence was 146 East 43rd St. in Manhattan. John worked as a day laborer at that time.[20]

John must have had a special relationship with my grandfather Edward because he was "best man" at Edward's wedding in 1904,[21] and, perhaps, because he was the oldest brother then living in NY.

By 1910, John had moved to his sister Maria's apartment at 590 3rd Ave, near the corner of East 39th Street. He worked as an elevator man in an office building. Timothy's orphaned children, Margaret and William, were also part of Maria's household at that time.[22] John never married, and I imagine he was very close to his siblings and his nieces and nephews, having lived with so many of them during his life.

John died in Manhattan at age 50. His death certificate explains that he died of an aneurism of the left common carotid artery at Presbyterian Hospital at age 46. (About ages on death certificates – they are only as accurate as the knowledge of the person providing the information to the undertaker. Documents closer to an event are more reliable, so John's baptismal record is more reliable than the death certificate.)

---

[16] NLI Gortnahoe baptisms film 02493-04, Catholic Parish Registers. http://registers.nli.ie/registers/vtls000632728#page/90/mode/1up.

[17] Catholic Parish Registers, the National Library of Ireland, Microfilm No. 02493/04, available on Ancestry.com. Since John was baptized on 22 September, he was probably born earlier that month.

[18] Certificate and Record of Death of John Doheny, 24 May 1911, City of New York Dept of Health, #17316

[19] 1900 US census, NYC, ED 579, Sheet 4A, 146 E 43rd Street, John emigrated in 1893 and brother Patrick in 1891.

[20] 1900 federal census, NYC, ED 579, Sheet 4A. 146 E 43rd Street

[21] Certificate and Record of Marriage of Edward J. Doheny and Catharine T. Greene, 28 Sept 1904, City of New York Bureau of Records, #2134

[22] 1910 Census, Manhattan, Ward 21, ED 1121, Page 20B.

John spent the last 17 days of his life in the hospital. How sad for Margaret and William to lose their uncle so soon after losing both of their parents. Several other Doheny family members lived in mid-Manhattan, relatively close to Presbyterian Hospital, so maybe they all took turns visiting John during his last days. He was buried in Calvary Cemetery, Queens.

Wikipedia says, "Calvary Cemetery is a Roman Catholic cemetery in Maspeth and Woodside, Queens, in New York City, New York, United States. With about 3 million burials, it has the largest number of interments of any cemetery in the United States; it is also one of the oldest cemeteries in the United States."

iii. James, son of William Doheny and Anne Scully

James was born in 1862. His sponsors were Michael Tierney(?) and Margaret Shearman. No other documents besides this baptismal record have been found so far.

23

It is not known when he died, if he survived childhood, whether he left Ireland, or if he married. There are many James Dohenys living in the United States in the early 1900s, but so far, none of them have been proven to be "our" James. Anne Murphy Heidel who shared many, many stories about her grandfather's siblings, did not mention a James Doheny.

If you are reading this book and believe you are descended from this James Doheny born in 1862 in Graigue, Tipperary, please contact the author so I can add your family stories to a supplement or future edition of this book.

---

[23] Catholic Parish Registers, the National Library of Ireland, Microfilm No. 02493/04, available on Ancestry.com. Since James was baptized on 5 July, so he was probably born either in June or early July.

iv. Maria, daughter of William Doheny and Anne Scully

Maria (the family always pronounced her name Mariah) was baptized on 29 Sep 1863. Her sponsors were James Scott and Mary Connell(?).

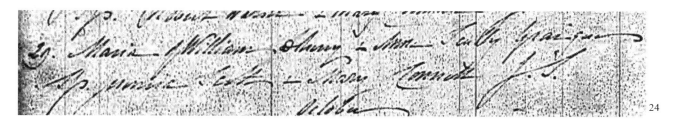

[24]

She emigrated about 1890 and worked as a dressmaker in Manhattan.[25] So, Maria, as well as Timothy, carried on some of the family's tailoring skills in their paid occupations in the USA. In 1905, Maria and her two brothers, John and Edward, lived together at 252 West 20th St., Manhattan. John's occupation was "elevator-runner," and Edward was a clerk. Edward was married the previous year, so it is unusual that he is enumerated with his sister in 1905. His wife, Katherine Greene is not with them, and she is not living with her siblings either. She just may not have been enumerated in the 1905 census for some undetermined reason.

The 1910 census gives Maria's address as 590 3rd Ave, Manhattan, and her brother John is still living with her. By this time, they also have the orphaned children of their brother Timothy living with them: Anna Margaret Doheny (15) and William Doheny (11).[26] By 1920, Anna Margaret and her brother William were living in a boarding house on their own in Trenton, NJ.[27]

Maria married James Barry in Sept 1922, and they lived in Manhattan.[28] My father said Aunt Maria's apartment was the first place he stayed after he ran away from an orphanage around 1922. (Then he went to Aunt Katie's and finally to Aunt Annie's.)

In 1925, Maria and Jim Barry were living at 243 39th Street,[29] the same apartment that Aunt Katie had before that.

In 1930, Maria and James Barry were living in the Bronx at 373 East 188th Street. James and Maria were retired by then; he was 68 and she was 63.[30] James died in Apr 1939.

---

[24] Catholic Parish Registers, the National Library of Ireland, Microfilm No. 02493/04, available on Ancestry.com. Since Maria was baptized on 29 Sep 1863, she was probably born in Sep.
[25] 1905 NYS Census, Manhattan ED 1, AD 5, page 2, 252 West 20th St. says Maria had been in the US for 15 years and she was a dressmaker.
[26] 1910 Federal Census, Manhattan NY, ED 1121, Sheet 20B
[27] 1920 US census, NJ, Mercer County, Trenton Ward 1, ED 50, Sheet 3-1A.
[28] Ancestry.com, New York, NY, Marriage License Indexes, 6 Sept 1922, James J Barry and Marie Doheny.
[29] 1925 NYS census, Manhattan, AD 12, ED 31, Block 1, Page 37. Maria and Jim are living at 243 E.39th St.
[30] 1930 Census, Bronx, New York City, ED 3-650 Sheet B-27.

In 1940, Maria and her brother Edward lived together at 223 Decatur Ave, Bronx,[31] then they moved to 2735 Marion Ave, Bronx. Cathleen Murphy McBride said, "When I was a child, it was: Uncleeddieandauntrye, one being as it were! I recall her as small, frail, humorous and old, as in wizened." Maria died of cardiac arrest and breast cancer on 10 March 1945. She was buried in Calvary Cemetery.[32] Her death certificate says she was 78, but she was really 82 when she died.[33]

Anne Murphy Heidel said, "I can picture Aunt Rye's apartment in the Bronx, and her sick in bed. The rooms were large with wood floors and lots of cabinets in the kitchen."[34]

v. Patrick, son of William Doheny and Anne Scully

Patrick, William and Anne's fifth child, was baptized 14 Jan 1865. His sponsors were Denis Leahy and Margaret Moriarty.

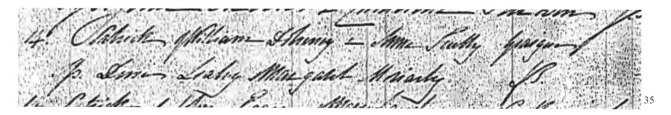[35]

He emigrated to New York in 1891,[36] soon after his siblings Timothy and Maria had left Ireland.

Below, you will see what a ship's passenger list looks like. It is likely that this Patrick Doheny is our relative, though his age should be 26, not 28. The record says Patrick Doheny, a 28 year-old male laborer from Ireland, travelled on the S.S. City of Chester and arrived in New York Harbor on 28 March 1891. The ship had picked up passengers at Liverpool, England and Queenstown, Ireland. Patrick said his last place of residence was Qtown (Queenstown). He travelled in steerage with one piece of baggage and was on a "protracted sojourn" to the U.S. with 462 other passengers.

---

[31] 1940 Census, Bronx, ED 3-1223, AD 23, Sheet 11A.
[32] Calvary Cemetery Records, Sect 23, Range 14, Plot D, Grave 20. Maria purchased this plot for her brother John in 1911. Maria was buried here 13 March 1945, and brother Edward on 8 April 1953.
[33] Certificate of Death for Maria Barry, 10 Mar 1945, Dept. of Health, Borough of Bronx, Certificate #2703.
[34] Excerpt from an email from Anne Murphy Heidel to the author dated 1 May 1999.
[35] Catholic Parish Registers, the National Library of Ireland, Microfilm No. 02493/04, available on Ancestry.com. Since Patrick was baptized on 14 Jan, he was probably born in Jan 1865.
[36] 1900 US census, NYC, ED 579, Sheet 4A, 146 E 43rd Street, Patrick emigrated in 1891.

Patrick followed Timothy's lead and moved to Bridgeport, CT. A Bridgeport City Directory in 1896 lists both Timothy and Patrick at 58 Johnson Street, and both of them worked in Warner Brothers industries. Patrick, specifically, was a laborer at Citizen's Gas Company.

Before Timothy's wife became pregnant with their second child, Patrick left their shared apartment. He moved to 59 Vesey Street, Manhattan, which was where his sister Maria lived.[38] While living there, he applied for US citizenship; this was 1898. Five years later, he became a naturalized citizen.[39]

Patrick met and married Bridget Corcoran, who was also an Irish immigrant. Their wedding took place on 24 Sept 1899 in Manhattan. Their witnesses were my grandfather, Edward Doheny, and Bridget's sister, Lizzie Corcoran. Patrick's residence was 59 Vesey Street and Bridget's was 402 East 21st Street.[40] They moved to 146 East 43rd Street, but didn't have their New York apartment to themselves. Patrick's brother John lived with them, as did Lizzie Corcoran and a boarder named Kate Holden. Patrick and John found work as "day laborers." This is all in the 1900 US Census.[41]

---

[37] New York Passenger Lists 1891; Microfilm Serial: M237, 1820-1897; Microfilm Roll: Roll 564; Line: 10; List Number: 387, available on Ancestry.com.
[38] Trow's Business Directory, Boroughs of Manhattan and Bronx, 1899-1900, p 316. Maria Doheny, h 59 Vesey Street.
[39] 1905 NYS Census, Yonkers, Westchester County, ED 4, Ward 5, page 81 says that Patrick is a citizen by then.
[40] City of New York Marriage Certificate # 14689, 24 Sept 1899, Patrick Doheny married Bridget Corcoran in Manhattan.
[41] 1900 US Census, Manhattan, NY, ED 579, Sheet 4A.

A year or so later, Patrick and Bridget moved to Westchester to an apartment at 8 Oak Place, Yonkers. Their daughter Annie Elizabeth was born there in September 1904. Also living with them in 1905 are Bridget's father, Richard Corcoran, and Bridget's younger sister, Elizabeth, a domestic servant. Patrick again found work as a day laborer.[42]

Only a year later, in Feb 1906, Patrick died unexpectedly at age 47, leaving behind his wife and little daughter, Annie Elizabeth.[43] Patrick's cause of death is unknown. And once more, a two-year old child was left without a father.

Annie Elizabeth seems to have been left an orphan before the age of 15, because in 1920 she is living with her father's brother Richard, his wife Katie, their daughter Anna Josephine, and Richard's brother Edward.[44] She was called Elizabeth while she lived there, probably to distinguish herself from her cousin Anna Josephine. Her mother Bridget probably died before Anna Elizabeth moved to Richard's family residence.[45]

Anne Murphy Heidel told me a little about Anna Elizabeth.[46]

> Elizabeth was the daughter of Patrick Doheny and his wife Bridget. She was a Doheny and lived with my grandparents, Richard Doheny and Katie Kelly, for a time, and later with Aunt Annie Doheny. My sister remembers hearing the aunts and our mother talking about her with great affection.

In 1920, when Anna Elizabeth was 16, she contracted tuberculosis, and Richard and Katie probably did not want their daughter Anna Josephine to be in danger of infection. For this reason, they sent Annie Elizabeth to live with Aunt Annie Doheny. Annie Elizabeth died in Nov 1922 at age 18 and was buried in Calvary Cemetery in the same plot as her father.[47] Just two months earlier, Aunt Annie had married Jim Farrell. I hope Annie Elizabeth was strong enough at that time to be able to share a little of the joy of that wedding.

\

[42] 1905 NYS Census, Yonkers, Westchester County, ED 4, Ward 5, page 81.

[43] Calvary Cemetery Records, Sect 19, Range 14, Plot T, Grave 17. Bridget bought this plot in Calvary to bury her husband on 18 Feb 1906. She is not buried there, though, and I haven't found her date of death.

[44] 1920 US census, NY, Manhattan, AD 12, ED 909, Sheet 7B, Elizabeth is living with Uncle Richard at 243 E.39th St.

[45] A Bridget Dahony died on 22 Feb 1910 in Westport CT, certificate # 77802. This MAY be Timothy's wife or Patrick's wife Bridget. Another Bridget Doheny, born about 1881, died 2 Feb 1910 in the Bronx. Death Certif # 728.

[46] Excerpt from an email from Anne Murphy Heidel to the author dated 1 Apr 1999.

[47] Calvary Cemetery Records. Patrick and his daughter Annie Elizabeth are buried in Section 19, Range 14, Plot T, Grave 17. Annie Doheny and James Farrell are also buried in this grave.

vi. *Richard, son of William Doheny and Anne Scully*

Richard was born on 16 Jul 1866 and baptized on the 17th. His sponsors were John Ahern and Margaret Shearman.

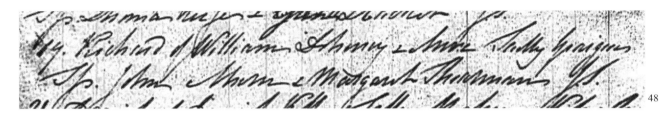

Read about Richard's life in Chapter Four.

vii. *William, son of William Doheny and Anne Scully*

William was born on October 22, 1867, in Graigue, Tipperary, Ireland, and baptized on Oct 26th. His sponsors were Richard Scott and Mary Shearman.

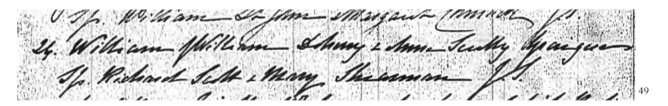

On the website RootsIreland.ie, there is a civil death record for a William Doheny, tailor's child, 3 months old, who died on 5 Feb 1868 in Graigue, Urlingford, County Kilkenny. These two records match the date of birth/baptism in civil and parish records, the father's name, occupation, place of birth, and the expected town where a death would be registered by the family of someone who died in Graigue.

---

[48] Catholic Parish Registers, the National Library of Ireland, Microfilm No. 02493/04, available on Ancestry.com. Richard Shinney [sic] was baptized on 19 Jul 1866. The record of his birth is held at the Office of the Superintendent Registrar of Births, Deaths and Marriages, Urlingford, Ireland.

[49] Ireland, Select Births and Baptisms, 1620-1911, available on Ancestry.com. William's birth was recorded in the civil records at Urlingford, Co.Kilkenny.

viii. Michael, son of William Doheny and Anne Scully

Michael was baptized on January 17, 1871, in Graigue, Tipperary, Ireland. His sponsors were John Morris and Bridget Hogan.

There is a record dated 27 Jan 1871 for a Michael Dohoney of Graigue who lived only 10 days, and I believe this is our Michael, since the dates and place match.

ix. Edward Joseph, son of William Doheny and Anne Scully

Edward Joseph was born on August 25, 1874, in Graigue, Tipperary, Ireland. His sponsors were Michael Doheny and Mary Anne Morris.

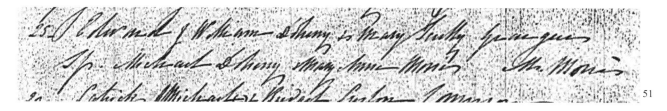

Read about Edward's life in Chapter Five.

---

[50] Catholic Parish Registers, the National Library of Ireland, Microfilm No. 02493/04, available on Ancestry.com.
[51] Catholic Parish Registers, the National Library of Ireland, Microfilm No. 02493/04, available on Ancestry.com.

x. Annie, daughter of William Doheny and Anne Scully

Annie was baptized on 22 Sep 1877. Her sponsors were Joseph Murphy and Ellen Scott. Annie seems to have sent word of her marriage back home to Ireland, because details of her marriage are entered right above her baptism record.

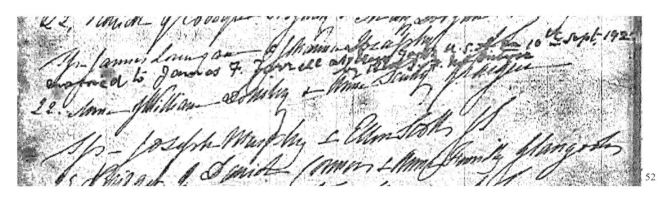

[52]

Annie never met her father because he died four months before her birth. She was ten or twelve when her siblings began to leave home for America. She was 16 when her mother died. That was 1893, and by that time, it was only Annie and two brothers, Edward and Richard, still living at home in Ireland. Then Edward left, and, finally, Richard brought her with him to America in 1895. Annie and Richard travelled on the ship Ohio which set out from the port of Queenstown and landed in Philadelphia 11 days later. They continued the voyage north to Manhattan. Each of them had $40 in their pockets.

In 1899, their brother Timothy suffered a tragic death on his job in Bridgeport CT at age 41. Then in 1906, Patrick died at age 47. In 1911, John died at age 46. In 1920, Richard died at 54. Out of 10 siblings, only three would live a relatively long life: Annie lived to be 75, Maria to 82, and Edward to almost 79.

To balance all this sadness, there were many happy family events to celebrate: marriages of siblings and the births of their children. Anna saw the marriage of her sister Maria to Jim Barry on 6 Sept 1922, and then she married the love of her life, James F. Farrell just four days later on 10 Sep 1922. She was about 45 when she got married. The 1925 census says Jim Farrell was a teamster.[53] Their marriage was recorded in New York, of course, but amazingly, also in the parish register of Gortnahoe.[54] [55]

---

[52] Catholic Parish Registers, the National Library of Ireland, Microfilm No. 02493/04, available on Ancestry.com.

[53] 1925 NYS census, Manhattan, AD 3, ED 14, Page 25, residence at 101 9th Ave.

[54] Ancestry.com, New York, New York, Marriage Index 1866-1937, 10 Sept 1922, Manhattan certificate # 22766.

[55] Ancestry.com, Ireland, Catholic Parish Registers, 1866-1915, there is a note right above Ann's baptism record that says she married James F Farrell on 10 Sept 1922, and their address was 101 9th Ave, Manhattan.

I met Uncle Jim Farrell on a few occasions. He was a very sweet man. He seemed very much to like having children visit him. I'm glad for that, because, as I mentioned before, Aunt Annie and Uncle Jim took in my father for a few years after he ran away from an orphanage. Actually, he had first stayed with Aunt Maria briefly, then Aunt Katie for a year, and then lived at Aunt Annie and Uncle Jim's apartment for about three years. While he was living with them, he graduated 8th grade at St. Bernard's School, located at 14th Street and 9th Ave., and attended two years of high school at the prestigious Stuyvesant HS on 2nd Ave and 15th Street. He left school at age 16, and after that he was on his own.

Aunt Annie's apartment was at 101 9th Ave, on the corner of West 17th Street. The West Side Docks were only two blocks away, and a group of boys that my father hung out with threw him in the river among the rats and debris, just for fun. My father said he had to sink or swim. I wonder what Aunt Annie said when he went back to her apartment.

The 1925 NYS census says that Annie's brother Edward also had an apartment at 101 9th Ave., where he lived with four of his children. However, my father always said that he "lived at Aunt Annie's." I am guessing that Aunt Annie was the person who was really caring for Edward's boys. The 1930 census says Edward was the only one in this apartment.[56] I surmise that the boys were all out on their own by then.

Between 1930 and 1935, the Farrells moved up to Inwood Park, which is at the northern tip of Manhattan.[57]

Anne Murphy Heidel said:

> Aunt Annie and Uncle Jim Farrell had a nice place. I remember going to Inwood Park with Uncle Jim, right outside their apartment. There were big trees all through the neighborhood. We also went to some small shops, I guess to pick up something for lunch. There was a bakery that Aunt Annie and Aunt Nora Kelly shopped at, called Cushman's. I remember when Aunt Nora visited us she would bring something from the bakery. [58]

Annie's sister Maria died in 1945. Their brother Edward had been living with Maria in the Bronx for a few years by then. After Maria died, Edward moved in with the Farrell's in Inwood Park.

Aunt Annie died in June 1952 at the age of 74. Though her cause of death was not on her death certificate, she had breast cancer, which probably at least contributed to her death. Edward remained living with his brother-in-law Jim Farrell until his own death the next year in April 1953.

Jim Farrell was the last of that generation. He died in 1964 at about age 90.

Cathleen Murphy McBride remembered this about Uncle Jim and Aunt Annie:

---

[56] 1930 US census, NY, Manhattan, AD 3, ED 31-285, 101 9th Ave. Annie and James Farrell and Edward Doheny.
[57] 1940 US census, New York, NY, ED 31-1973, says the Farrells had lived at 603 Isham St since at least 1935.
[58] Excerpt of email to the author from Anne Murphy Heidel on 1 May 1999.

"Uncle Jim was the sweetest man I knew as a child. He would play dolls with me and included me in his daily ritual of feeding the squirrel that came to his fire escape window. I believe he earned his living by delivering bread. When Aunt Annie died, he wrote to tell me, and his handwriting was like beautiful calligraphy. Aunt Annie was quiet and somewhat shy, always very loving, and a strong hugger! She was always delighted to see us, and it made me look forward to every visit."

The reverse side of this photo says, "Our neighbor Mrs. Lynch's brother, Annie D. Farrell and James Farrell. Picture taken at 603 Isham St., August 1951."

Chapter Three

Timothy DOHENY (1858-1899)
Bridget MAHER (1872-ca.1910)

..1 William Doheny (ca.1837 – 1877)
.. +Anne Scully (ca.1838 – 1893)
..... 2 **Timothy A. Doheny (1858 - 1899)**
..... +Bridget Maher (1872 – ca.1910), m.1893
.... 3 Anna Margaret Doheny (1894 - 1982)
.... +Pearce Shepherd (1901 - 1969), m. 25 Nov 1929
.... 3 William E Doheny, Sr. (1898 - 1956)
.... +Irene S. Eeck (1904 - Unknown), m. 1925
.... 4 William E. Doheny Jr. (1925 - 2013)
.... +Patricia (1930 - 1993)
.... 4 Donald G. Doheny (1932 - 2013)
.... +Pauline E Bierylo (1933 - 1997), m. Apr 1954
.... +Joan (1932 - 2009), m. Jun 1971

Timothy A. Doheny was born in Graigue just a little more than nine months after his parents, William and Anne, were married. He was baptized on December 14, 1858. His sponsors were Cornelius Doheny and Ellen Purcell.

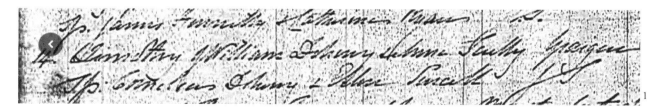

He learned his father's trade as a tailor and was one of their only children to have found employment as a tailor in the USA. He seems to have been the first of his siblings to emigrate to the USA. He first appears in USA documents in 1890 in the Bridgeport, CT city directory of 1890-1891. He would have had to submit his name and occupation the year before, so he was probably living in Bridgeport in 1889. Another clue regarding his arrival in the USA is found in his naturalization papers. Since those papers are dated 22 March 1894, Timothy needed to have been a resident of the

---

[1] Catholic Parish Registers, the National Library of Ireland, Microfilm No. 02493/04, available on Ancestry.com. Timothy was baptized on 14 Dec 1858, so he was probably born in December.

USA by March 1889; immigrants had to have lived in the USA for 5 continuous years before they could be naturalized.

I found no clues about why Timothy settled in Bridgeport CT instead of Manhattan, as his other siblings would do, but he quickly found a job in Bridgeport in a tailor shop about 1.5 miles from his residence.[2] He probably walked to work, which was across the Pequonnock River, and that could be a nasty walk in the winter.

In 1893, Timothy married Bridget Maher, also an Irish immigrant. He got a new job at 341 Main St., which was about the same distance from his former residence. Some of their joy was dampened when Timothy learned that his mother had just died.

Timothy and Bridget's first child, Anna Margaret, was born the next year, 1894, and she may have been named after Timothy's mother, Anne Scully.

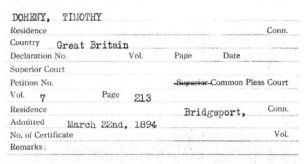

In 1894 Timothy celebrated another important milestone in their family life; he achieved US citizenship.[3] Though there was no literacy test in naturalization law of the time, Timothy could be proud of the fact that he could read and write. He swore allegiance to his new country and had to pass an oral civics exam before a judge. Typically, civics tests were delivered in open court, and they tended to be impromptu, so the prospective citizen did not know what the questions would be.[4] At the time, wives became citizens automatically when their husbands were naturalized.

The next year, in 1895, Timothy's brother Patrick came to live with them and found work as a laborer at Citizen's Gas Co., a company owned by the Warner Brothers,[5] not the Hollywood Warner brothers. However, these Warner Brothers were also millionaires and friendly with some of the most powerful people in America, including John D. Rockefeller and Theodore Roosevelt. The Warners owned and operated many major businesses in Bridgeport. One of these businesses was a corset factory. In 1896, the apartment was getting tight for three adults and a toddler, so they all moved to 58 Johnson Place., and Timothy started working for the Warner Brothers in their corset factory as a painter. In 1897, Patrick moved to Manhattan. In 1898, Bridget became pregnant with her second child. Timothy's family moved to 213 Railroad Ave.,[6] and William was born in December 1898.

---

[2] 1890 Bridgeport City Directory says he lived at 164 Helen St and worked at 92 State St, Bridgeport.

[3] National Archives at Boston, Naturalization Record Books, 12/1893 - 9/1906; NAI Number: 2838938; Record Group Title: Records of District Courts of the United States, 1685-2009; Record Group Number: RG 21.

[4] https://www.uscis.gov/history-and-genealogy/history-and-genealogy-news/origins-naturalization-civics-test

[5] Bridgeport CT 1896 City Directory.

[6] Bridgeport CT 1899 City Directory.

Suddenly, everything turned upside down. Timothy died tragically on 26 Dec 1899, the day after Christmas 1899. He was 41, nearly the same age at which his father had died. The announcement of Timothy's death actually made it into several east coast newspapers.[7] It read:

A Painter's Peculiar Death

Bridgeport, Dec 26. – Timothy Doheny, a painter at Warner Brothers' corset factory, was killed in a peculiar way this morning. Doheny was painting near a large shaft. The hub of a pulley caught in the clothing on his back and tightened up so quickly around his neck that his breath was shut off. He was 34 years old [sic] and leaves a wife and two small children.[8]

After Timothy died, Bridget and her two children moved several times.[9] Their apartment in 1906 at 35 Hawthorne Ave, Ansonia, a section of Bridgeport, was a little larger, and Bridget took in two boarders, probably to help pay the rent. One man was an apprentice "horseshoe'r " and the other man worked in the Warner corset factory where Timothy had died.[10]

Timothy & Bridget's Addresses in Bridgeport Directories			
1890	Timothy Doheny	164 Helen	Tailor Emp192 State Street
1891	Timothy Doheny	164 Helen	Tailor Emp192 State Street
1892	Timothy Doheny	164 Helen	Tailor Emp192 State Street
1893	Timothy A Doheny	164 Helen	Tailor Emp 841 Main
1894	Timothy A Doheny	164 Helen	Tailor Emp 841 Main
1895	Timothy A Doheny	164 Helen	Tailor Emp 841 Main
1896	Timothy A Doheny	58 Johnson Place	Emp W. Bros. Co.
1899	Timothy A Doheny	213 Railroad Ave	Emp W. Bros. Co.
1900	Bridget Doheny, widow Timothy	h 599 Myrtle Ave	
1901	Bridget Doheny, widow Timothy	rooms 33 West Ave	
1902	Bridget Doheny, widow Timothy	h 8 Vanstone Court	
1903	Bridget Doheny, widow Timothy	h 8 Vanstone Court	
1904	Bridget Doheny, widow Timothy	h 8 Vanstone Court	
1905	Bridget Doheny, widow Timothy	removed to Derby	
1905	Bridget Doheny, widow Timothy	h 35 Hawthorne Ave, Ansonia CT	
1906	Bridget Doheny, widow Timothy	h 35 Hawthorne Ave, Ansonia CT	

After 1906 Bridget disappears from the public record, so I am guessing that Bridget died between 1905 and 1910. The best clue for this is that, by 1910, her two children Anna Margaret and William

[7] www.newspapers.com found the announcement in the Asbury Park Press, NJ; Deutsche Correspondent, a German language newspaper in Baltimore MD; Hartford Courant, CT; The Brandon Union, VT; Wilkes-Barre Times Leader, PA.
[8] Hartford Currant, CT
[9] The Bridgeport City Directories list her as Widow of Timothy at 599 Myrtle Ave. in 1900, 33 West Ave. in 1901, then 8 Vanstone Court in 1902 to 1904, and finally 35 Hawthorne Ave. in 1905 and 1906.
[10] 1900 federal census, CT, Fairfield County, Bridgeport ED-10 Sheet 4A

are living with her sister-in-law, Timothy's sister, Maria Doheny, in Manhattan.[11] By 1920, Margaret and William were living in Trenton, in a boarding house with ten other working people, mostly firemen. He was an auto mechanic at 21, and she, at 23, was a stenographer at a factory.[12]

Anne Murphy Heidel told me a little about Anna Margaret and her brother Bill.[13]

> Margaret Shepherd, when I knew her, lived in East Orange NJ. Her husband was Pearce Shepherd. He worked for an insurance company as an actuary and was a gentleman and a most delightful man. (Cathleen Murphy McBride added, "Pearce was dignified and quiet; he doted on Margaret.") They had no children of their own, but Margaret helped her brother raise his boys after Bill was divorced. Chances are Bill remarried.

> Margaret and Pearce had the most beautiful apartment I had ever seen. They also rented a house on the Jersey shore every summer. One summer, my sister and I got to spend a couple of weeks there. I have fond memories of that time. Margaret was a lovely person. I remember that she was taking college classes, probably just for fun. I don't think she wanted for anything. She was tall and very attractive and had the most beautiful laugh. I suspect she was in her teens when her parents died, so I don't think she was able to get much education. Maybe she didn't finish High School.

> Her brother Bill worked for the post office and was a very nice man also. He had two sons, William and Donald. Both of Bill's sons lived in NJ some years ago.

According to Margaret's Social Security Application, she worked as a secretary in an insurance company until 1929. Which one is not noted on the application. Somehow, she met Pearce Shepherd, who we know from several sources was an actuary in an insurance company.[14] [15] [16] Margaret married Pearce Shepherd in Nov 1929 in Manhattan,[17] and the couple took up residence at 17 Summit St., East Orange NJ in a very pretty four-story apartment building that still advertises large 1-2-3-bedroom rentals. For those interested, there is a photo of the building on Google Maps.

On her Social Security Application, Margaret did not give her correct age. She said her birthday was 4 Oct 1900, but it really was 4 Oct 1894. She also wrote her mother's first name incorrectly. Margaret wrote down Beatrice Maher, but it really was Bridget, which threw off some of my initial research. The SS application was dated 1941, and it said that Margaret was then working for Hahne

---

[11] 1910 Census, Manhattan, Ward 21, ED 1121, Page 20B. Maria Doheny Head, John Doheny brother, William E Doheny 11 nephew, Anna M Doheny 15 niece.
[12] 1920 US census, NJ, Mercer County, Trenton, ED 50, Sheet 3-1A. Margaret and William resided at 14 Southard St.
[13] Emails to the author from Anne Murphy Heidel dated 18 Feb and 22 Feb 1999.
[14] 1930 Census, Manhattan NY, AD 8, SD 21, ED 31-228, Sheet 15B, Margaret and Pearce lived at 166 Second Ave.
[15] 1940 Census, East Orange, Essex County NJ, Ward 2, S.D.11, ED 7-96A, Sheet 1B, 17 Summit St., Pearce completed 4 years of college and Margaret completed 2 years of college.
[16] https://prabook.com/web/pearce.shepherd/1054837 Pearce's illustrious career is outlined on this website. There is at least one inaccuracy on the page, though. The date of his marriage should say 1929, not 1919.
[17] Ancestry.com New York, NY Extracted Marriage Index, 1866-1937, Anna M Doheny married Pearce Shepherd in Manhattan on 25 Nov 1929.

& Co. on Broad St. in Newark, NJ, which was about 3.5 miles from their residence in East Orange. Perhaps she used public transportation, or maybe she had a car to get to work.

About Hayne's, Wikipedia says Hahne's was a major department store in Newark; it was five stories high and had an atrium in the center. The atrium rose to the fourth floor. Hayne's even had two restaurants. Its motto was "The Store with the Friendly Spirit." Hayne's closed in 1987.

As an actuary, Pearce was probably doing well financially. The 1940 census says his annual salary was $5,000. There is a record of a cruise the couple took through the Panama Canal in March 1952 on the "Trafalgar." [18] The passengers were examined by a physician in Hong Kong and cleared for the trip through the Panama Canal, so this may have been part of an around-the-world trip. Two other passengers were also from East Orange, and their names are right above the names of Margaret and Pearce; it is my guess that they were friends or even in-laws.

In 1964, Pearce Shepherd was Senior Vice President and Chief Actuary of Prudential Insurance Company of America and was named Chairman-Elect of the Health Insurance Council, a prestigious national organization.[19] In 1965, he was a US Senate witness on private pension plans and represented the US Chamber of Commerce. He spoke on behalf of profit-sharing and extending and protecting private pension plans.[20]

Pearce and Anna Margaret continued to live in East Orange for many years. They both died in NJ: Pearce in Montclair NJ in 1969 and Margaret in Rumson NJ in 1982. She was almost 88 years old.

Here are some interesting facts about Pearce's life from his obituary that was published in *The New York Times* on 9 Sep 1969:

- Pearce Shepherd retired in 1966 as senior vice-president and chief actuary of the Prudential Insurance Company.
- He died at age 67 at his home at 18 Trinity Place, Montclair NJ.
- Pearce was a former president of the Society of Actuaries and Home Office Life Underwriters Association and former chairman of the Health Insurance Council.
- He was born in Chicago and graduated in 1924 from the university of Chicago, where he was a member of Phi Beta Kappa.
- Before joining Prudential in 1932, he was with a consulting actuary firm in Chicago and with the North American Reassurance Company in New York.
- In 1943, Pearce became senior vice president at Prudential, and in 1959, he became chief actuary.
- He was the former president of the Robert Treat Council of the Boy Scouts in Newark.
- His brother, C. O. Shepherd, was actuary of Travelers Insurance Company, and his brother, Bruce E. Shepherd, was chief actuary of the Life Insurance Association of America.

---

[18] Ancestry.com, New York, Passenger Lists, 1820-1957, Pearce and Margaret Shepherd, ages 50 and 49, left from Cristebel, C.Z. on the 18th Feb and arrived at the port of New York on 30 March 1952. Ship: M.S. Trafalgar. There were only nine cabin passengers and 43 crew members.

[19] https://heinonline.org/HOL/LandingPage?handle=hein.journals/inslj26&div=60&id=&page=

[20] https://www.aging.senate.gov/imo/media/doc/publications/351965.pdf

Timothy and Bridget's second child, William (Bill), joined the US Army Air Service in 1917 and served in WW I as a corporal in the 20th and the 11th Aero Service Squadrons in France. He was probably 18 or 19 years old when he enlisted. He was living with Margaret in Trenton NJ when he enlisted, and he wrote Margaret's name down as his contact person.[21]   This photo is on the Wikipedia page of the 11th Aero Squadron, Day Bombardment Group. They are posing with Dayton-Wright DH-4s at the Maulan Airdrome, France, in November 1918.[22]

Airplanes were quite primitive at the time, and according to a Defense Department document of the time, Aero Squadrons operated "in advance of the independent cavalry in order to locate the enemy and to keep track of its movements. Contact with the enemy once gained will be maintained thereafter continuously... During combat the aero squadron will operate around the flanks and over and to the rear of the enemy's position, for the purpose of reporting his dispositions, the approach of reinforcements, or the beginning of his withdrawal from action." [23]

After World War I, William Doheny Sr. married Irene Peck in Philadelphia. That was early in 1925.[24]   Then they lived in Brooklyn[25] for a while, and they had two sons, William Jr. (1925-2013) and Donald (1932-2013). William Sr. worked as a mail clerk for a railroad, according to the 1930 and 1940 censuses. By 1940, they were living in Elizabeth, NJ.[26]   These censuses mention that Irene and her two sons were all born in New Jersey, though William Jr.'s obituary (see below) says he was born in Brooklyn. Their birth certificates are needed to solve the slight discrepancy.

William Jr. married Patricia Van Duyne in Crawford, NJ, in 1954. They had several children.

Here are excerpts from William Jr.'s obituary published in the NJ Star-Ledger on 15 Feb 2013:

> William E. "Bill" Doheny Jr., 87, of Salisbury, N.C., passed away on Feb. 10, 2013. Mr. Doheny was born in Brooklyn, N.Y., on Dec. 17, 1925, the son of William E. and Irene Doheny. He graduated from St. Mary High School, Elizabeth, N.J.; proudly served in the U.S. Navy as a medic during World War II, and graduated from Cornell University. He was employed as a chemist with Boyle-Midway Inc., Cranford, N.J. A

---

[21] Amazon.com U.S., Army Transport Service, Passenger Lists, 1910-1939
[22] Photo by Air Service, United States Army - Air Service, United States Army photograph, Public Domain, https://commons.wikimedia.org/w/index.php?curid=26212584
[23] https://media.defense.gov/2010/Oct/13/2001329759/-1/-1/0/AFD-101013-008.pdf page 23.
[24] Ancestry.com, Philadelphia, Pennsylvania, Marriage Index, 1885-1951 William E Doheny married Irene S Peck in Philadelphia. Their marriage license number is 510067 and digital GSU number is 4141671.
[25] 1930 US census, NY, Kings County, Brooklyn, ED 24-1344, Sheet 6A, residence was 1970 51st Street.
[26] 1940 US census, NJ, Elizabeth, Union County, ED 23-88A, Sheet 64B, residence was 1136 Freemont St.

longtime resident of Cranford and Sea Bright, N.J., and Titusville, Fla., he is survived by six children, 13 grandchildren, and four great-grandchildren. He was preceded in death by grandson David Muller. In lieu of flowers, donations may be made in the name of William E. Doheny to the North Carolina State Veterans Home-Salisbury, P.O. Box 599, Salisbury, N.C. 28145.[27]

Donald, William Sr's second son, married Pauline Bierylo in 1954 in Elizabeth NJ, and they had a son. The marriage ended in divorce, and Anne Murphy Heidel said, "I think Donald remarried because he was pretty young at the time of the divorce."

Cathleen Murphy McBride wrote to me about her memories of Margaret Shepherd and her brother Bill Doheny:

Margaret had a delightful laugh, (not unlike Aunt Annie's). She and Pearce had a beautiful apartment in New Jersey, and five cats. They had no children of their own, but were very generous with her nephews William and Donald. Margaret's brother Bill was divorced, and may have remarried. Bill was quiet and shy, I thought, but very thoughtful and sweet.

The Shepherds used to rent a house at Lavalette, NJ, and invited Anne and me to spend time there when we were small. Donnie, about my age, was there as well, and we had great fun with him. Anne laughed at him most of the time, to his great delight. I rode around on the bar of his bike as he pedaled the streets of the town. We fished and swam and had a wonderful time living right on the ocean.

That was the summer my grandmother had her stroke, and mother came to tell us, and took Anne home with her. I stayed another week and went home with Bill who brought me to work with him and turned me over to mother on their lunch break. He was living alone in New Jersey at the time in a bleak little apartment, but he did his best to entertain a little girl he barely knew, taking me for ice cream and bringing out a box of costume jewelry that I assumed had belonged to his wife and let me go through it and take anything I wanted.

---

[27] http://obits.nj.com/obituaries/starledger/obituary.aspx?n=william-e-doheny-bill&pid=163073738

Chapter Four

Richard DOHENY (1866 – 1920)
Catherine KELLY (1864 – 1944)

1 William Doheny (ca.1837 – 1877)
+Anne Scully (ca.1838 – 1893)
..... 2 **Richard Doheny** (1866 - 1920)
..... +Catherine Kelly (1864 - 1944), m. Oct 1899
.... 3 Anna Josephine Doheny (1901 - 1970)
.............+James Murphy (1902 - 1981), m. Jun 1932
.... 4 Cathleen Marie Murphy (1933 - 2019)
.... +Living McBride
.... 4 Anne Murphy (1938 - 2019)
.... +Living Heidel

Richard was born on 16 Jul 1866 and baptized on the 17th. His sponsors were John Ahern and Margaret Shearman.

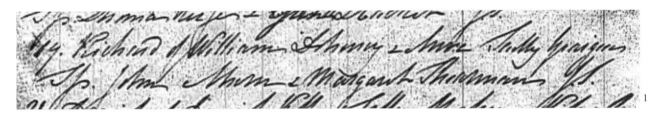

Richard, 11 when his father died, continued learning tailoring from his older brothers.

He had watched Timothy, Maria and Patrick leave Ireland a few years before. Then John left a month before his mother died. In 1893, Richard was present at his mother's death in Graigue, and he is the one who registered her death in Urlingford,[2] probably because he was the oldest of Anne's children still living at home.

I imagine there was some serious ambivalence among the remaining surviving siblings, Richard, Edward, and Annie. Should they stay, or should they leave? Edward made his decision to leave in

---

[1] Ireland, Select Births and Baptisms, 1620-1911, available on Ancestry.com. Richard's birth was recorded in the civil records at Urlingford, Co.Kilkenny, and in the parish register in Gortnahoe.
[2] www.rootsireland.ie   Civil Death Record for Anne Dohoney, 8 Sep 1893, widow of Tailor. Her son Richard of Graiguepaudeen was the informant.

early 1895. Then Richard and Annie left a few months later, after selling the family cottage and property to their next-door neighbor, a farmer who also had the name Doheny.

Richard, now almost 29, and his sister Annie, almost 19, sailed on the S.S. Ohio out of Queenstown, Ireland, and arrived in Philadelphia, PA in April 1895.

The S.S. Ohio had a regular run to Philadelphia from Liverpool, England, with a stop in Queenstown, Ireland, to pick up additional passengers, before she crossed the Atlantic on a seven to 11-day journey. The S.S. Ohio occasionally stopped in New York Harbor first, but not on this run.

So, Richard and Anne's ticket took them first to Philadelphia and then on to New York. They said they each had $40 in their possession. On the ship's passenger list, Richard listed his occupation as tailor from Graigue, Ireland. They were bound for New York and intended to stay with their sister Maria in New York City. The ship's passenger list even gives us Maria's address: 203 Henry Street, which is in Manhattan's Lower East Side.[3] It appears that they were counting on Maria to take care of them in New York City, just as she had in Graigue when she helped her widowed mother with the younger children. The Henry Street address was a boarding house run by a young family for 17 working men and women in their 20s, 30s, and 40s, according to the 1900 census. Maria, Richard and Anne lived on Henry Street just for a little while; then moved to Vesey Street.[4]

This image of the SS Ohio is in the public domain and found in Wikipedia. The S.S. Ohio was an American made iron passenger/cargo ship, built in 1872. She was a transatlantic passenger ship until 1898, so she was nearing the end of her service for the English and Irish emigrants when Richard and Anne took their voyage to America in 1895. The Ohio was among the first ships to be fitted with compound steam engines, and was refitted in 1887 with a

new, smaller, triple expansion steam engine, quite innovative for the time. She and her four sister ships were built by the Pennsylvania RR Company, and named after the four states serviced by this Railroad – the states of Pennsylvania, Indiana, Illinois, and Ohio.[5]

Richard married a woman named Catherine Kelly. He may have known her back in Ireland, because she was also from Gortnahoe, from the very next cluster of homes called Longfordpass.[6] Richard and Catherine, who was known in our family as Aunt Katie, were married on 3 Oct 1899 in

---

[3] Ancestry.com, Pennsylvania, Passenger and Crew Lists, 1800-1962, S.S. Ohio left Ireland on 4th April and arrived at Philadelphia on 14 April 1895.
[4] Manhattan Directory of 1900 shows a Richard Doheny, porter, at 59 Vesey Street, which was Maria's address in 1899.
[5] https://en.wikipedia.org/wiki/SS_Ohio_(1872)
[6] Ancestry.com, Ireland Catholic Parish Registers, 1655-1915. Catherine was the daughter of Patrick Kelly and Mary Cahill. Her residence was Longfordpress, Gortnahoe. She was baptized in the parish of Gurtnahoe-Glengoole, County Tipperary, Ireland on 24 Nov 1864.

Manhattan.[7] Richard's brother John was his "best man,"[8] perhaps because he was Richard's oldest brother.

Their first residence was 109 60th Street, Manhattan.[9] Even though they were newlyweds, Richard's brother Edward lived with them. Richard and Edward were both building porters. "Porter" was a general term for different sorts of work at that time. "Porter" was higher in rank than "helper." They might have worked in a store or a warehouse. Richard and Edward each were listed as "porter - 'Bldg' " on the 1900 census. Working as a porter was a common occupation for Irish immigrants.

The next year, 1901, Richard and Catherine's daughter Anna Josephine was born. Richard's brother John was Anna Josephine's godfather.[10] Anna Josephine was baptized at Church of St. Paul the Apostle, 60th St and Columbus Ave, NYC. Her godparents were her father's brother John and her mother's sister Nora Kelly.[11]

This photo is ca. 1910.

In 1910, Richard's family lived at 40 East 40th Street, Manhattan, according to the census. In 1910, Richard was employed as a porter in a dry goods company. Catherine was working as a "caretaker in a private house." Their address was around the corner from Park Ave. The other homes on the block seem to be large, expensive residences in the early 20th century. No one else besides our family is enumerated at their address, so perhaps Richard's family were caretakers of the home at 40 East 40th Street, in the absence of wealthy owners.

From 1916 to about 1923, Richard's family residence was 243 East 39th Street, Manhattan. Richard's brother Edward lived with them again for part of the time between 1917-1920, because Edward's family was breaking up. Sometimes Edward's children Gerard, Lawrence and Bernard would live with them, too. My father said he attended St. Gabriel's School while he lived with Aunt Katie. St. Gabriel School was at E. 36th and 2nd Ave., practically around the corner from their residence. Richard and Katie were also caring for his brother Patrick's orphaned daughter, Anna Elizabeth, at the same time. They all called her Elizabeth, probably to distinguish her from Anna Josephine.

---

[7] Ancestry.com, New York, NY Marriage Index 1866-1937. Richard Doheny married Catherine Kelly on 3 Oct 1899 in Manhattan. Certificate 16457.
[8] Excerpt of email to the author from Anne Murphy Heidel on 1 May 1999.
[9] 1900 US census, NY, New York, Manhattan, ED 448, Sheet14B.
[10] Letter to the author from Anne Murphy Heidel dated 10 Jan 1999.
[11] This is documented in the Hughes Family Tree on Ancestry.com

The 1920 census was in January, and it says that Richard and Catherine were still considered aliens; Richard had submitted his intention-to-become-a-citizen papers, but was not naturalized yet. Perhaps Richard was ill by January 1920, because the census says that he is not working. His age was 53. His daughter Anna and brother Edward were the household members who were working. Anna Josephine, age 18, was a typist at Western Union, having dropped out of High School after one year,[12] and Edward was a clerk at Metropolitan Life Insurance Co.

Richard died in August 1920. Around the same time that Richard was dying, Anna Elizabeth, only 15 years old, contracted tuberculosis. As much as she loved her, Catherine probably thought it would be better for her own daughter Anna Josephine if Anna Elizabeth were cared for by someone else. Richard's sister Annie agreed to take her in. Anna Elizabeth would die at Aunt Annie's two years later.[13]

Richard's widow Katie began her own naturalization process on 2 May 1921.[14]

By 1925, Richard's widow Katie and his daughter Anna J. had moved to the Bronx. (Aunt Maria and Uncle Jim Barry moved into Katie's old apartment on E. 39th St.[15]) In the 1930 census, Katie called herself a "decorative seamstress," but she said she was not working in 1930. She was 66, and Anna J., at age 29, was still at home. Anna J. had been promoted to "supervisor in the telegraph industry" by 1930.[16] (Anna J. would get my father Bernard a job at Western Union around that time.) She was commuting from the Bronx to the main Western Union office in Manhattan.

Cathleen Murphy McBride said:

> "Mother worked in the main Western Union office near Wall Street during most of our growing up years. I went to work with her a couple of times. During World War II, she moved to the personnel department and worked off Fifth Ave., near the Public Library. It was within sight of the Empire State Building because she was there the Saturday that there was a dramatic accident, I think a plane crashed into it, and the elevator plunged many floors."

Cathleen Murphy McBride also commented on her grandmother, Katie Kelly:

> "It is interesting that my grandmother, who grew up on a farm and had no special training that I know of, worked as a seamstress in an upholstery shop at some point in time. I remember her tackling one of our chairs when I was young. She made all my mother's clothes, and her own, I presume. My sister Anne inherited some of that talent. She made the wedding dresses for her daughters, among many other projects.

---

[12] 1941 US census, Queens, New York City, SD 45, ED 41-453, Sheet 3B.

[13] Death Certificate for Annie Elizabeth Doheny, NYC Dept of Health, #8329, 20 Nov 1922. Annie's residence was 101 9th Ave where Aunt Annie and Uncle Jim Farrell lived.

[14] New York, NY County Supreme Court Naturalizations, Vol 484, Page 59, 2 May 1921. Catherine Doheny was living at 243 East 39th St, Manhattan when she petitioned to become a US citizen.

[15] 1925 NYS census, Manhattan, AD 12, ED 31, Block 1, Page 37. Maria and Jim are living at 243 E.39th St.

[16] 1930 US Census, Bronx, NY, SD 26, ED 3-667. Katie and Anna J. lived at 2964 Perry St.

"My grandmother must have been a warm, welcoming lady, because she not only had Elizabeth, Eddie and John living with her, she also brought over four or five Kelly nieces of hers to live with her and my mother. They said you could always get a card game and a cup of tea at her place! Her place seems to have been all over Manhattan and the Bronx. As children, when we'd be out driving, Mother would say, 'I used to live over there.' She said it so often, that my father suggested that they had kept one jump ahead of the rent collector. When we knew my grandmother, she had aged and probably had a few small strokes, and she was slow and quiet."

Anne Murphy Heidel remembered my grandfather Edward living with her family at some point. Her family continued to give a home to other people; she said that her "godfather Pat Fennaly moved in after Uncle Eddie moved out." She also remembered a brief visit sometime between 1950 and 1956 by Fr. Richard Doheny of California.[17] (Father Richard is the person who put the author in touch with the Pastor at Gortnahoe in 2000.)

Anna Josephine married James Murphy (his photo is at left) in a June Wedding in 1932 in Flushing, NY. Anne Murphy Heidel said, "My parents' marriage witnesses were John Sheehan, a friend of my father's, and Mary Moore, referred to as mother's cousin. Mary Moore's mother was called Auntie Nannie (Nancy?), and I believe she was a Greene, possibly related to your grandmother Katharine Greene."[18] James Murphy worked as a "truck chauffeur" for an "electric power and light company in 1940."[19]

Anna Josephine and James Murphy had two daughters, Cathleen and Anne, my two 2nd cousins who shared so many memories with me. They both died in 2019.

Cathleen Murphy McBride was a Maryknoll sister for several years. She served in the Philippines. I never met her, unfortunately, but we corresponded. She was the only one of William Doheny and Anne Scully's descendants, whom I know of, who entered religious life besides me. She left Maryknoll and married Owen McBride in 1972.

---

[17] Excerpt from an email from Anne Murphy Heidel to the author dated 1 Apr 1999.
[18] Katharine Greene's only sister was Helen V. Greene. There is no evidence they had another sister. My father Bernard also spoke of a Mrs. Moore, and he thought she was his father's sister, but that cannot be right either; Edward's only sisters were Maria Doheny Barry and Annie Doheny Farrell. Perhaps Mrs. Moore was a Kelly or Murphy relative.
[19] 1940 US Census, NY, Queens, SD 45, ED 41-453, Sheet 3B, residence was 20-40 147th St.

To the right is a photo of Anne Murphy Heidel. I'm glad she stayed in close contact with my parents after her own mother, Anna Josephine, died.

Richard Doheny's wife, Catherine Kelly, died in 1944 in Flushing, Queens County, while she was living with her daughter Anna Josephine.[20]

Anna Josephine Doheny Murphy died in 1971 in Hyde Park, Dutchess County, while she was living with her daughter Anne Murphy Heidel.[21]

Cathleen Murphy McBride died on 12 Jul 2019 in Braintree, MA.

Anne Murphy Heidel died on 28 Sep 2019 in Sugar Land, TX, in the care of three of her children, who also live in Sugar Land.

---

[20] New York, NY, Extracted Death Index, 1862-1948, available on Ancestry.com. Catherine Kelly died 9 Oct 1944 in Queens.
[21] Social Security Index, available on Ancestry.com. Anne Doheny Murphy died in Oct 1971 in Hyde Park, NY.

Chapter Five

Edward J. DOHENY (1874-1953)
Katharine T. GREENE (1878-1933)

1 William Doheny (ca.1837 – 1877)
 +Anne Scully (ca.1838 – 1893)
..... 2 **Edward Joseph Doheny I** (1874-1953)
..... +Katharine Theresa Greene (1878-1933), m. Sep 1904
.... 3 Catharine Doheny (1905-1905)
.... 3 Edward Joseph Doheny II (1907-1972)
.... 3 Thomas J. Doheny (1908-1908)
.... 3 Francis William Doheny (1909-1973)
.... 3 Gerard J Doheny (1910-1933)
.... 3 Lawrence Aloysius Doheny (1912-1978)
.... 3 Bernard Greene Doheny (1913-1989)

My grandfather was a handsome man, of medium height and build, with striking blue eyes. He had gray hair by 44 years of age.[1] But, as you can see from this photo, his gray hair made him look all the more distinguished.

Edward was the ninth child of William Doheny and Anne Scully. His mother was 36 when he was born on 13 August 1874[2] in Graigue, County Tipperary, Ireland. He was baptized a week and a half later, and his godparents were Michael Doheny and Mary Anne Morris.[3] [4] [5]

---

[1] WWI Draft Registration card, dated 12 Sep 1918, gave this physical description of Edward.
[2] On his citizenship papers, Edward said his birthday was August 13, 1875. The day is probably correct, but not the year.
[3] Ireland, Catholic Parish Registers, 1655-1915, Ancestry.com. Edward was baptized 25 Aug 1874 in Graigue in the Diocese of Cashel and Emly.
[4] Civil Birth Record, www.rootsireland.ie -- Edmund Dohoney, born 25 Aug 1874 in Graigue, Fennor in the district of Urlingford, Co. Kilkenny. Father was William Dohoney; mother was Anne Scully. Father registered the birth on 3 Sep 1874. William gave the registrar Edward's date of baptism, not his date of birth. "Edmund" is a transcription error.
[5] Catholic Parish Registers, the National Library of Ireland, Microfilm No. 02493/04, available on Ancestry.com.

Edward's father died at the young age of 40 when little Edward was only two years old. Though he grew up without a father, Edward graduated from 8[6] grade and then worked with other members of the family as the town's tailors. Edward's mother died at age 55 – when Edward was 19. He emigrated to New York the next year, following many of his siblings. Edward traveled down to the port of Queenstown, which is present day Cobh, the Cork city harbor. Queenstown was the embarkation point for thousands and thousands of the Irish during the mass migrations of the 19th Century. At Queenstown, he boarded the S.S. Britannic I for a two-week transatlantic journey and arrived in NY Harbor on 16 March 1895.

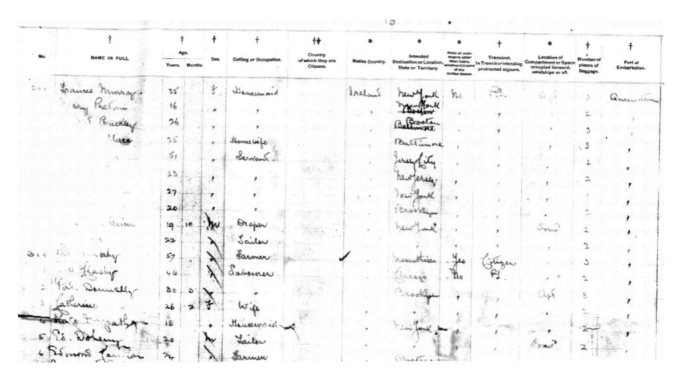

The various columns in the Britannic's passenger list (above) say that Ed Doheny, tailor, 20 years of age, intended to sail to New York "for a protracted sojourn." He occupied a forward space of steerage and had with him 2 pieces of baggage. [7][8] Edward seems to have kept up his tailoring skills after he arrived in the United States, because Uncle Larry told my sister Elizabeth that his dad "would sew his shirts by hand, sitting crossed legged on a table."

Descriptions of travelling in steerage (3rd class) paint a grim picture, especially when a ship hit rough seas and bad weather. The Britannic I carried 380 third-class passengers on Edward's voyage and 50 cabin passengers. "The steerage accommodations were located on the two lower decks and consisted of large dormitory-style cabins capable of sleeping up to 20 passengers lined against the

---

[6] 1940 US Census, NY, Bronx, S.D 23, ED 3-1333, Sheet 11A.

[7] S.S. Britannic, NY Passenger List, Film M237 Roll 638, Ancestry.com, image 145/867

[8] Father Richard Doheny of Fair Oaks, California told me in a phone conversation in 2000 that all the Doheny boys were tailors in Ireland. He said his parents owned the property right behind our family's home, and we were all cousins. He put me in touch with V. Rev. O'Rourke of Gortnahoe, Thurles, Tipperary. Father Richard Doheny died 4 March 2006, and is buried in Fennor Cemetery, Gortnahoe, Tipperary. His obituary is online.

hull, with an open space running along the center line of the ship where passengers could congregate. These accommodations were divided into two main sections at either end of the ship, berths for single men in the bow and berths for single women, married couples and families in the stern."[9]

This image of the S.S. Britannic I of the White Star Line is from an old advertising card. The image is used with permission of Norway Heritage. Go to www.norwayheritage.com for a detailed history of this ship. The S.S. Britannic I sailed back and forth between Liverpool, Queenstown and New York from 1874 to 1899. Then she was Boer War transport and was finally scrapped in 1903.

Edward lived with his brother Richard and his wife Katie in Manhattan after he arrived in New York.[10] He found a job as a porter, like his brother Richard,[11] and applied for US citizenship. Five years later, on 26 June 1900, Edward became a naturalized citizen, renouncing his allegiance to the "Queen of the United Kingdom of Great Britain and Ireland" and swearing allegiance to the United States of America at the US District Court in Manhattan.[12]

In 1904, Edward began work at Metropolitan Life Insurance Company. He would work there as a clerk for 40 years, retiring on 29 Dec 1944. The 1940 census[13] mentions that his annual salary was

---

[9] https://en.wikipedia.org/wiki/SS_Britannic_(1874)
[10] 1900 Census, New York, NY, ED 448, Sheet 14B, 109 60th St, Richard (porter), wife Katie, and Edward lived here.
[11] 1910 Census, New York, NY, Ward 21, ED 117, 42 E 40th St. Richard was a porter in a dry goods company.
[12] Edward's Naturalization Papers are in the Appendix, should you like to see them.
[13] 1940 Census, Bronx, NY, ED 3-1333, Sheet 11A, 2653 Decatur Ave.

$1,464. Though Edward was a heavy drinker, he was apparently always able to go to work, and we have a lovely commemorative photo of his retirement illustrating the appreciation of his supervisors.

In 1999, Anne Murphy Heidel gave the author the decanter and the two cordial glasses seen in this photo.

The reverse side of the photo is stamped: "Photo Bureau, M.L.I.Co., Dec 29 1944" followed by someone's handwritten notation: Mr. Edward J. Doheny / Retired / After 40 years with / Metropolitan Life Ins. Co. / died April 5, 1953 / Age 79 years.

Perhaps Edward sought the job at Met Life because he had "met someone." Here is what might have happened: One of Edward's early addresses was 101 9th Ave., the same apartment building as Jim Farrell.[14] It is possible that Jim knew Catherine Farrell Greene and was instrumental in introducing Edward to her daughter Katharine. Though I have not definitely established a kinship relationship between these two Farrell families, both Farrells were from County Longford, Ireland. Edward married Katharine T. Greene on September 28, 1904, in Manhattan.[15] Edward's brother John Doheny and Katharine's sister Helen Greene were their witnesses. (At the time of their marriage, Edward was living with his brother John and sister Maria at 252 W 20th St, Manhattan.)

Before the wedding, Katharine lived at 287 Prospect Park West, Brooklyn with her mother, her brother Francis, and her sister Helen. The ceremony was not in the bride's Brooklyn parish, which seems a little unusual. It took place at St. Francis Xavier Church, W 16th St, downtown Manhattan (perhaps for the convenience of the Doheny family, who all lived in Manhattan?). The couple's first child, Catharine, was born seven months after the wedding, but sadly only lived one day. Was Katharine pregnant at the time of their marriage, or was their baby born prematurely? In any case, the couple endured their first deep sorrow. Two more of their children died young: Thomas at two months and Gerard at age 23.[16]

Children were born in quick succession: Edward Jr in 1907, Thomas in 1908, Francis in 1909, Gerard in 1910, Larry in 1912, and Bernard in 1913.

---

[14] 1905 Manhattan City Directory. Addresses would have been collected sometime during the prior year.

[15] Marriage Certificate (civil) for Edward J. Doheny and Katharine T. Greene.

[16] Calvary Cemetery records, Section 32, Range 6, Plot T, Grave 6. Edward bought the grave for Catharine, age 1 day, who was buried on 10 April 1905. Other internments in this grave are Thomas J Doheny (2 mos.), buried 23 Oct 1908, Katharine Doheny (54), buried 15 May 1933, Gerald Doheny (22), buried 5 Jan 1934, and Edward J Doheny II (65), buried 28 Aug 1972.

Bernard is the child that Katharine is holding in the photo at left, so the date is 1914.

Bernard always said his mother was a nurse. (I found a photo of a 1910 nurse's uniform that looks identical to the cap and apron our grandmother is wearing, but on civil records Katharine is described as houseworker.)[17]

Katharine with Francis, Gerard, Larry, and Ed. Perhaps the day is Ed's First Communion at age 7 in 1914. Location is uncertain.

The family life of Edward Doheny and his wife Katharine Greene can be described as tragic in many ways. The two never attained a stable family life. Fewer than ten years into their marriage, Edward left, or was asked to leave, the household. My father was about 2 years old when the family broke up, which mirrors Edward Sr's own experience of being left without a father as a 2-year-old.

My sister Elizabeth said, "I can imagine there was discord in the house due to his drinking. He was kicked out regularly but it seemed that Katharine would take him back fairly regularly, with the result being many children. The story that I remember is that Aunt Helen especially did not like our grandfather Edward."

Katharine did her best as a single mother. Her sister Helen and brother Frank Greene were living with her, perhaps to help raise the children.[18] (I imagine Helen being a difficult person to have in the house. She lived with my own family while I was in high school, and she tended to be strict and bossy around my mother and us girls.)

Katharine's mental health began to deteriorate, maybe after having so many children with no husband at home, and having adult siblings sometimes interfering. Madeline Hendrickson told me that Katharine's son Francis (who was Madeline's common law spouse) told her this story: "He and his mother were travelling on the subway when she became ill – disoriented – mentally ill. He was

---

[17] Kings Park Register of Deaths says "houseworker." 1915 NY State Census, June 1, Kings County, AD 16, Ward 24, ED 60, p15, says "housework." 1920 US Census, Kings County, S.D.3, ED 710, Sheet 18A says "housewife."
[18] 1915 NY State Census, June 1, Kings County, AD 16, Ward 24, ED 60, p15. Katharine is enumerated with her five boys, her brother Francis, and her sister Helen at 647 19th St, Brooklyn. Edward is not enumerated with the family. He was probably living with his brother Richard's family at 243 E39th St., Manhattan. Both Edward and Richard are at that address in a 1917 Manhattan Directory.

about 11 or 12, I think.[19] I can imagine what a trauma that must have been for a frightened insecure child. He mentioned how he and his brothers were placed in a Staten Island orphanage – how his mother was placed in Kings Park Hospital and eventually died there. He never spoke much of his father."[20]

Katharine spent 7 years, 5 months, and 15 days in Kings Park Hospital before she died on 12 May 1933.[21] That calculates to an admittance date of 28 Nov 1925. There may have been an earlier stay, too, because she was enumerated at Kings Park Hospital on 1 June 1925 in the NY State census.[22] Hospital records say that she died of pulmonary tuberculosis. The hospital's information administrator could not locate her psychiatric records for me.[23]

Katharine's obituary in the Brooklyn Daily Eagle:

> DOHENY—KATHARINE T. DO-HENY (nee Greene), on May 12, 1933. Funeral from home of her sister, Miss Helen V. Greene, 530 2d St., Brooklyn, Monday, May 15; mass of requiem 10 a.m. at St. Francis Xavier Church. Interment Calvary Cemetery.

Bernard apparently was never told that his mother was sent to a state psychiatric hospital. Maybe the adults just told him she had died because they thought he wouldn't understand, and they didn't expect her to get better. In any case, he never saw his mother again and didn't know she lived until 1933. (I uncovered her date of death long after Bernard himself had died.)

When Katharine couldn't take care of her children, her oldest son ran away from home, and then the rest of them were sent to an orphanage, Mount St. Michael's Home on Staten Island. The Home was staffed by the New York Congregation of the Sisters of Mercy.[24] About 370 boys and girls between the ages of 3 and 15 were in the care of these sisters.[25]

---

[19] Francis was born 7 Nov 1909, according to his birth certificate, so this event may have been around 1920.

[20] Letter from Madeline Hendrickson to the author dated 15 Apr 1999.

[21] Verified Transcript of Register of Deaths at Kings Park State Hospital.

[22] Katharine is enumerated in the 1920 census at home with all of her children on 1 Jan 1920, so her hospitalization began after 1920 and before Jan 1925. Bernard was 7 in Oct 1920.

[23] Letter to the author from Deborah Strube, Health Information Management Administrator, Pilgrim Psychiatric Center. Ms. Strube said she had made a thorough search for Katharine's psychiatric records, but she found none.

[24] There are photos of the Sisters of Mercy on the Facebook page of St-MikesKidz.Community. My father never mentioned that the habit I wore as a Brooklyn Sister of Mercy reminded him of the ones worn by the sisters who staffed the orphanage.

[25] 1925 NY State Census, AD 2, ED 31, Richmond County, Ward 5, pages 11-19, lists the names of all the children in the orphanage.

Mount St. Michael's Home
1380 Arthur Kill Rd.
Staten Island, NY

Photo from NY Public
Library collection.

The home closed in 1978.

Bernard related that he and his brothers hated the orphanage, and they ran away from Mount St. Michael's many times.[26] My sister Elizabeth said, "I remember Daddy telling us a story that he tried to run away every day - he only made it to the back field before they caught him - until they either stopped chasing him or didn't catch him. He was in there with Uncle Larry and Gerard. He said they served rice three times a day in every kind of way... especially rice pudding!" My sister Anne says that, to this day, she won't eat rice pudding or bread pudding because of this story.

In 1925, all the boys except Edward Jr are enumerated with their father in Manhattan in the same building as Aunt Annie and Uncle Jim, who were probably their actual caregivers; Bernard said he lived with various aunts and uncles after they ran away from the Home, and the Home wouldn't take them back. They are not enumerated at Mount St. Michaels in the 1925 state census.

It is interesting to note that the Dohenys had a long history of taking in needy relatives. Edward lived with his sister Annie before they were both married. In 1920, as his marriage was breaking up, Edward moved in with his brother Richard, his wife Katie, and their daughter Anna Josephine. There is also an orphaned niece Elizabeth living there. Elizabeth's real name was Annie Elizabeth, and to distinguish her from Richard and Katie's daughter Anna, they called Annie Elizabeth by her middle name. Annie Elizabeth was the daughter of Patrick Doheny and Bridget Corcoran who had both died before 1920. Earlier, Patrick had himself been taken in by an older brother Timothy. Maria took in her unmarried brother John plus two orphaned children of Timothy named William and Anna Margaret. In the 1930s and 1940s, Edward lived with his sister Maria and her husband Jim Barry in the Bronx. He also lived with Katie, Richard's widow, again. Near the end of his life, Edward lived with Jim Farrell near Inwood Park in upper Manhattan. Aunt Helen Greene lived with Bernard's family in the 1960s.[27]

Anne Murphy Heidel wrote this about her Granduncle Edward:

---

[26] Taped interview of Bernard Doheny by the author on 30 June 1988.
[27] Various census reports, city directories, and death certificates document this willingness to "take in" relatives.

"Uncle Eddie lived with us for a period of time in the 1940s. I remember him well. His boys came occasionally. Sometimes they were upsetting visits for my mom, my sister Cathleen, and me. When we talked about those days, we thought that the relationship between father and sons was ambivalent. Probably for good reason. At any rate, I was frequently his companion on trips around town, and I was fond of him. He had beautiful white hair, and I remember that he dressed up in a suit and tie to go to the store! He suffered the curse of the Irish - the damn bottle. Because of it he left our home." [28]

Edward's grandniece Cathleen Murphy McBride wrote:

"Uncle Eddie definitely was his own person and a man of style. My father (James Murphy) earned his living working as a truck driver and later operated a crane in the yard, and he dressed and behaved accordingly. Uncle Eddie usually wore a dress suit and vest in the house and a jacket when the occasion demanded. As a kid, the difference was noticed by me with curiosity. He used to tell me about his work with the insurance company and how they paid for him to spend time at a sanitorium for TB. He was proud of that care as if it were a real treasure he secured, as indeed it was. His artistic talents came to the fore there with all the lovely craft projects he made: the beaded hotplates and a willow framed tray with butterflies and flowers made of dried flowers and feathers, it seems to me.

"I often wondered if my grandfather Richard was like him, though I think he didn't look like him. It's hard to know; I only saw photos of him when he was young, but I knew Uncle Eddie for 18 years in his old age. Once he got a check from the IRS, his tax return, for one dollar. He was so tickled, he framed it. He could look so fierce to a little girl because he was heavy and had a deep voice. But then he had this pug-ish smile, which he shared now and then, and it spoke of a merry heart. He was very devoted to my mother, and she to him.

"He lived with us, for about a year, a good while after my grandmother Katie had died, and her back bedroom was empty. Arrangements and reasons for them were never discussed with children in those days, so I don't know why he needed a place. I had the sense that he missed the city in our place in Flushing. He was an urbane gentleman!"

Sometime between 1944 and 1950, Edward contracted tuberculosis, and spent a year or so in a rest home in Plainview, according to Bernard's wife Grace. The institution was called The Nassau County Sanitarium.[29] There was a large staff at the institution, and someone offered classes in beading. Edward made beaded glass hot pads for some relatives. He gave us one, and my mother used it all the time. (Whenever it needed repair, I restrung it.) Anne Murphy Heidel said, "I have a

---

[28] Letter from Anne Murphy Heidel to the author, 10 Jan 1999.

[29] The Sanitarium (var. Sanatorium) at 1535 Old Country Road was situated within the angle formed by Round Swamp Rd and Old Country Road, Plainview. https://en.wikipedia.org/wiki/Old_Bethpage,_New_York says it was built in the early 1930s. The large complex of Georgian style buildings was used as a TB ward until the 1960s. In 1976, it became a drug and alcohol rehabilitation center and housed a branch of the Cornell Cooperative Extension. In 1999, Charles Wang of the New York Islanders bought the property.

tray that Edward made when he was at the TB recuperation home in the country. After Edward recovered from TB, he went back to live in Inwood with his sister Annie and Jim Farrell.

Edward Doheny died at age 78 on April 5, 1953 after a short stay at a rather good nursing home run by the Little Sisters of the Poor in Manhattan.[30] He was the last of his generation to survive. He is buried in Calvary Cemetery, Woodside NY.[31] The cause of death is not on his death certificate, but he likely died of a heart attack, the cause of death of several of his children.

Neither Edward nor Katharine lived to see the successes that their sons achieved, in spite of all they had gone through as children – Edward Jr. in business, Francis as a New York State Assembly-man, Larry as a proud deli owner, and Bernard providing a home in the suburbs for four daughters.
The brothers were all very intelligent people; they loved to read, and could engage in discussions about almost anything.

Cathleen Murphy McBride shared this personal memory: "Uncle Eddie sometimes worked as a waiter for the Players Club in Manhattan where all the big male actors came to refresh themselves before and especially after a show. I think he took on some of their airs from the contact! He spoke of John Barrymore as if they had gone to different schools together, as they used to say." [32]

Grace Doheny was very fond of her father-in-law, and visited him many times before and after she was married. She had only good things to say about him. I met my grandfather just once, probably when he was in the nursing home. The room was very small and dark, and Edward was propped up in a comfortable chair with a lap blanket around him. The impression that stayed with me was of a man who had suffered, but who had been able to keep his warm smile and kind eyes.

Edward accumulated a remarkably large number of addresses in his life.

Date	Address	Source
1874	Graigue, Ireland	Edward's Baptismal record
1895-07-11	158 Clinton St, Manhattan	Edward's Application for US Citizenship
1900-06-26	109 W 60th St, Manhattan	Edward's Naturalization Certificate and 1900 US Census. Edward is living with Richard and Katie.
1904-07	101 9th Ave.	1905 Manhattan City Directory (Same address as Jim Farrell.)

[30] Certificate of Death for Edward Doheny, Dept of Health & Vital Records, New York, NY.
[31] Calvary Cemetery Records, Sect 23, Range 14, Plot D, Grave 20, right next to Richard and Katie.
[32] E-mail from Cathleen Murphy McBride to the author, 11 July 2000.

1904-09-28	252 W 20th St, Manhattan	Edward and Katharine's Marriage Certificate and 1905 NYS Census. Edward is enumerated with his siblings Maria and John. Katharine is not with them, and she is not enumerated at her mother's house in Brooklyn.
1909-11-07	236 E 21st St, Manhattan	Francis's birth Certificate
1910-04-27	287 9th Ave (Prospect Park West), Brooklyn	1910 US Census. Edward, with his wife Katharine, their sons Edward Jr, Francis, plus Francis Greene and Helen Greene. This was Katharine's mother's residence. She had died in 1909.
1912-02-27	653 19th Street, Brooklyn	Lawrence's birth certificate
1913-10-11	523 6th Ave, Brooklyn	Bernard's birth certificate
1915-06-01	647 19th Street, Brooklyn	1915 NYS Census. Edward is not living with his family, but Katharine, her five boys, plus Francis and Helen Greene are living here. Edward may be living with his brother Richard. Edward, Richard and Katie weren't found in the 1915 census.
1916 to 1920	243 E 39th St., Manhattan	1917 and 1918 Manhattan City Directories. Edward, clerk, at same address as his brother Richard, porter. Also Edward's 1918 WWI draft registration card and the 1920 US Census
1920-01-10	243 E 39th St., Manhattan	1920 US Census. Edward is living with his brother Richard's family. His wife Katharine, five boys, and Helen Greene are living at 220 Greenwood Ave., Brooklyn
1924 to 1931	101 9th Ave, Manhattan. (His apartment was at the same address as Uncle Jim and Aunt Annie.)	1924 Manhattan Voter List, 1925 NYS Census, 1930 US Census, and 1931 Manhattan Voter List. In 1925, four sons are enumerated with him. His wife Katharine is in Kings Park State Hospital, Smithtown, LI, and his oldest son Ed Jr seems to be on his own. According to the 1930 census, Edward is living alone in his apartment. It cost him $15 a month; he did not have a radio. Gerard 19 and Bernard 16 were living in a boarding house at 138 Ft Greene Place, Brooklyn, and both were working as messengers for Western Union. Their cousin Anne, daughter of Richard & Katie, had gotten them a job. Francis, 20, was in the Navy living at 79th St., Brooklyn. Lawrence and Edward Jr addresses are unknown.
1935 to 1940-04-01	2653 Decatur Ave, Bronx	1940 US Census. Edward is living with his widowed sister Maria Barry (Jim did 1939) and in the Bronx since 1935.
1945-03-10	2763 Marion Ave, Bronx	Death Certificate for Maria Barry. Edward was still living with Maria Barry at the time of her death. He is the informant on her death certificate.

Late 1940s	Plainview, NY	Edward contracted tuberculosis and spent a year or so at a rest home called The Nassau County Sanitarium, Plainview, Long Island.
1952-06-29	603 Isham St., Manhattan	After Maria died in 1945, Edward moved in with his sister Annie and Jim Farrell. Annie died in 1952. The address 603 Isham St. is on Edward's 1953 death certificate as his usual place of residence.
1953-04-05	Little Sisters of the Poor Nursing Home, Manhattan	Edward's Death Certificate. The informant for his death certificate was his son Francis of 603 Isham St, so Francis also lived with Aunt Annie and Uncle Jim at this time.

Manhattan
Residences
1895-1935

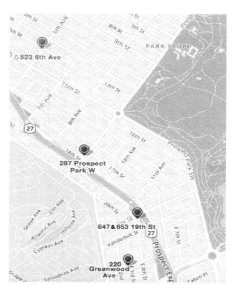

Brooklyn Residences 1910-1915

Inwood and The Bronx 1935-1953

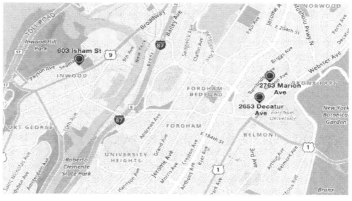

Chapter Six

Edward J. DOHENY II
(1907 – 1972)
Catherine Idola TALBOTT
(1910 – 1976)

Edward J. Doheny II was warmly welcomed into the world by his parents Edward and Katharine Greene Doheny on the fair day of 10 May 1907.[1]

<table>
<tr><td>1 William Doheny (ca.1837 – 1877)</td></tr>
<tr><td> +Anne Scully (ca.1838 – 1893)</td></tr>
<tr><td>..... 2 Edward Joseph Doheny I (1874-1953)</td></tr>
<tr><td>..... +Katharine Theresa Greene (1878-1933), m. Sep 1904</td></tr>
<tr><td>......... 3 Edward Joseph Doheny II (1907-1972)</td></tr>
<tr><td>........ +Catherine Idola Talbott (1910-1976), m: Jul 1939</td></tr>
<tr><td>.............. 4 Edward Joseph Doheny III (1942-2016)</td></tr>
<tr><td>.............. 4 Richard J Doheny (1945-2013)</td></tr>
</table>

He was born during the week of a major longshore-men strike along the waterfront in Manhattan and Brooklyn that everyone in the city was talking about. 10,000 longshoremen had walked off the job, emotions were running high, and ordinary people wondered how it would end. A couple of days before Edward was born, the longshoremen were tipped off that shipping agents were recruiting workmen from the Italian quarter of Brooklyn as strikebreakers. As a result, about 500 longshoremen plus their sympathizers from the neighborhood Brooklyn sugar refineries rioted along Metropolitan Ave just the day before Edward was born. They attacked 300 Italian strikebreakers, and seriously wounded some of them. Elsewhere, in Manhattan, there were smaller outbreaks.[2] People were just hoping their neighborhoods wouldn't have any rioting. Edward and Katharine were living at 236 E 21st St, Manhattan at the time, not that far from all the action.

Edward was actually Katharine's second child. The first baby, a girl named Catherine, lived only one day, so the healthy little baby Edward was a great joy to the young couple.

For 15 months, Edward was the center of everyone's attention. Then he had a little brother named Thomas. Thomas was born in August 1908 but only survived until October. Edward was too young to understand, but his parents were deeply affected by losing two babies in three years. Knowing how much kin try to reach out to one another during times of loss, I imagine the Dohenys and Greenes of Manhattan and Brooklyn did what they could to console the young parents.

---

[1] The New York Times, 10 May 1907, Weather report: "Fair to-day, cooler to-morrow; fresh west to northwest winds."
[2] The New York Times, 9 May 1907, "Strikers Riot on Water Front, Bricks Rain off Roofs", page 1.

Edward   Gerard
Francis   Bernard   Lawrence

When little Edward was about three, the family moved to Brooklyn. Edward would have four more brothers.

Edward, as the eldest, was the first to recognize all the trouble his father was causing because of alcohol abuse. His family became unstable when he was about eight years old; his father was in and out of their home, and then his mother Katharine became mentally ill when he was about 13.

This affected his schoolwork, and Edward dropped out of school after grade 10;[3] he even ran away from home (according to a story my father Bernard told me). It is unknown where he went or how he supported himself at that time, but his siblings were sent to an orphanage on Staten Island. I imagine Edward felt very lonely.

In spite of all that, Edward grew up, secured a good job, and led a relatively successful life.

Edward met Catherine Idola Talbott, and they married on 1 Jul 1939. He worked as a clerk in a publishing house. Idola, as we always knew her, worked as a clerk in a brokerage. They lived in a nice apartment building at 1026 President Street, Brooklyn,[4] just a block away from the entrance to the Brooklyn Botanic Garden.

Ed and Idola had two boys: Edward III who was born in Jan 1942, and Richard who was born in Mar 1945.

Idola was prone to depression when her children were young. In 1949, she was hospitalized briefly, and my father told my mother that we were going to take care of Idola and her boys so Edward could go to work and not lose his job. My mother was tasked with nursing Idola back to health. This was when we lived in the Quonset Huts in Canarsie, Brooklyn. The Quonset Huts were erected in several USA cities to provide temporary housing for returning veterans of World War II.

---

[3] 1940 US Census, Brooklyn, NY, SD 5, AD 11, ED 24-1311, Sheet 4B. Edward and Idola both said they had completed two years of HS.
[4] Ibid.

The steel Quonset huts were about 20 ft wide, 50 ft long, and 9 ft high. Each was supposed to house a family of no more than four until the family had enough money to find better housing. We already had a family of four, and now added Idola and her two boys. We lived in very tight quarters during this time in our lives!

Edward and Idola drank a lot. It is interesting to note that their sons Edward and Richard swore they would never drink alcohol, or at least never get drunk. I believe they kept this promise for their whole lives.

Edward II died of a heart attack on 23 Aug 1972 in Brooklyn. His Social Security death benefit was not collected until May 1976, the same month that Idola died.[5] Maybe the family collected both benefits at the same time.

The Children of Ed and Idola

Edward J Doheny III was born in Brooklyn in 1942. He served three years with the U.S. Army with part of this time spent in Viet Nam. Edward married Helen Steil a very loving and talented woman in 1982 in St. Therese Church, Aurora, IL, and they had two sons. Their sons now have sons, so the Doheny name goes on through them.

Edward wrote to me about his profession:

"I am a Certified Hazardous Materials Manager (CHMM) and a member of the Academy of Certified Hazardous Materials Managers (ACHMM). The Academy promotes responsible management of hazardous material by industry, academia and governmental agencies / department.

"A CHMM must be knowledgeable in the Federal regulations governing the environment, transportation, storage, safe use and disposal of all the hazardous materials that make our modern society possible.

"To become a CHMM, a person must have a degree in hard science or in an environmental program from a recognized college or university. My degree was in chemistry. The person must also have worked in a safety, health, transportation or environmental position for at least three years (or without a degree, at least 11 years). Then that person may apply to take a four-hour test on all aspects for Federal regulations impacting hazardous material management, science related to waste remediation/destruction, and ethics. A passing grade is required for each part. Fail one part, you have failed the entire test. The latest data from the Academy indicates about 1 in 3 who take the test fail.

---

[5] Social Security Index, available on Ancestry.com

"Once you pass the test and are accepted for membership, every year you must attend at least 20 hours of continuing education in the CHMM areas of responsibility. Also, a CHMM must be recertified every five years (i.e., prove you are fulfilling all of the requirements of a CHMM). "When a CHMM retires, that person is fully qualified for life in a monastery!"

Edward III was retired from Brenntag Pacific in Portland, Oregon. He died of Parkinson's Disease on 21 Apr 2016 in Vancouver, Washington.[6]

Edward II with Edward III

Oct 11, 1942

Francis Doheny with Edward Doheny

Edward III with his mother

Front: Francis Doheny, Edward III, Frank Greene, Idola
Rear: Ally (Friend of Helen Greene), Bernard Doheny,
Mary (friend of Helen Greene), Grace Vogelbach

Edward III in May 1943

[6] Obituary for Edward J Doheny III, https://www.hamiltonmylan.com/obituary/3678752

Ed and Idola's second son was named Richard. He was born in Mar 1945 in Brooklyn.

Richard married in 1969.[7] He had two girls and a boy with his first wife.

Richard worked in the IT department of Montefiore Hospital in the Bronx for many years, and that was where he met his second wife. They had a little girl. Richard died of a heart attack on 19 Apr 2013 in Ardsley, Westchester County, New York;[8] his daughter was about two years old.

Richard also fathered a son before he was married. I "met" his son through AncestryDNA. This man is a college professor of computer science, and I told him his father was a college graduate and had worked in a technical field. He would have been very proud if he had known this man was a technology professional, too.

Richard was interested in family history, and he visited Ireland in 2000 to do some research. He spoke with the parish priest of Gortnahoe, V. Rev. John J. O'Rourke, who gave him a tour of the church and the graveyard. He pointed Richard in the direction of the farm where our Doheny ancestors once lived, and Richard spoke with one of the descendants of the Doheny family who had inherited the property. This person was Father Richard Doheny's brother John.

The story has come full circle.

---

[7] New York, NY, Marriage License Indexes, 1907-1995, License #12182. Index is available on Amazon.com.
[8] http://www.tributes.com/obituary/show/Richard-J.-Doheny-95733113

Chapter Seven

Francis W. DOHENY (1909-1973)

1 William Doheny (ca.1837 – 1877)
 +Anne Scully (ca.1838 – 1893)
..... 2 Edward Joseph Doheny I (1874-1953)
..... +Katharine Theresa Greene (1878-1933), m. Sep 1904
.... 3 **Francis W. Doheny** (1909-1973)

My Uncle Frank loved to argue! Not surprising, since he was an attorney and a New York State Assembly-man.

He was the most intellectual of Edward J Doheny's five sons. Frank went to Regis HS in Manhattan on scholarship, joined the Navy and became an officer, went to Columbia University on the G.I. Bill, earned a law degree, was a politician for a while, studied the piano as an adult, took up birding as a serious hobby, and even taught in an inner-city elementary school.

My earliest memories of Uncle Frank were of him babysitting for us. I was 6 or 7 at the time; he was in his early 40s. He had decided to take piano lessons as an adult, and he entertained his three little nieces on our old upright piano. He may have been instrumental in us getting the piano. My sister Anne would one day become a very proficient pianist; her early practicing was on that piano.

Frank and my Uncle Bob Chess (not really an uncle, but our closest family friend) got along really well. It was a lot of fun to hear them discuss politics. They were both staunch liberal-Democrats and were highly informed about current events. They could feed off each other, and their discussions were by turns very serious and very hilarious. My parents always voted Republican, and they tended to be more conservative than either Frank or Bob. My father could hold his own in the discussions, but my mother got very upset when the arguments became heated. She withdrew, usually to the kitchen. As a teenager preparing to enter the convent, I could hold my own, too, in an argument with him about religion. He encouraged me to argue with him, which I think helped to develop my critical thinking skills.

During most of his adult life, Frank considered himself an atheist, or at least an agnostic. But he had a conversion near the end of his life. He and his partner Madeline Hendrickson visited Brazil around 1971. Madeline's sister was a Carmelite nun in Brazil. Frank met the Carmelite monastery's chaplain, and they got into deep discussions about religion and life. The chaplain asked him to read "The Hound of Heaven" by the English poet Francis Thompson. All of Frank's angst seemed to be reflected in that poem.

> I fled Him, down the nights and down the days;
> I fled Him, down the arches of the years;
> I fled Him, down the labyrinthine ways
> Of my own mind; and in the midst of tears
> I hid from Him, and under running laughter.
> …
> Ah, fondest, blindest, weakest,
> I am He Whom thou seekest!
> Thou dravest love from thee, who dravest Me.

The last line means, "You drove love away from yourself because you have driven my love away from you." Frank said this poem brought him back to the Catholic Church.

Frank never married, but he did have at least three long-term relationships with intelligent, kind women who were his match in many ways. He only lived with the last of these women, Madeline Hendrickson, whom we considered our aunt. Madeline was born on 10 Mar 1919 in the Bronx. The story Frank told was that the rules governing Social Security at the time would mean a great reduction in their income if they became legally married. Everyone in my family recognized them as husband and wife, a common law marriage, if you will. Even though I remember Uncle Frank describing their relationship as platonic, none of us really believed that. At Madeline's home in Northport, Uncle Frank had his own room upstairs. I saw his room once, and he kept it very neat and tidy.

Frank and Madeline visited Ireland, and they travelled to Gortnahoe, Thurles, and Cashel, where they found some Doheny cousins. Here is what Madeline wrote to me on 15 Apr 1999:

Dear Catherine,

On our trip to Ireland we stayed at Cashel in Tipperary. Then drove north to Thurles. There was another town I can't remember & can't find on my map. I would recognize it if I saw the name. It wasn't Urlingford. We drove out from Thurles - there were no street names - except rarely and then in Gaelic. We stopped at a small group of homes at a crossroads - went into a house with a sign in the window advertising "Tea." Frank asked about his family from a lovely 16 year old waitress - she was related to him!

She came with us and directed us to the "house on the hill." I think they called it "the priest's house." The priest's parents lived there in an earth-floored kitchen with a blazing fireplace. The rest of the large house was unused. Their son was the priest who lived in America. (Father Richard Doheny) He was at the races - home on vacation. Later that evening he came with a friend to visit us at the "Bishop's house," then an inn in Cashel. He worked at an orphanage in California. I can't remember his name or the city he lives in. But he was handsome and charming and Frank's cousin.

The young girl then took us to another home not too far off. A small farm. The house looked about the size of a double garage - concrete. The lady of the house was about our age and there was also a very garrulous aged woman so thrilled to meet people from America she couldn't stop talking. She was in bed. I do remember how hospitable they were - laid out the best they had for us. Wish I could remember the young girl's name. I remember how I wished we could have taken her back to the USA with us. She was so beautiful and so shy. The area seemed very poor. These were also relatives.

You know they pronounce the name DAH-heny.

About Frank's papers -- Anything he had I gave to Bob Ferrari. I didn't examine them – I thought they were mostly financial records. There were no photos. (I contacted Bob Farrari, but he said he no longer had any of Frank's papers.)

Frank's childhood was very painful for him, so I never pried into it. He mentioned how he and his mother were traveling on the subway when she became ill -- disoriented -- mentally ill. He was about 11 or 12, I think. I can imagine what trauma that must be for a frightened, insecure child. He mentioned how he and his brothers were placed in a Staten Island orphanage. How his mother was placed in Kings Park State Hospital and eventually died there. He never spoke much of his father.

He said you are all related to the wealthy Doheny's of California. There is a Doheny Blvd. named after him - in Los Angeles, I think. He said he once had to deliver a message to this VIP Doheny. He handed it over to him but his reception was cool at the least. I don't know if he knew the contents of the message.

Frank went to Regis HS and had a scholarship to Fordham - it paid only tuition. He needed fare money for travel from Brooklyn and money for food and lodging. He became discouraged and quit. Took jobs as vacuum cleaner salesman, etc., etc. - rode a freight south - was starving. He said a black man shared some collard greens with him - how good they tasted. In desperation, he joined the Navy. When he retired (as a Chief Pharmacist's Mate) he went to Columbia University on the G.I. Bill and then Columbia Law School.

He said many times he had considered suicide. Your father always seemed so serene and well adjusted, yet they suffered the same hardships.

Frank was a most remarkable man.

I went bird watching with Frank and Madeline when I was in my mid-twenties. I was still in the convent, and had no money, so they very generously treated me to the entire long weekend. It was held at Gurney's Inn, on the south fork of Long Island. I remember the food was delicious, and much fancier than any other food I had ever eaten. Out of respect for me being a religious, Madeline, her friend Marian, and I stayed in one room, and Frank and Marian's boyfriend were in another room.

It was quite a challenging weekend. We visited the Walking Dunes and had guided tours of many other great birding sites on the east end of the island, all led by naturalists. The weekend taught me that birdwatching meant far more than trying to identify as many species of birds as possible. It was really all about ecology and the environment. The naturalists we met were constantly pointing out the beauty of the "web of life" in every ecosystem we visited. It was the first time I heard people talk about the over-population of deer on Long Island, and how disease was spreading among deer and other animals including humans as a result. Actually, it was the first time I heard humans described as an animal species.

I learned some very good outdoor habits: wear a sun hat, stay hydrated, tuck your pants legs into your socks, and, of course, carry your binoculars everywhere. You can probably see that my weekend with Frank and Madeline was a highly significant one in my life. I got to know Frank and Madeline much better, and I got to know more about life in general.

As an aside, I'll mention that Frank had prostate problems, and we had to give him cover many times during the bird walks so he could go behind a bush.

I stayed close to Madeline for the rest of her life. Here is a photo of us in 1990. Madeline died on 12 Jul 2006 in Northport, Suffolk County, NY.

There is a brief biography on the back of Frank's 1955 campaign photo.

★ **VOTE FOR** ★
FRANCIS W.
DOHENY

FOR ASSEMBLYMAN
THIRD ASSEMBLY DISTRICT
New York County

Liberal Party Candidate
★ **DEMOCRATIC PARTY CANDIDATE** ★

Endorsed by: A.F.L.-C.I.O. Labor Organizations; West Side Veterans Groups; West Side Civic, Fraternal and Social Organizations.

Preferred by Citizens' Union

EDUCATION

Regis High School; Fordham University; Columbia University; Columbia Law School.

BACKGROUND

Born and raised in Manhattan; Veteran, World War II as Chief Warrant Officer, U. S. Navy.

Practicing Attorney in New York; Member of New York State and Federal Bars.

Former Research Counsel to Democratic Leader of New York State Assembly.

VOTE FOR

FRANCIS W. DOHENY
★ **ASSEMBLYMAN** ★

Frank is on the right in this photo. (Seated is Governor Averell Harriman, Governor of New York State from 1955 to 1958. After Harriman's defeat by Nelson Rockefeller in the 1958 election, Harriman, as a core member of the group of foreign policy elders known as "The Wise Men," helped negotiate the "Partial Nuclear Test Ban Treaty" during JFK's administration.)

Francis was born on 7 Nov 1909 in Manhattan. Soon after that, the family moved to Brooklyn and his younger brothers Gerard, Lawrence and Bernard were born in quick succession. Francis's early life was greatly affected by his father's drinking and his mother's poor mental health. He was sent to an orphanage on Staten Island with his three younger brothers, and after they ran away too many times, and the orphanage wouldn't take them back, the boys lived with various aunts.

Francis sharp mind and intelligence helped him weather the poor conditions of his early childhood, and, while he lived with relatives, his brilliance enabled him to attend and graduate from Regis High School in Manhattan, an elite Catholic institution on the upper East Side, run by the Jesuits. The school even now offers tuition-free education to gifted Catholic boys who could not otherwise afford to attend a Catholic High School. The *Huffington Post*, 23 Jan 2014, said Regis High School is consistently ranked in the top five high schools in the nation in regard to SAT/ACT scores. Enrollment is limited to about 135 male students.

At left is a photo of Frank in the Navy, dated 21 Mar 1944. He retired from the Navy in 1948. At right is a photo of Frank's graduation from Columbia Law School in 1953.

From 1956 to 1962, Francis practiced law; he was a member of the New York State and Federal Bars. He was elected to the New York State Assembly from the Third District of Manhattan, and he served as Research Counsel to the Democratic Leader of the State Assembly. Frank lived at 813 9th Ave, near the corner of W 54th St., in an area of the city known as Hell's Kitchen.

Here is Frank shaking hands with President John F Kennedy. The photo is dated 12 Oct 1960.

Frank was a man of the highest ethical standards, and he had a strong commitment to the poor of New York. That is why he entered politics. He told me that service to the party machine got in the way of serving the people of New York and his district, and he became disillusioned about politics. He didn't continue to run for office and, instead, decided to become an elementary school teacher to work directly on behalf of poor children. He taught for a few years in PS 20 in the Lower East Side. This school is now called the Anna Silver School which "has a strong commitment to the arts, sparkling facilities, and dual language programs in both Mandarin-English and Spanish-English," according to this website: https://insideschools.org/school/01/01M020.

Frank only lived to be 63. He died of a heart attack on 16 Aug 1973 in the Veterans Administration Hospital, Northport, Suffolk County, New York. He is buried in Long Island National Cemetery in East Farmingdale, Suffolk County, New York, section 2R, grave 5919.

Frank's obituary in the New York Times:

FRANCIS W. DOHENY, EX-ASSEMBLYMAN, 63

Special to The New York Times

NORTHPORT, L. I. Aug. 17— Former Assemblyman Francis W. Doheny, who also had been a Navy man, a lawyer and a teacher, died yesterday in the Veterans Administration Hospital here. He was 63 years old and lived at 47 Northwest Drive.

Mr. Doheny, a Democrat, represented the Third Assembly District of New York City's West Side from 1958 to 1962. Earlier he was research counsel to the minority leader of the State Senate.

He was born in Brooklyn and served 20 years in the Navy, retiring as a chief warrant officer in 1948.

After leaving the Navy, he earned a B.S. degree in 1951 from Columbia University and a law degree in 1953. He practiced law in Manhattan from 1955 to 1962, when he became a teacher at Public School 20 on the lower East Side. He retired three years ago.

Surviving are two brothers, Bernard and Lawrence.

The New York Times

Chapter Eight

Gerard J. Doheny (1910-1933)

When my father died, we discovered a news clipping in his wallet about his brother Gerard's death. He had kept the clipping in his wallet since 1934. It is from *The Brooklyn Daily Eagle*, 4 Jan 1934, and appeared on the front page and was continued on page 2.

Search for Atlantis Ends in Boy's Death

Four Adventurers, One a Brooklynite, Who Tried 'to Regenerate' Themselves Off the Florida Coast Didn't Reckon With Malaria

The body of young Gerard Doheny of 11 W. 103d St., Manhattan, was brought back to New York today, from Florida, marking the tragic conclusion of a once rose-colored expedition in the interest of "human regeneratoin through biologic living."

Four hopeful adventurers had set out on the expedition on Nov. 11 last. Besides Doheny they were Irving Rosenzweig, 24, of 529 McDonald Ave.; Victor F. Peterson of Moline, Ill., and "Captain" John L. Mott, formerly of 111-25 Jamaica Ave., Richmond Hill.

Naturopathic Idea

They set out with not much money but high hopes and some fantastic ideas. Chief among their stock of ideas was a sort of "naturopathic" one that living the simple life and eating no meat, eggs, milk or vegetable would "regenerate" men, causing them to live for hundreds of years. Their plan was to find a comfortable little tropical island somewhere off the south of Florida and live the simple life there.

In addition, according to a dispatch today from Tampa, Fla., "Captain" Mott told the police there that they were planning to locate the lost Atlantis—fabled continent which sank in the Atlantic millenniums ago—and set up a col-

Continued on Page 2

Quest for 'Life' Fatal to Boy

Continued from Page 1

ony of devotees of thet simple life there.

But the whole thing went astray. They got as far as Old Town, Fla., then Cross City and finally Tampa. On Dec. 27 the four were found in a Tampa rooming house, Doheny and Petersen suffering from malaria, weak from lack of sustaining food. They were rushed to a hospital, and Doheny died there on Dec. 31. Rosenzweig, threatened with malaria, forsook his "simple life" tenets sufficiently to take some quinine.

At the Rosenzweig home in Brooklyn members of his family pooh-poohed the Atlantis portion of the account from Miami, but they said that Irving had for years been interested in "biological living." A brother, Abraham, said that the expedition was an outgrowth of a "healthy camp" at Flanders, N. J., directed by a Dr. Walter Siegmeister, who propounded the theories of simple living by eating only fruits and refraining from love or haircuts.

The Doheny Boy's body was brought to the Delaney Brothers' Funeral Parlor, 341 2d Ave., Manhattan, and preparations were made for a funeral at 11 a.m. tomorrow. A brother, Bernard Doheny, employed in a telegraph office did not come to work today, and he and other members of the family could not be reached either at home or at the funeral director's.

Search for Atlantis
Ends in Boy's Death

Four Adventurers, One a Brooklynite, Who Tried 'to Regenerate' Themselves Off the Florida Coast Didn't Reckon With Malaria

The body of young Gerard Doheny of 11 W. 103d St., Manhattan, was brought to New York today, from Florida, marking the tragic conclusion of a once rose-colored expedition in the interest of "human regeneration through biologic living."

Four hopeful adventurers had set out on the expedition on Nov. 11 last. Besides Doheny, they were Irving Rosenzweig, 24, of 529 McDonald Ave., Victor F. Peterson of Moline, Ill., and "Captain" John L. Mott, formerly of 111-25 Jamaica Ave., Richmond Hill.

Naturopathic Idea

They set out with not much money but high hopes and some fantastic ideas. Chief among their stock of ideas was a sort of "naturopathic" one that living the simple life and eating no meat, eggs, milk or vegetable would "regenerate" men, causing them to live for hundreds of years. Their plan was to find a comfortable little tropical island somewhere off the south of Florida and live the simple life there.

In addition, according to a dispatch today from Tampa, Fla., "Captain" Mott told the police there that they were planning to locate the lost Atlantis - fabled continent which sank in the Atlantic millenniums ago - and set up a colony of devotees of the simple life there.

But the whole thing went astray. They got as far as Old Town, Fla., then Cross City and finally Tampa. On Dec. 27 the four were found in a Tampa rooming house, Doheny and Peterson suffering from malaria, weak from lack of sustaining food. They were rushed to a hospital, and Doheny died there on Dec. 31. Rosenzweig, threatened with malaria, forsook his "simple life" tenets sufficiently to take some quinine.

At the Rosenzweig home in Brooklyn, members of his family pooh-poohed the Atlantis portion of the account from Miami, but they said that Irving had for years been interested in "biological living." A brother, Abraham, said that the expedition was an outgrowth of a "healthy camp" at Flanders, N.J., directed by a Dr. Walter Siegmeister, who propounded the theories of simple living by eating only fruits and refraining from love or haircuts.

The Doheny Boy's body was brought to the Delaney Brothers' Funeral Parlor, 341 2d Ave., New York, NY, and preparations were made for a funeral at 11 a.m. tomorrow. A brother, Bernard Doheny, employed in a telegraph office did not come to work today, and he and other members of the family could not be reached either at home or at the funeral director's.

According to Gerard's death certificate, he had worked at Western Union for the previous seven years as a clerk, and 15 Nov 1933 was the last day he worked there. So, this adventure that ended in his death was only about a month and a half long. Gerard's death certificate says his official address was 2735 Marion Ave, Bronx, even though the newspaper clipping says his last NY residence was 11 W. 103rd St, Manhattan.

I don't know which relative was living on Marion Ave in 1933. Neither the 1930 nor the 1940 US census lists any name that I recognized on Marion Ave. However, this address does appear later on Aunt Maria's 1945 death certificate. My grandfather Edward was living there with his sister Maria when she died in March 1945.

In 1930, my father Bernard (age 16) lived with Gerard (age 19) at 138 Ft. Greene Place, Brooklyn, with ten other lodgers, all members of the working poor. Gerard and Bernard were both employed as messengers for Western Union in 1930.[1]

My father said he felt very close to Gerard, and his death was a big blow to him.

Here is a photo of Gerard when he was very young, maybe 4 years old, in 1913 or 1914.

Gerard J. Doheny was born on 12 Oct 1910 in Brooklyn, New York. He died of malaria and malnutrition on 31 Dec 1933 in Tampa, Hillsborough County, Florida. He was buried on 05 Jan 1934 in Calvary Cemetery, Woodside, NY, in the same grave as his two older siblings, Catharine and Thomas, and his mother Katharine Greene Doheny who had predeceased him by a few months. Gerard's older brother Edward II would also be buried in this grave in 1972.[2]

---

[1] 1930 US census, Brooklyn, Kings County, AD 10, SD 28, ED 24-49, Sheet 5A.
[2] Calvary Cemetery Records for Section 32, Range 6, Plot T, Grave 6, New Calvary.

Chapter Nine

Lawrence A. DOHENY (1912-1978)

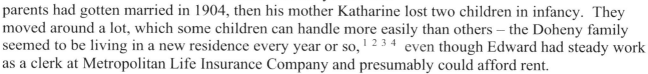

1 William Doheny (ca.1837 – 1877)
 +Anne Scully (ca.1838 – 1893)
..... 2 Edward Joseph Doheny I (1874 – 1953)
..... +Katharine Theresa Greene (1878 – 1933), m. Sep 1904
…...... 3 **Lawrence A. Doheny** (1912 – 1978)
……. +Catherine Doonan (1928 – 2017)

On a calm, cold and clear day, 27 Feb 1912, Lawrence was born to Edward Doheny and Katharine Greene. Here is a photo of Larry in his mother's arms when he was a toddler.

Calm is not an adjective for Larry's early life, however. Rather, there was a considerable amount of turmoil in his youth. His parents had gotten married in 1904, then his mother Katharine lost two children in infancy. They moved around a lot, which some children can handle more easily than others – the Doheny family seemed to be living in a new residence every year or so, [1] [2] [3] [4] even though Edward had steady work as a clerk at Metropolitan Life Insurance Company and presumably could afford rent.

Edward, Larry's father, had a drinking problem, which deeply affected the family from the very beginning. Sometimes Edward lived alone or with his own siblings, then came back and rejoined his family. Larry's family life would later mirror his father's life in several ways. Larry drank and had to move out of his home several times, though he always supported his family financially and did his utmost to maintain a relationship with his children.

When Larry was a boy of about eight, his mother became disoriented and mentally ill. She was sent to Kings Park State Hospital, which was miles away in Suffolk County, a difficult trip from Brooklyn in those days. It is possible that her husband and children never saw her again. She was there for 7 ½ years before she died at Kings Park.

---

[1] 653 19th Street, Brooklyn, in 1912 when Lawrence was born, according to Lawrence's birth certificate.
[2] 523 6th Ave., Brooklyn, in 1913 according to Bernard's birth certificate.
[3] 647 19th Street, Brooklyn, according to the 1915 NYS census, and Edward I is not living with his family.
[4] 220 Greenwood Ave., Brooklyn, from about 1916 to about 1920 when the boys were sent to an orphanage.

Larry and his brothers Bernard, Gerard and Frank were placed in an orphanage on Staten Island called Mount St. Michael's Home around 1920. They "escaped" from the orphanage many times until the staff stopped looking for them. My sister Anne remembers Uncle Larry telling her that the orphanage served them bread pudding or rice pudding several times a day, so, to this day, Anne won't eat either one of them.

After they left the orphanage, Larry and his brothers lived with one aunt after another. Anne said, "Daddy rarely spoke about his life before he met Mother, but he did tell me that one time after running away, he and Larry stole sweet potatoes from a street vendor because they had nothing to eat. Considering their early life, it is amazing that the brothers did so well." Larry would have done even better, she said, "had he not been overtaken by his alcoholism and all it brings with it."

The brothers all attended school while they lived with their aunts. Larry finished one year of high school in an academic program at a Catholic High School. He left school in 1927.[5] Only Frank would graduate from High School.

By their middle teens, Edward II, Gerard, Larry, and Bernard were all out on their own and supporting themselves somehow. Before being drafted into the army at age 30, Larry worked as a clerk,[6] and before that he worked as a sheet-metal-worker's helper for W.E. Stewart of Syracuse NY. (It is not clear that he actually worked in Syracuse, though.) He "cut, shaped, folded, and installed sheet metal furnace castings and pipes used as replacement parts in defective furnaces. He did metal roof repairs."[7]

Military Service

Larry was 5 ft 4 in, had blue eyes and brown hair, and weighed 120 lbs when he was drafted in May 1942 into the Army Air Forces.[8] His processing was done at Fort Jay, Governors Island, New York. About Fort Jay, Wikipedia.org says, "During World War II, Fort Jay was the headquarters of the First Army in the early part of the war, and later the Eastern Defense Command (EDC), responsible for all Army units and defense coordination in the northeastern United States, and in the east coast states from Maine through Florida. These were primarily coast defense, anti-aircraft, and fighter assets."

---

[5] Lawrence Doheny's Honorable Discharge papers say he attended Cathedral HS, NYC. The name of the school confused me because Cathedral HS was founded in 1905 as an all-girls high school, and it remains an all-girls school to this day. There is a Cathedral Preparatory School and Seminary in Elmhurst, Queens, for boys who think they want to become priests, but I don't recall Uncle Larry ever mentioning he once wanted to be a priest. Anyway, his discharge papers say he attended Cathedral HS, NYC.

[6] Lawrence Doheny's WWII enlistment record, available on Ancestry.com

[7] Lawrence Doheny's Honorable Discharge papers offer us this description of a sheet-metal-worker's helper.

[8] Lawrence Doheny's Honorable Discharge papers. Larry's Army Serial Number is 32 334 854.

Both Larry and my father Bernard gave Aunt Helen Greene's address as their home address when they entered military service: 130 Lenox Rd., Brooklyn, NY.

The photo is of Lawrence, Bernard and Francis. The reverse side is stamped, "Bluebird Photo Art Studio, 73 Sands St., Brooklyn, N.Y." It possibly was taken in Aug 1943 at the time my parents were married in Brooklyn. My father was on a one week leave from basic training for his marriage and brief honeymoon. This was before Bernard was promoted to Master Sergeant, thus no stripes. Frank was my father's "Best Man," so he was in Brooklyn at that time. Larry is not in the wedding photos, and no photos of the guests were taken of the wedding guests except for Grace's parents and Grace's sister Jeanie; thus, I can't prove the date of the photo.

Larry was in the Army for 3 ½ years and reached the rank of Staff Sergeant. His MOS (Military Occupation Specialty) was "Platoon Sergeant qualified to use a BAR (Browning Automatic Rifle) and an M1 Rifle." Carrying a BAR was no easy feat, in light of his small frame. A BAR weighs about 20 lbs and is about 47 inches long. It is gas operated with a range of over 4,000 yards, though its effective range is more like 1,500 yards. It can deliver up to 650 rounds per minute,

firing single shots or bursts of 2 or 3 shots. It can be fired from the shoulder or mounted on a bipod.[9] He also had to carry his regular back pack. I don't know if he also had to carry his own ammunition.

His Separation Papers say that he participated in the invasion of Normandy, but the actual day he landed on the beach is not noted. The Normandy invasion lasted for 85 days (starting on D-Day, 6 June 1944 and lasting until August 1944) as the allied troops reclaimed the coast and then pushed the German occupiers out of France.

Larry was injured twice during the Normandy Campaign; once on 15 July 1944 and again on 24 July 1944.[10] His wounds are briefly described in something called "WWII Hospital Admission Card Files" available on Ancestry.com. His first admission was for a bullet wound to the base of the thumb. He was also treated for acute sinusitis and an infection in his ankle. In a second hospitalization, he was treated for trench foot. After each treatment, he was sent back into battle.

---

[9] https://www.britannica.com/technology/Browning-automatic-rifle

[10] His Separation Papers have this quote, "Purple Heart, GO 42, Hq 4, Inf 18 July 1944 w/OLC GO 10 92 GH, 11 Aug 1944." Having consulted a military friend, I think this means: "Purple Heart, General Orders Number 42, Headquarters 4th Infantry Division, awarded on 18 July 1944, with Oak Leaf Cluster (meaning a second award) General Orders Number 10 (92 GH may be an acknowledgement by a higher headquarters of the Division's General Orders 42) awarded on 11 Aug 1944."

Larry had four different assignments during World War II:

- 3 months as a private in Basic Infantry (521)
- 2 years as a PFC Rifleman (745) (It was during the last 2 months of this period that he was wounded.)
- 8 months as a Platoon Sergeant (745) with the rank of Staff Sergeant (from Sep 44 to May 45, in the campaigns in Luxembourg and Germany)

> "Served with the 4th Infantry Division in combat in the ETO (European Theatre of Operations). Led the men in action against the enemy in Normandy, Luxembourg and Germany. Awarded the combat infantry badge for service against the enemy."

- During his last 6 months in the Army, Larry was a Distribution File Clerk (055) with the rank of Staff Sergeant (These were the 6 months between the end of the war in May and when he went home in November.)

Besides his Purple Heart, he received the American Service Medal, the European-African-Middle Eastern Service Medal, the World War II Victory Leaf, and the Good Conduct Medal.

The war ended in Europe in May 1945, and the eastern war against Japan ended on 2 Sep 1945. Thousands of US servicemen were anxious to get home. My father Bernard was able to connect with Larry before they got their orders to go home. Bernard was able to go home in October; Larry had to wait until 9 Nov 1945 before he was allowed to leave Europe.

In 1944, privates in the army received $50 a month, and staff sergeants received $96 a month. In Nov 1945, Larry received $300 in separation pay. He elected to pay $7.20 per month after "separation" for Veterans Administration insurance. He would receive money each month for his war wounds, especially the damage to his hand, but I don't know the amount.

A Successful Deli Business

After he left the Army, Larry bought and operated a delicatessen business, probably on the G.I. Bill. It became a big gathering place for all the men in the family. All the Doheny brothers and Bernie's brothers-in-law would meet in Larry's deli every Friday night to play cards till the wee hours. He gave his delicious potato salad recipe to my sister Anne, who shared it with our sister Betty.

> Scrub some red skinned potatoes and boil them for about 20 min. Don't overcook. Drain the water and cut the potatoes inside the pot so they stay hot. Pour equal amounts of oil and apple cider vinegar over the hot potatoes and mix. Add a diced small yellow onion and 4 or 5 diced celery stalks. Mix with a fork and add some mayonnaise if you like. Serve warm or cold.

It was a very successful deli, and when Larry met and married Catherine "Bobby" Doonan, he was able to pay for a honeymoon in Bermuda. [11]   He also made enough money to support a family. They had two girls whom Larry loved dearly.

My sister Betty recalled:

> Mom told me that Bobby demanded that Uncle Larry spend more time with her and the kids. When he hired someone to run the deli business in his absence, the employee robbed him blind. Uncle Larry ended up losing the business and went into debt. But for his business being stolen out from under him, Larry could have had a very successful career.

Anne adds this:

> I remember hearing the grownups talk about how owning and operating a deli is the kind of business that takes a lot of hard work and time to make it stay successful. I learned that after a while, Uncle Larry gave in and hired a helper; I think it was a series of helpers over a period of time. It turns out that the last of those helpers robbed him blind, and Uncle Larry lost the business. I don't know if that was before or after Bobby and he were separated. Once he was separated, his drinking got much worse – he was a binge drinker. Then he would get sober and stay that way for a while before going on another binge.

When he lost the deli, Larry became an elevator operator somewhere in Manhattan or downtown Brooklyn. He also had jobs as a building maintenance man and a doorman.

Larry married Catherine Doonan in early Jan 1950 in Brooklyn, NY. (His marriage license was dated Dec 29, 1949,[12] so they were probably married very shortly after that.). Bobby was born in 1928, so she was 16 years younger than her husband. Bobby died in 2017 in Nassau County, New York.

Anne said she was always fascinated by the adult's conversation at the dining room table. "If I was quiet, everyone forgot that I was there, nearby, listening." That's how Anne picked up this information:
- Uncle Larry met Bobby while he was going out with her mother.
- The fact that Bobby's mother was living with Larry and Bobby was more than a "difficult dynamic" operating in their family life. "Impossible dynamic" is more accurate.
- It was also Anne's impression that our mother liked Bobby and disliked Bobby's mother. She said, "I am pretty sure that Mother thought that Bobby's mother liked her drink and was a drinking companion of Uncle Larry's even after Bobby and he were married."

---

[11] Departing Passenger and Crew Lists, 1914-1966, available on Ancestry.com. The record says Lawrence A. and Kathleen D. Doheny, ages 37 and 21, of 304 Beach 90th St, Rockaway NY, with 3 bags weighing 34 lbs, were on their way to Bermuda on Jan 5, 1950 aboard Pan American Airways.
[12] New York, NY, Marriage License Indexes, 1907-2018, available on Ancestry.com.

Betty said, "My sisters and I were told that Larry was first attracted to Bobby's mother; she was his drinking partner. But when he met Bobby, he dropped the mom and fell in love with Bobby. She became pregnant, and they got married."

Bobby's mother lived with Larry and Bobby in Rockaway (maybe it was Bobby's mother's home that they all were living in). Anyway, Bobby's mother ruled the roost, as the saying goes. Bobby wasn't allowed to do anything without her mother's permission, and her mother intruded into Larry and Bobby's marriage.

Based on my family's direct observations, Larry loved his daughters dearly. But he was often prevented from seeing them, which pained him deeply the rest of his life.

Anne said:

> Larry didn't walk out – Bobby threw him out. I don't know exactly when that happened, but it wasn't when his daughters were toddlers because they were all still living together during our childhood. It is possible that there were earlier, shorter separations that we don't know about, but they became truly separated when his daughters were children, as opposed to toddlers.
>
> After the separation, Larry often tried to visit, but Bobby made it difficult for him to exercise visitation rights. If he was drinking, I can certainly understand her not allowing him to take them on his own, rather than visiting them at Bobby's house, but it was my impression that she didn't want that either.
>
> I do know that Uncle Larry persisted in his efforts to see the girls, and constantly, throughout his life, tried to stay on the wagon, sometimes succeeding for months, and especially when he had something to strive for – like seeing his children (or, much later, going on vacation with my own family).
>
> When he was able to have the girls, he sometimes brought them out to our house in Plainview.
>
> I remember an impression of his feelings of tremendous sadness and loss as far as his children were concerned. I remember at one point him finding out that he had been paying alimony for years after Bobby's situation had changed. (She may have remarried.) But Bobby had not told him he was no longer responsible for paying alimony. That hurt him deeply. And made Mother pretty angry that Bobby could do that – but I do seem to remember that she thought it was probably Bobby's mother who put her up to it.

Betty said, "Uncle Larry always payed child support, and that would be in keeping with his character. I remember hearing that Bobby remarried, but no details. Larry was not a violent drunk, rather a crying drunk, but my suspicion is that alcoholism was the reason he was kept away from his children."

I remember taking the subway from downtown Brooklyn to the Rockaways and visiting Larry's family a couple of times before we moved to Plainview in 1954. We even stayed overnight, sleeping on the floor. Kids can sleep anywhere! I remember going to Rockaway Beach where my feet got cut up on all the sharp shells on the beach, and I remember I did a lot of crying over that. I was about 7.

More of Betty's recollections:

Uncle Larry was the "fun" uncle. (Photo at left is Larry and Betty, 1961.) He was the one who brought us toys. He brought things for us to all play with together like shuffle board, badminton, and croquet. (I can't imagine Mom and Dad buying us those things in the middle of the summer.) He brought us wind-up toys. We played cards after dinner whenever he visited. He bought my refrigerator before I bought my house. (He said he wanted there to be enough room in it for cold beer.)

Betty told me that, as a kid, she thought it strange that we didn't call Bobby, Aunt Bobby.

The last time Betty remembers spending time with Larry's children was around 1963. Uncle Larry took his daughters and Betty ice skating at Rockefeller Center. Something happened that gave Betty a feeling that stuck with her as an odd behavior for him. He seemed to reprimand one of them over something that was no big deal, and Betty had the feeling that he did it because he wanted to act like a father. (Did he learn that from our parents who reprimanded us for the smallest infraction?) Uncle Larry never reprimanded any of us.

Uncle Larry spent nearly every weekend at our house in Plainview when I was in HS. And he was a doting, loving uncle to my sister Anne and her two children. Larry was Anne's godfather.

Anne said:

> Up until the year before he died, when his alcoholism was getting much worse, he spent many of his weekends at my house and took many vacations with our family.

> That was actually the worst time of his drinking – he would say he was coming for the weekend, and then not show up (many times). He was in and out of rehab during that entire time, trying to stop drinking, but couldn't. We rarely saw him during his last two years. The last time he checked himself in to the hospital was the week before he died. I got the call from the hospital and went in to see him, but he was in a bad way. I think he knew I was there, but, unfortunately, even after all those years, I didn't understand that his alcoholism was a disease. I was exasperated with him for what I thought was his decision to drink instead of looking forward to the trip we had planned

up to Schroon Lake in a couple of weeks with the kids. I gave him a piece of my mind – not knowing if he could hear me or not, and I'll always be sorry for that.

Larry also smoked a lot. Mother complained about his smoking and the damage he did to some of our furniture. She was afraid he would set our house on fire. The dining set he inherited from Aunt Helen, and then gave to me, still has a cigarette burn on the table top.

He even smoked in bed, apparently, and on this occasion, fell asleep and dropped the cigarette on the mattress. The mattress smoldered. Neighbors saw smoke coming out from around the apartment door and called the fire department. The firemen had to break down the apartment door to get in, and when they did, the apartment burst into flames, charring his body, and melting every bit of plastic in the apartment. The firemen told us the smoke from the smoldering mattress probably killed him long before the fire erupted. Mother, Daddy and I drove into Manhattan and were allowed in to the apartment to try to retrieve anything we could. I found a metal salt and pepper shaker on the windowsill, which I gave to Anne, who still has them. Daddy and I had to identify Larry's body at the Belleview morgue, an experience I will never forget.

Betty said, "A very generous and thoughtful thing Uncle Larry did for me was to send me money when I was in California. He figured correctly that I might be low on cash. Around the same time, Anne sent me money. Mother sent me a check, too, but it was only to be used to buy a plane ticket home. I sent it back to her after I got a job. Once, Uncle Larry thought his oldest daughter had called him, but hung up without speaking with him... maybe wanting to find out if he was still alive. It could have just been a wrong number, but Uncle Larry was hoping it was his daughter."

In conclusion...

Anne said:

> I want to make sure this is known about Uncle Larry. He was not perfect by any means, but he was the most generous person I have ever met in my life. Not only generous, but thoughtful. In 1954, right after we moved to Plainview, Uncle Larry remembered that I wanted a Halloween mask and knew there wasn't a cent extra in our house at that time. He showed up with a Halloween mask for me (and assorted other little wind-up toys and candy for everybody, as usual). That was the norm with him.
>
> Later, when I bought my own house, he put in a fireplace (which I wanted, but never asked for, or even expected to have – he just heard me wishing for one). He offered me money several times when he knew I needed it for my children. I never accepted those offers, but it was a comfort knowing I had his support, and also sometimes knowing he needed support more than I did, but that was his way.
>
> As an alcoholic, Uncle Larry made many pretty bad mistakes, I'm sure, but his memory deserves to give him credit where credit is due, which is in very many places.

Through AncestryDNA, I got in touch with a grandson of Larry and Bobby. He told me that his mother looked her father up long ago, but he was already deceased. Anne said, "It makes me cry that Heather looked him up but found that her father was already deceased. I'm sure that it would have given him the greatest joy to be in touch with her again."[13]

The last place Larry lived was a beautiful high-rise apartment called Harborview Terrace at 530 West 55th near 10th Ave. It had a great view of Manhattan's West Side. It was bright, and he was very happy to be there. The location is Hell's Kitchen, also known as the Clinton neighborhood. Harborview Terrace is run by the NYC Housing Authority for the elderly and disabled and has 195 units. Larry was among its first residents. The building is not kept very well these days. Druggies living with elderly relatives apparently rule the complex; a NY Times article said that the law-abiding residents cannot get the housing authority to do anything about it. In the Senior Center downstairs, the workers fear for their lives.

Larry died in his apartment on 24 May 1978.[14] [15] His death certificate was issued at Belleview and signed by a very famous forensic pathologist, Michael Baden, who was involved in JFK's autopsy and, more recently, was involved in Jeffrey Epstein's autopsy. I thought Larry's death certificate would say that the immediate cause of death was heart attack caused by smoke inhalation, as the firemen had told us. Instead, it says that Larry died of natural causes due to chronic alcoholism and a fatty liver, but doesn't reference the smoke, and it says an autopsy was *not* done.

My father Bernard, who was Larry's last surviving sibling, arranged for a wake at the Thomas Dalton Funeral Home in Hicksville, NY, near our home in Plainview. Larry was buried on 31 May 1978 in the Long Island National Cemetery in Farmingdale, Suffolk County, New York.[16]

Summer 1963 – Grace, Margo, Catherine, Anne, Larry on a boat trip the Hudson River to Bear Mountain, NY. (Betty may have taken the photo.)

---

[13] Email from Larry's grandson on 16 Apr 2018, "I know my mother looked him up long ago, and he was already deceased."
[14] Verified in Social Security Records. Social Security Number 051-09-2689.
[15] Lawrence Doheny, Death Certificate, New York City Dept of Health, Borough of Manhattan, Certif#156-78-108715.
[16] He is buried in Grave 1623-A, Section 2T.

Chapter Ten

Bernard G. DOHENY (1913-1989)
Grace D. VOGELBACH (1918-2005)

1 William Doheny (ca.1837 – 1877)
 +Anne Scully (ca.1838 – 1893)
..... 2 Edward Joseph Doheny I (1874 – 1953)
..... +Katharine Theresa Greene (1878 – 1933), m. Sep 1904
.... 3 **Bernard Greene Doheny II** (1913 – 1989)
…..... +Grace Dolores Vogelbach (1918 – 2005)
.... 4 Catherine Grace Doheny (the author)
.... 4 Anne Marie Doheny
.... 4 Elizabeth Grace Doheny
.... 4 Margaret Doheny

This chapter will sound much more personal than the rest of the book because this chapter is about my own family. I have included many first-hand stories and far fewer footnotes than in other chapters since I am the source. The voice sometimes varies between first-person and third-person.

Bernard Greene Doheny was the youngest of Edward J. Doheny and Katharine T. Greene's seven children. He was born on 11 Oct 1913 when the family was living in Park Slope, Brooklyn.[1]

Bernard's father Edward was a clerk at Metropolitan Life Insurance Company. (One of Bernard's granddaughters, Grace Anne Murphy, would work there, too, many years later.)

Baby Bernard was baptized when he was two weeks old. The family's parish was Holy Family parish on 13th St, Brooklyn, about three blocks from their home. Bernard's godparents were Helen Greene and Francis Greene, his mother's siblings. I can imagine Bernard's baptism day and the whole family taking part - Katharine pushing her new baby in a carriage, Edward carrying Larry, only a year and a half old, and Helen Greene and Frank Greene shepherding Gerard, Francis and Edward Jr. to the church for the baptism.

As mentioned in earlier chapters, Edward Sr. had a drinking problem, and he was not living with his wife and children by the time Bernard was two years old. In 1915, Katherine and her children lived at 647 19th St, in the Windsor Terrace section of Brooklyn, but Edward Sr. is not there.[2] (In other

---

[1] The address on Bernard's birth certificate is 523 Sixth Ave, Park Slope, Brooklyn.
[2] 1915 NY State census, Kings County, ED 60, Page 15

censuses, I have found Edward Sr. living with one of his siblings when he was not enumerated with his own family.)

A year before my father died, I interviewed him and taped the stories he told of his childhood. The audio is about one half-hour long. I put it on a CD and gave copies to my sisters so we could all hear Daddy tell these stories in his own voice. Excerpts from the tape are interspersed throughout this chapter.[3] (B = Bernard, C = Catherine, G = Grace)

B: The first thing I recall clearly is riding a buckboard down a hill on 18th Street in Brooklyn. Down at the bottom of the hill was a picket fence, and I don't know which brother was driving, but he hit the picket fence, and I went up and got speared by the pickets at the top. An iron picket fence. I must have been bleeding like a pig when they got me home.
C: Did they bring you to a doctor to get you fixed up, or did they fix you up at home?
B: No, my mother, she fixed it up. She was a nurse.[4]

Bernard must have been about five when this occurred, because they had moved again by the time he was ready to start school; he was five when he started First Grade at Immaculate Heart of Mary School on Ft Hamilton Parkway, only one block from their new address at 220 Greenwood Ave. near E. 3rd St, also in Windsor Terrace. He excelled in school, in spite of the turmoil at home.

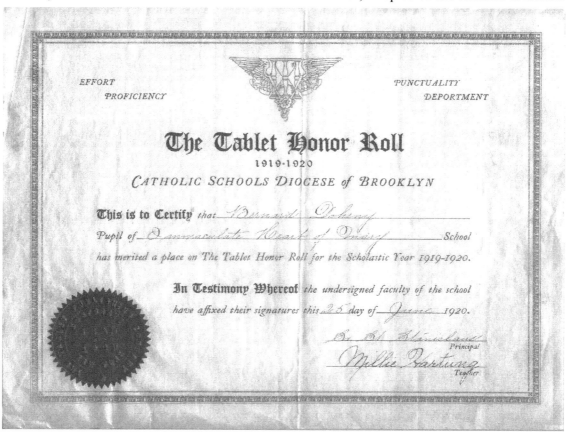

---

[3] Taped interview, 30 Jun 1988, at Bernard & Grace's home, 526 Carmel Road, South Venice, FL.
[4] Katharine is wearing the uniform of a nurse, but census records and her death certificate say she was a homeworker.

Bernard earned this prestigious Tablet Honor Roll certificate at the end of First Grade. (The Tablet was a long-running newspaper published by the Roman Catholic Diocese of Brooklyn.)

Family life was slowly crumbling around Bernard and his siblings. His father was seldom home, and he was living more or less permanently in Manhattan with one or the other of his siblings. Aunt Helen Greene, a public-school teacher, was living with her sister Katharine and the five boys in a small Brooklyn apartment, and she helped take care of them in the evenings and on weekends. Katharine's own mental health was beginning to decline. Bernard's eldest brother Edward decided to run away from home, and soon after that Bernard and the rest of his brothers were sent to live with relatives and subsequently placed in an orphanage called Mount St. Michael's Home, on Staten Island, NY. My father said he hated the orphanage and ran away several times.

Bernard's memories about his First Communion, living on Greenwood Ave., and the orphanage:

G: When did you make your First Holy Communion? That was another story you used to tell us about.

B: Oh, yeah, that was when we were living on Greenwood Ave. On Communion Day you had to get all dressed up, and I wasn't allowed out of the yard, so I wouldn't get dirty. I had to stay in there until everything was over.

G: I thought it was the day before, when, after you went to confession, and you weren't allowed to be bad or anything...

B: No, it was when I was all dressed up.

C: You mean after the First Communion. Then you came home, and you weren't allowed out because you had to stay dressed up.

B: Right, yeah.

G: Were you with your mother then?

B: Yes.

B: I recall going to the stable on Ft Hamilton Parkway when we lived on Greenwood Ave; it was after practice for a play at school. The play was about a wooden horse and a jockey. And going to the stable with my horse, they gave me a ride on a horse. So that was about it at that time.

C: So, you lived on Greenwood, and what?

B: Greenwood Ave. and Third Street, before that it was on 18th Street. I forget what the side streets were.

C: And who was living at home at that time?

B: We were all at home at that time. Edward hadn't run away until a couple of years later.

C: Where were you living when he did that?

B: On Greenwood Ave.

C: So, you lived on Greenwood for a long time, then.

B: Yeah, quite a while. From there we moved, or I did, with Larry and Gerard, moved over to Manhattan with Aunt Katie, my father's brother's wife.

C: What uncle was that, do you remember?

B: No, he had died before that.

C: Do you remember any of your father's brothers or sisters' names?

B: Aunt Maria (pronounced Mariah), Aunt Annie, and another one. I forget... Her married name was Mrs. Moore. For a while, there, we went between Aunt Katie's and Aunt Annie's over on 9th Ave.

C: 9th Ave in Manhattan?

B: Right, and 17th Street.

C: So, you were in school by then.

B: Yeah. We went to the home, Mount St. Michael's on Staten Island, and from there, Larry and I ran away about three times before they kicked us out.

C: They were really strict, I bet, in those years, right?

B: Yeah... very strict.

G: I remember you told me that one time you got to the police station. What was that about the police station?

B: Unh... I know... One time, I got picked up by, must have been a policeman. In the car, a bee stung me on the nose. That was where I almost drowned, as well. They had a swimming pool, and, uh, you know, playing around, I got thrown into the pool, and sunk down to the bottom, and they had to come in and pull me out.

G: What? Was that at Mount St. Vincent's?

B: That was at Mount St. Michaels.

G: Mount St. Michaels's, at least?

B: Yeah

C: Who went in? Work people?

B: The kids.

C: How old were you then?

B: About ten, I guess.

C: OK, when you finally got kicked out of the home, how old were you then?

B: Aaah.

C: Still in grammar school?

B: Yes. Oh, I must have been, uh, about 11.

C: 11, that's like 5th or 6th Grade.

B. Aunt Maria lived in the apartment that Aunt Katie had before that on E. 39th St. And, uh, I went to school at St. Gabriel's on 36th Street and Second Ave. in Manhattan. And between there and St. Bernard's over on 14th Street near Ninth Ave, that was where I graduated from.

C: Then where did you go to High School?

B: Eh, Stuyvesant, it was there near Second Ave., Second or Third Ave., and 15th Street in Manhattan.

C: So, you went to Stuyvesant High School in Manhattan?

B: Right, until they kicked me out of there. [laughter]

C: Why did they kick you out? Hooky, or what?

B: No, it was, uh, chemistry. I just couldn't remember all the, uh, symbols and all the names. I turned in a paper with zero.

G: Gee, you never told ME that. I thought I was the only one who got zeroes!

C: And that was enough to get you kicked out of high school in those days?

G: He probably went to work!

B: Yeah, I went to, uh, Western Union. I was a messenger. Down on Hudson Street in Manhattan. It was on the West Side down below 14th Street. And then I went to the main office where Anne Doheny worked, and she probably helped me get in to there.

G: You were a roller skater there, too, right?

B: Right.

Merging Bernard's memories with public records, here is the chronology of his early life:

- Jan 1920, Bernard's father is enumerated with his brother Richard's family on E. 39th St, NYC.
- Jun 1920, Bernard finished First Grade. He is not yet 7.
- Aug 1920, Bernard's Uncle Richard Doheny died.
- Oct 1920, Bernard turned 7. Aunt Katie, now a widow, has taken in Gerard, Larry and Bernard. She is also caring for another orphaned niece (Annie Elizabeth, the daughter of Edward's brother Patrick), plus her own daughter Anna Josephine. All those children in her household were probably a great strain while she was mourning the loss of her husband. And Annie Elizabeth had come down with tuberculosis by 1920. Bernard, Larry and Gerard were soon sent to live with Aunt Annie at 9th Ave and 17th St, Manhattan.
- Sep 1922, Aunt Annie married Jim Farrell (not a relative of the Greene family, as far as I can determine); Bernard, Larry, Gerard and Francis were placed in the orphanage on Staten Island. The boys ran away several times.
- ca. 1923 to 1925, Bernard lived with Aunt Maria who had moved into Aunt Katie's apartment on E. 39th St. (Aunt Katie and Anna Elizabeth moved to the Bronx). There Bernard attended St. Gabriel's School on 36th and 2nd Ave. for a little while.
- Early 1925, Edward's wife Katharine is sent to Kings Park State Hospital, and her children never see her again.

- Jun 1925-1928, Francis, Gerard, Lawrence, and Bernard are back living with their father in an apartment in the same building as Annie and Jim Farrell. Annie, though, is probably the one taking care of them. While living at this apartment, Bernard attended St. Bernard's School on 14th St. near 9th Ave. and graduated from elementary school there. Then he attended two years of High School at Stuyvesant High School, an elite scholarship public school. It was a half hour walk to high school, 1 ½ miles away, at 15th St and 1st Ave. (I tried to get my father's permanent record card, but the secretary of Stuyvesant High School put me off, saying those records no longer exist, or were lost when the school moved to Battery Park some years ago.)
- Jun 1928, Bernard is asked to leave Stuyvesant High School. He is 14 and now has to survive on his own. The 1930 census shows him living with his brother Gerard at 138 Ft Greene Place, Brooklyn, in a boarding house for poor working men. Gerard and Bernard are both working for Western Union in 1930.

For the next ten years, Bernard lived on the West Side of Manhattan.[5] He worked at Western Union as a clerk typist, which included general office work such as classifying correspondence, messages and reports. He operated mimeograph, multigraph, ditto and other office machines.[6]

Bernard Meets Grace

G: And then, what else happened at Western Union?

B: That's where I met little Gracie Vogelbach. [laughter]

C: What was that like?

B: …in the dark room…

G: Oh, you didn't meet me in there. [laughter] You met me out… out at the "drop."

C: Did you kiss her in the dark room, Daddy?

B: Aaah, maybe. [laughter]

C: Mother says you met her at, uh…

G: T&R

C: Testing and Regulating at Western Union. And, both of you were on roller skates at that time?

G: No.

C: Mother was, but Daddy wasn't?

G: No, I was typing, and Daddy was typing. I think it was on a holiday.

C: It was holiday time? How long did you know each other before you got married?

G: 1942, wasn't it, Bernie?

C: OK, in 1942 you met each other.

B: No, it was before that.

C: When did you go into the Army?

G: When did the war break out?

C: '41

B: '41

G: Oh! So, it must have been before that. It must have been '41 then, I guess, because it was soon after that, that, uh, you were called in to the war. It was in October that I met you. I remember going out with Jimmy Mack right before that. Remember? I was in the middle of…

C: Oh, Yeah, breaking up with him. So, so, anyway, after you met each other, what kind of dates did you ask mother to go out with you on?

B: So, uh, it was mostly roller skating, huh?

G: Except when you were mad at me, or when I was mad at you, you'd make up by taking me to the movies. And I wouldn't like it anyway because it had loud, loud music. I remember him taking me to the Strand. He probably had to borrow money to get there, and I hated it.

C: Can you remember any of those details? You know, borrowing money for dates, or…

G: Ooooooh, he can't… How can he…

C: All right, well, Mother, you can tell me those things then. Daddy, how about, where were you living at that time? [long pause] Do you remember? Where?

G: Up in New York, 84th Street or something like that. Where was it, Bernie?

---

[5] 1940 US census, NY, Manhattan, AD 9, ED 31-746, page 3B, address was 200 W. 95th St. Bernard is a lodger with the Sweeney family. That census said he lived in Manhattan in 1935, too.

[6] Bernard's Separation Papers described his civilian work before he was drafted.

B: Yeah, it was up in the 80's.

C: On the east side or the west side?

B: The west side... 94th... 95th?

G: Ah, yeah, that's right.

C: So, it was up in Harlem, then?

B: No, Harlem started up around 110th.

C: So, you lived there, you worked downtown Manhattan. And you would just take mother out just on Friday night, or on Saturday night, or what? Any night of the week, it didn't matter?

B: Umnh

C: And what did you like about Mother when you first met her? [laughter]

B: I liked her wiggle, huh? [laughter]

C: Did you talk more then, or did you let her do the talking?

B: Noooo, I couldn't get a word in edgewise then, either. [laughter]

C: So, how did you get to know her, how did she get to know you?

B: Well, she keeps saying that it was when I was in the Army sending the letters...

C: So, did you ask mother to marry you, or did you just... did the two of you, um, just mutually agree that this was going to be the next step?

G: [saying something in the background]

C: OK, come 'ere, Ma, come 'ere. Sit down over here.

G: No! I'm not going to sit down, I've got things to...

C: OK, just stand over here...

G: Noooo… You asked me how much did a man have to earn before he could marry me. What did I say? He'd have to have a thousand dollars in the bank. [laughter]

C: So, is that what you did?

B: Noooo, we didn't get that thousand until after I got in the Army.

G: It was on Virginia's kitchen floor that he proposed to me.

C: So he knelt down... ?

G: He knelt down and proposed to me.

C: Ahhh. What were the words?

G: I don't remember that... [expressed as, I'm not going to tell you that] [laughter]

Bernard was drafted by the US Army in 1942. My sister Betty remembers Daddy saying that the Army didn't accept him until after he had an operation for one undescended testicle. He had the operation and went on to father four children. He was inducted into the Army on 13 Oct 1942, two days after his birthday. Two weeks later, he entered active service. He gave his Aunt Helen Greene's address, 130 Lenox Rd., Brooklyn, as his home address. Grace's parents were against her marrying a soldier; they said he might be killed in action, leaving Grace a young widow. But Grace and Bernard did get married, and her parents attended the wedding. They married on 21 Aug 1943 at Our Lady of Refuge Church, Brooklyn, NY. Their witnesses were Bernard's brother Francis and Grace's sister Jean.

Their honeymoon was at Beaver Brook Camp. Here is how Grace described it:

The walls only went up about…eh…well…about eight feet, I guess. But then there was about a foot in between that and the roof. And these little rooms were just like cubbyholes. And there was only one bathroom on the floor there. And there were all these little cubbyhole rooms. So, you could hear everything that went on in the next room. And we didn't realize that it was like that until we looked up later on, you know. Gosh it was dark in there, it was very dark. We didn't have an electric light or anything in that place. It was a camp. Can you imagine that? I made reservations at a camp. And Daddy said, "What!? Beaver Brook Camp!" We had to get up with a bugle and go to bed at sundown. Oh, I tell ya! It was so black up there. You couldn't see your fingers in front of you.

When they returned to Brooklyn, they rented a room at 1617 Dorchester Rd. in Flatbush, where Grace would live until Bernard returned from the war.

Bernard arrived in England on 30 Jan 1944, after 8 days at sea. After D-Day, which was 6 June, he waited in England until his company crossed the English Channel to participate in the Allied invasion. The 258th Artillery landed on Utah Beach on July 4 at 12:30pm. Bernard participated in

campaigns in Ardennes, Normandy, Northern France, Rhineland, including the Battle of the Bulge. He was qualified to use a Springfield Rifle and a carbine. Bernard said, thankfully, he was never in a situation where he had to shoot a person.

Bernard's rank was Master Sergeant, serving as Sergeant Major in the headquarters company of 258th Field Artillery Group. He would be in England, France, Belgium, Holland and Germany as part of the XIX Corps of the First Army. He "supervised and directed the work of several departments of a headquarters organization in the preparation of correspondence, records, reports, and orders. He coordinated reports from various field artillery battalions." Mother told us that he was briefly also a chaplain's assistant, but that is not part of his service record on his separation papers.

Germany surrendered on 8 May 1945, but Bernard did not leave Europe for another five months. He was very anxious to get home, as he said in one of the two letters to his wife that still exist. Bernard left Europe on 17 Oct 1945, spent seven days at sea on the return voyage, and finally received his Honorable Discharge at Fort Dix, NJ, on 29 Oct 1945. His separation pay was $300, travel pay was $3.95, and he used that to get back to Brooklyn.

Bernard told me this story: "In the army, when we were getting ready to come home, I had to go and pick up our travel orders. It was about 50 miles away. We got down there all right, picked up the orders, and on the way back to the outfit, the driver hit a hole in the road, and, uh, we were lucky to get out. And in getting out, he landed on top of my legs, and I had bruises on both legs for the next, uh, about 6 months. That was the closest I came to getting injured in the war."

After WW II, a New Job and a Family

After Bernard returned from the war, he went job hunting, and in 1946 found work as an accounting clerk at Goldman Sachs Co., an investment banking firm in the financial district of Manhattan. He worked there until his retirement in 1979. He was a very valued internal accountant. At his retirement party, his boss said that Bernard never made an arithmetic error in all his 33 years at Goldman Sachs. His last job there was actually checking the company's computer calculations!

I was born while we lived on Dorchester Rd. I was named after Daddy's mother Katharine, though the spelling is a little different. My crying apparently disturbed the peace of the two "spinsters" who owned the house, and we were asked to leave that apartment.

So, we moved to the Quonset Huts, near Seaview Ave in Canarsie. The city had authorized Robert Moses to buy hundreds of surplus Quonset Huts from the US Army and put them in Canarsie, and several other places in New York City, to temporarily house returning World War II soldiers and their families. Mom's second child Anne was born while our family lived in Canarsie. The best thing about the huts is that our family started a lifelong friendship with Laura and Bob Chess while we lived there.

Mom and Dad followed the family tradition of taking in relatives who had nowhere to go. Bernard's sister in-law Idola needed care after a hospitalization in the late 1940s, and stayed with us in the huts for a couple of months with her two boys. This was the first of the instances when Mom was not consulted. Daddy and his brothers simply told her that Idola would be living with us for a little while. The Quonset Huts were designed for families of four, and now we had seven people living together. A similar thing would happen when we lived in Plainview. "The Boys," meaning Daddy and his brothers, decided Aunt Helen would live with us when she developed dementia. More about that later.

Living conditions were quite primitive in the huts. Food shopping entailed walking a mile to the grocery store while pushing the baby carriage, a couple of times a week. There were also walks with the carriage to a depot that sold cooking/heating fluid for the tanks that you see in the photo above. Mom put the fuel cans in the carriage, too, and wheeled them back to our hut. These chores had to be done in all sorts of weather. We did not have a car, bus stops were a long walk away, and cabs were beyond our budget.

In 1949, our family moved to a New York City housing project at 414 Baltic Street, Brooklyn, known as the Gowanus Apartments. Daddy commuted to his job by walking 15 minutes to the subway station at Hoyt and Schermerhorn in downtown Brooklyn, boarded the A train for a 10-minute ride to Fulton St., and then walked five minutes to Goldman Sachs at 20 Broad Street.

Here is a sketch of the floorplan of our apartment; I believe it was about 800 square feet. Betty was born while we lived at 414 Baltic St. Her crib was in Mom and Dad's room.

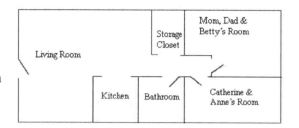

The Gowanus Apartments were in a section of Brooklyn known at the time as South Brooklyn, now just called Gowanus. We were two blocks away from the Gowanus Canal, which was an open sewer designed to relieve sewage and storm water from South Brooklyn. It smelled awful when the wind blew our way. (The EPA designated it a Superfund site in 2008, and the canal is supposed to be cleaned up by 2022.)[7]

The Gowanus Apartments had two terrific playgrounds with swings and monkey bars, and mom brought us there frequently. The playgrounds were my favorite part of living there.

Our parents were worried about the high crime rate in South Brooklyn. A story was that the parish priests included self-defense training as part of their altar boy training so that mothers would allow their sons to serve Mass in the mornings. Mom and Dad worried about our safety, too, though nothing bad ever happened to any of us while we lived in Brooklyn.

In 1951 and 1952, our extended family was worried about Grandpa Vogelbach who had had several strokes, so Mom and her sisters took turns helping their parents out in Holbrook, Long Island. One week a month, our family would take a subway ride to Jamaica Avenue Station on a Saturday morning, then a very slow Long Island Railroad out to Holbrook, followed by a half mile walk to Grandma and Grandpa's house. Daddy would stay with the family until Sunday afternoon and go back to Brooklyn by himself. The next Saturday he would come out to Holbrook again. On Sunday, we'd all return to Brooklyn, and repeat it all the next month.

Not much happened during the week out in Holbrook that I can remember, but the weekends were great. Two families were always there together; the one that was coming and the one that was going. One weekend it was the Dohenys and the Blacks, and next weekend it was the Martins and the Dohenys. There were woods to explore, chickens to feed, snow to play in, and in the summer, a sprinkler to run through, and a lily pond with goldfish to watch, and always cousins to play with.

The Blacks and Dohenys both had children who had to begin school in the fall of 1952. Virginia Black said her family would move permanently to Holbrook in time for the start of that school year. Grandpa Vogelbach, died in October 1952, and since

---

[7] https://www.epa.gov/newsreleases/pilot-project-advances-epas-cleanup-gowanus-canal-superfund-site-brooklyn-ny

Virginia lived there, she continued to care for her mother. Virginia's children were enrolled in St. Joseph's School in Lake Ronkonkoma.

I had skipped kindergarten in 1951, since I would have had to miss a week of school every month, but now I was required to start first grade. My parents fervently believed they were supposed to send their children to a Catholic school so they would get a thorough education in Catholicism. They tried to enroll me in our parish's elementary school, St. Agnes on Degraw Street, but, probably because of the tremendous population increase from the new Gowanus projects, there were already 70 children in the first grade, and the pastor said they just could not admit me. I went to public school for the first two months of first grade while my mother banged on the convent door once a week to beg the principal to let me in the school. In November, the principal relented, and I left a very enjoyable public education environment and entered the forbidding halls of St. Agnes School. Another new admission and I made 72 children in the 1-A class. In public school there were many pre-reading activities; I learned the "The Itsy-Bitsy Spider;" and the atmosphere was sociable, light, and happy. Catholic school was dark, severe, strict, and demanding. When I started first grade, Anne was enrolled in the public school kindergarten, and finished a year there before she, too, was enrolled in St. Agnes for first grade.

Around this time, the housing authority notified us that we no longer qualified for subsidized housing; Daddy's salary, plus his overtime, meant he was making too much money each month for us to live in the Gowanus Apartments. He faced a conundrum. He needed to avoid our eviction, yet we couldn't survive on his regular salary, so he needed to work overtime just to break even. It was time to go house hunting. Bernard bought a used car for $200, a 1936 Oldsmobile coupe (I liked its running boards), and every chance we got we drove to the suburbs to look for a house.

AUG. 1952.

Three of my parents' friends from church were in a similar predicament. Sometimes they all went house hunting together. The Millers were the first to pick a place. They bought a split-level home in Morton Village in Plainview, Long Island. Soon the Swanstroms, Liguoris and Dohenys each bought a home in Morton Village. When my father tried to get a V.A. mortgage, they wouldn't count his overtime money, so he was denied, unless he could provide a down payment. All of my parents' friends got a V.A. mortgage without a down payment because their base salary was high enough. Grandpa Doheny died in April 1953 and left each of his sons $1,000. Daddy used it for a down payment on a home that cost $9,999. They then secured a 30-year V.A. mortgage. Mom said, "That was something else, wasn't it? Well as I said, everything seems to have worked out fine during our whole married life. I mean, whenever we were in a pinch, something came up."

On 8 April 1954, we moved to 162 Morton Blvd, Plainview, Long Island, and the Swanstroms and Liguoris were our next-door neighbors for the next 25 years.

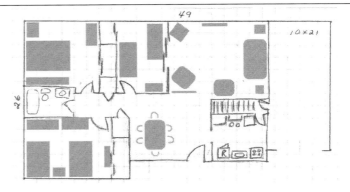

Though it was more difficult for Daddy to commute to work now, he never complained, because living in Plainview meant his children could grow up in a single-family home with a big backyard and a full basement to play in. There were lots of other children on the block, and all the mothers looked out for the safety of their own and everyone else's children. Dad's commute to work, though, was about two hours each way.

We bought our first telephone in 1954. It was needed so Daddy could call Mom to tell her which train he was taking home. For as long as I lived at home, Mom emphasized that the phone was for necessary calls only. We were always required to ask permission to use the phone. (We also had to ask permission to turn on our little 10" black and white TV. I believe it was a gift from Frank Doheny.) When we lived in Brooklyn, we had no phone. If Mom or Dad needed to make a call, they walked to a nearby candy store and used the pay phone there, or in an emergency, they asked Tim and Florence Commander in the apartment next door if they could use their phone.

The home on Morton Blvd. was modest, but it served us well. To the left is a photo Daddy took on the occasion of Anne's First Communion in 1955. In the photo are Uncle Eddie Black, John and Greg Black, and Anne and Betty.

Mom had to learn how to drive so she could pick her husband up at the Bethpage Long Island Railroad station. The car she learned on had manual transmission and a long stick shift on the floor. Mom claimed that she got her license on the first try because the inspector felt sorry for her.

Our home in Plainview was a magnet for the Doheny brothers, Larry especially. He took the train out to Plainview probably once a month while we were growing up. He and Daddy got along really well. We saw him get drunk sometimes and cry over things in his life, but we also had great times with him playing badminton, croquet, various card games, and in general having a really good time when he came out to visit us.

Right after we moved to Plainview, Muriel Liguori asked Mom to mind her two boys when they got home from school so she could go to work. Mom was not enthusiastic about this. She had just taken care of her sister Joan's boys for many months before we moved to Plainview while Joan worked at a dry-cleaning store in our Brooklyn neighborhood. Mom was pregnant with her fourth child. She relented, though, and Muriel paid her $8 a week, which really wasn't enough to give the boys supper every night, she told me. Mom also began to feel resentful that she had no time to work on setting up her new home. She said she was even a little jealous that neighbors were buying new rugs and curtains while all of her time was being consumed with caring for lots of children, some of them not her own. She said, years later, that she knows she lost her patience too often with the children. Mom said, "That was the worst time in my life, I think." [8]

Margo was born in the fall of the year we moved to Plainview. Daddy joked, "Grace had another baby every time we moved, so we better stay put now."

The photo at left was taken the day Mom and Margo came home from the hospital. We all wanted to hold the baby, and Anne was chosen for the honor.

Here is what it was like to live in a home with six people and one toilet. We were always worried about the septic tank overflowing. Our neighborhood did not have sewers until the 1970s, and we watched people on the block constantly dealing with collapsed front lawns and overflowing septic tanks. So, the rules at our house were: one shower per week, and wash dishes with the least amount of water possible. Bob Chess had a sign in his vacation house at Brant Lake, "Yellow let it mellow. Brown flush it down." Mom asked us to follow that practice at home, too, and we were also supposed to deposit any lightly used toilet paper in a wastebasket instead of flushing it down. On the good side, our regular household of six people never experienced a problem with the septic tank!

Around 1961, Aunt Helen Greene began to show signs of dementia. The Doheny brothers decided that Helen should live with Bernard's family. Mom was not consulted, and said later that she resented this. But, as Anne said, "Mom was the first to tell people that she had big shoulders." Aunt Helen lived with our family until about 1965 when she began doing bizarre things like running out of the house half-naked and locking herself in the bathroom for what seemed like hours. Mom put a porcelain pot outside our one bathroom for the convenience of anyone who really had to go. When Aunt Helen fell down the basement steps, Mom and Dad had to make the difficult decision to place her in a nursing home. The first nursing home restrained her in a straight-jacket and overmedicated her, so Mom and Dad moved Aunt Helen to the more pleasant Bronx State Hospital. She died there in 1968.

My sisters and I attended a variety of elementary schools. Again, this was because Mom and Dad felt obligated to send their children to Catholic school. I attended the local Plainview public schools from 2nd to 6th grade, and then I attended St. Patrick's School, Huntington, for 7th and 8th grades. Anne went to public school for one year, then commuted to St. Martin of Tours, Bethpage, for the rest of elementary school. Betty went to public school for kindergarten, then St. Martin's for 1st to 3rd grades; then, when our local parish, St. Pius X, opened its own school, she went there from 4th to 8th grades. Margo went to kindergarten in the local public school, then attended St Pius X for the rest of elementary school. For high school, we all commuted to Queen of the Rosary Academy in

---

[8] From a taped interview on 30 June 1988 in South Venice, Florida. Disk 2, track 9.

Amityville, 15 miles away. Every year we bit our nails waiting for the school budget to pass with enough money to provide bussing to private schools within a 15-mile radius from a taxpayer's home.

I'm sure each of us could critique our elementary and high school experience, and I'll include my own critique here. I loved public school. I enjoyed the small class sizes of about 25, art and music classes, gym, lots of social opportunities, relaxed, nurturing teachers, and collaborative learning. Catholic school was the exact opposite: rote learning, class sizes over 50, straight rows, enforced silence, no art, music or gym classes, and austere nuns. When I became a teacher myself, I was determined to teach the way I was taught in public school, and I hope my students enjoyed school more than they would have if I ran a strict Catholic school classroom.

When all of her children were in school, Mom had more time to herself and decided she wanted a part time job. She tried a factory job winding electromagnets, but found it mind-numbing. That job only lasted a couple of weeks. Mom was always a people-person and was much happier in her next job; she was invited to be the cook at St. Pius X Convent from 1964 to 1968. After that, she was an Office Manager and Secretary at Center Tool Company, Plainview, where she could use her excellent secretarial and organizational skills. She and Daddy intended to use her money for vacations – cruises, especially, but to leave the country, she would need a passport. That posed an unexpected problem.

Grace Vogelbach was born at home during the flu pandemic of 1918 when doctors were otherwise occupied. Family members ran to find a doctor when she was about to be born, and two doctors surprisingly showed up! While the doctors argued about who would go upstairs to attend the birth, baby Grace was born, with her grandmother Susannah Beyers assisting. It seems Mom's birth was never recorded at the Health Department. Years later, when Mom applied for a passport and found that she needed a birth certificate, her sister Virginia had to write a letter swearing that Grace was her sister, and that she had been born in Brooklyn on 19 Oct 1918.

Retirement in Sarasota

Daddy retired from Goldman Sachs on 19 Jan 1979. My parents' lives changed drastically with Daddy home all day. Mom was the social one who always had a million chores, activities, and hobbies, but Daddy didn't. Mom was afraid that their unequal ways might be bad for their relationship in retirement and tried to get her husband involved, but without much success. She was also afraid he might get in the habit of drinking too much beer. She knew there was a family tendency for this. They both liked warm weather, so they began to talk about moving to Florida. All their children were on their own, so there were no big obligations keeping them on Long Island.

So, Mom and Dad drove to St. Petersburg, FL to visit old friends, and after the visit, drove a little farther south to Sarasota. They stayed overnight in a motel in Venice and visited local homes that were for sale. A knowledgeable real estate agent steered them to relatively new homes built by the best construction company at the time. They found a five-year-old home that was in mint condition. The sale went smoothly, and they returned to Long Island to start packing. Mom was dealing with pain from a yet undiagnosed urethral pre-cancer, and the stress of packing resulted in her becoming very ill on moving day. They left anyway, as planned, on 1 Dec 1979. Two days later they were in their new home at 526 Carmel Rd., South Venice, FL.

Mom said their life in retirement on Carmel Rd. was like a 10-year honeymoon. She declared that she and Daddy fell in love all over again. They bowled together and went dancing at the American Legion and the VFW Halls. They loved their parish at Epiphany Cathedral, Venice. They went to the beach several times a week and did star-gazing to their heart's content; light pollution in South Venice was very mild in the 1980s. Mom went to crafts every week at the Venice Community Center. They made good friends with people on their block, and their children and grandchildren flew or drove down to see them a couple of times a year. Every Sunday, they spoke with their daughters on the phone.

Daddy had cataracts removed. He also developed atherosclerotic heart disease, but his mental faculties did not appear to be affected. Mom had a spinal operation to correct a painful disk problem the year before Daddy died, but life in general was good for most of their years in Florida. Around Jan 1988, Daddy developed sideroblastic anemia. He needed more and more frequent blood transfusions until they no longer helped him. His health slowly deteriorated, but I never heard him complain about pain or his increasing weakness. Margo and her family decided to move to Florida around this time; one of their many reasons was to be of help to Mom and Dad.

A few weeks before Daddy died, his doctor recommended that family members try to come down to say goodbye. When I went down, the only symptom my father mentioned to me was that he couldn't get his legs to relax. Two weeks after I went back to New York, Daddy died peacefully at home in the care of hospice; that was 18 May 1989. He had all of his mental faculties to the end and had gotten all of his affairs in order. Mom and Dad had both arranged their own funerals, which I think was the most considerate and kind gift they could have given us. The Lemon Bay Funeral Home arranged to ship Daddy's body up to Patchogue, Long Island. The wake was at Ruland Funeral Home, and the Mass of Burial was held in Betty's parish, Mary Immaculate, Bellport. Both were packed with relatives and friends of my family from their days on Long Island, as well as in-laws, friends and colleagues of their children. Daddy was buried in Calverton National Cemetery, Suffolk County NY, on 22 May 1989.

Mom's widowhood lasted about 15 years. She stayed active in all of her usual activities and enjoyed her social life. She flew to New York a couple of times a year to visit her sisters, her New York friends, and her children and grandchildren. She even had a boyfriend by the name of Charles Spiro to dance with and go to social events with.

As she aged, Mom developed Type II diabetes, glaucoma, high blood pressure, and high cholesterol. In 1999, she had a stroke in her left ear that left her totally deaf on that side. She was fortunate to have had a very talented internist by the name of Dr. Hicks, one of the few geriatric physicians in Sarasota. He was constantly adjusting Mom's medications because as one condition got worse, the meds for her other conditions would go out of balance. When Mom was in the last few months of her life, Dr. Hicks told me that he considered Mom to be one of his successes because, in spite of all that was medically wrong with her, she lived to be 87. Mom died in the Hospice House in South Venice on 5 Nov 2005 after several small strokes. Her daughters and granddaughter Grace were with her when she died. The night Mom died, Venus was shining brightly just below the moon on a very clear night. She would have loved seeing that!

Bernard Doheny and Grace Vogelbach had four children, five grandchildren (Gerard and Grace Murphy, Christina Maines, and Maureen and Michael Gundlach), and Grace lived to know her first great-grandchild, Angelo Corsini.

Here are Bernard and Grace's obituaries:

Bernard G. Doheny

Bernard G. Doheny, 75, 526 Carmel Road, Venice, died May 18, 1989.

He was born Oct. 11, 1913, in Brooklyn, N.Y., and came to this area 10 years ago from Long Island, N.Y. He was an accounting clerk with Goldman, Sachs and Co. investment bankers in New York City and a member of Epiphany Cathedral, Veterans of Foreign Wars and American Legion. He was an Army veteran of World War II.

Survivors include his wife, Grace; four daughters, Catherine of Bayside, N.Y., Anne Murphy of Medford, N.Y., Elizabeth Gundlach of Bellport, N.Y., and Margaret Maines of Bayport, N.Y.; and five grandchildren.

Services will be on Long Island. Burial will be in Calverton National Cemetery on Long Island. Lemon Bay Funeral Home, S. Venice Chapel, is in charge.

Compiled from notices in Sarasota Herald-Tribune on 13 Nov 2005 and Newsday on 11/20/2005

Grace D. Doheny

DOHENY-Grace,, 87, , died peacefully in her sleep on Nov 5, 2005, at Hospice House of Venice, FL.

Grace was born on Oct 19, 1918 in Brooklyn NY, graduated from Girl's Commercial High School and moved to Venice FL in 1979 from Plainview NY with her husband, Bernard. She was a member of Epiphany Cathedral Parish, VFW 8118 Aux., South Venice Civic Association Women's Club, Senior Friendship Center and the Moose Club of Englewood. She loved to bowl, golf and play cards with her many friends. She was the beloved sister of Joan Martin of Brooklyn; mother of four daughters, Catherine Dente of Sarasota, Anne Schuessler and Elizabeth Gundlach, both of New York, Margaret Maines of Northport, FL; she had five grandchildren, a great-grandson and two step-great-granddaughters. Funeral services were held in Bellport, NY. Lemon Bay Funeral Home, Venice Chapel, is in charge. Grace was laid to rest next to her Bernie in the National Cemetery in Calverton.

Chapter Eleven

John Farrell (early 1800s)
Mary Kane (early 1800s)

Why are there whole chapters about the Farrell and the Greene families? Because they are part of my family's Irish lineage. My Irish grandmother, whose ancestors were Greenes, Farrells and Kanes, married into the Doheny Family. As more of us take DNA tests, these chapters may help connect us to far-flung relatives.

John Farrell and Mary Kane are the earliest ancestors I have found so far for Katharine T. Greene, the wife of Edward J. Doheny. (Katharine and Edward are the subjects of Chapter Five.)

The Farrell family lived in County Longford. All of their eight known children were baptized in the Roman Catholic Parish of Ardagh and Moydow.

..... **1 John Farrell (ca.1800 – ca.1870)**
..... **+Mary Kane, married ca.1830**
.... 2 Patrick Farrell (1831 – Unknown)
.... 2 Mary Farrell (1833 – Unknown)
.... 2 Stephen Farrell (1834 – Unknown)
.... 2 Margaret Farrell (1837 – Unknown)
.... 2 Thomas Farrell (1839 – Unknown)
.... 2 Eleanora Farrell (1841 – Unknown)
.... 2 **Catherine Farrell** (1843 –1909 in Brooklyn, NY)
.... +Francis Greene (ca.1845 – 1884 in Brooklyn, NY), married ca.1874 in NY
.... 3 **Katharine T. Greene** (1878 in Brooklyn, NY – 1933 in Smithtown, Suffolk, NY)
.... **+Edward Joseph Doheny** (1874 in Tipperary, Ireland – 1953 in New York, NY), m: 1904 in NY
.... 3 Francis Joseph Greene (1880 in Brooklyn, NY – 1959 in Blue Point, Suffolk, NY)
.... 3 Helen V. Greene (1884 in Brooklyn, NY – 1968 in Bronx, NY)
.... +William Keenan, married 1889 in Brooklyn, NY
.... **2 Denis Farrell (1848 – 1924 in San Francisco, CA)**
.... +Anne Ward (1848 – 1916 in San Francisco, CA)

The first Irish record I found that mentions our ancestors John Farrell and Mary Kane is a baptism record for their son Patrick. Patrick is probably their first child. His baptismal date is 18 Mar 1831;[1] John and Mary probably were married before June 1830. IF Patrick was their first child, AND if the family followed the usual naming custom, then John Farrell's father was named Patrick.

---

[1] Ancestry.com, Ireland, Catholic Parish Registers, 1655-1915, Ardagh and Moydow, Longford, Ireland. John Farrell and Mary Kane are recorded as the parents of Patrick Farrell, baptized 18 Mar 1831. Patrick's sponsors were Thomas and Anne Farrell, and perhaps John had a brother named Thomas.

There is evidence that the family was from the small (ca. 90 acres) townland of Lissanisky[2] in the civil parish of Ardagh in County Longford.[3] Coincidentally, Lissanisky is just a bit west of Edgeworthstown, the place of birth of many members of the Greene Family.

Lissanisky is on Logainm.ie: Lissanisky.

Map

It is located at 53° 41' 9" N, 7° 41' 12" W.

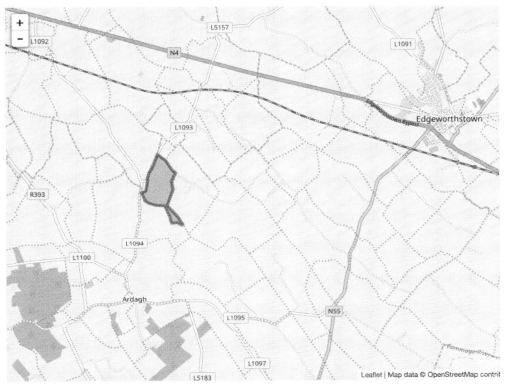

Area

Lissanisky has an area of:

- 367,758 m² / 36.78 hectares / 0.3678 km²
- 0.14 square miles
- 90.88 acres / 90 acres, 3 roods, 20 perches

Griffiths Valuation (1847-1864) lists only five occupants in Lissanisky: two Peter Farrells, two John Farrells and one John Kane.[4] We are probably related to all of them. I wonder if, perhaps, everyone else died or moved away during or after the Famine?

---

[2] Ancestry.com, Ireland, Select Births and Baptisms, 1620-1911, names Lissanisky, Longford, Ireland, as the birthplace of all of Denis Farrell (youngest son of John Farrell and Mary Kane) and Anne Ward's children.

[3] https://www.townlands.ie/longford/

[4] http://www.askaboutireland.ie/griffith-valuation/index.xml?action=doNameSearch&PlaceID=879335&county=Longford&barony=Ardagh&parish=Ardagh&townland=%3Cb%3ELissanisky%3C/b%3E

John Farrell and Mary Kane had at least eight children in 17 years.

		Baptized	Date of Emigration	Date and Place of Death
i.	Patrick	18 Mar 1831	unknown	unknown
ii.	Mary	1 Feb 1833	unknown	unknown
iii.	Stephen	24 Dec 1834	unknown	unknown
iv.	Margaret	16 Jul 1837	unknown	unknown
v.	Thomas	29 Jan 1839	unknown	unknown
vi.	Eleanora	12 May 1841	unknown	unknown
vii.	Catherine	19 Jul 1843	ca.1867	11 Dec 1909, Brooklyn NY
viii.	Denis	17 Mar 1848	1887, Philadelphia	29 Oct 1924, San Francisco CA

Actual Baptismal Records of John and Mary's children were found in the Roman Catholic parish of Ardagh and Moydow, County Longford, Ireland:[5]

i. Patrick Farrell, baptized 18 Mar 1831. Sponsors were Thomas and Anne Farrell. [6]

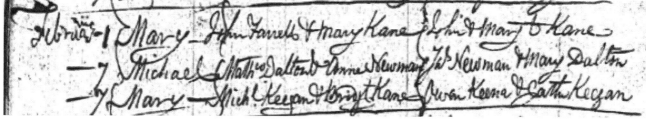

ii. Mary Farrell, baptized 1 Feb 1833. Sponsors were John and Mary T. Kane. [7]

iii. Stephen Farrell, baptized 24 Dec 1834. Sponsors were Peter Farrell and Ellen Kane. [8]

[5] https://www.ancestry.com/search/collections/irelandcatholicparish/
[6] Ancestry.com, Ireland Catholic Parish Registers, 1655-1915, Ardagh and Moydow 1793 - 1842 (image 69/149)
[7] Ancestry.com, Ireland Catholic Parish Registers, 1655-1915, Ardagh and Moydow 1793 - 1842 (image 76/149)
[8] Ancestry.com, Ireland Catholic Parish Registers, 1655-1915, Ardagh and Moydow 1793 - 1842 (image 82/149)

iv. Margaret Farrell, baptized 16 Jul 1837. Sponsors were Thomas Keenan and Betty Kane. [9]

v. Thomas Farrell, baptized 29 Jan 1839. Sponsors were Mick Farrell and Mary Dowd. [10]

vi. Eleanora Farrell, baptized 12 May 1841. Sponsors were Mich Brady and Anna Kays. [11]

vii. Catherine Farrell, baptized 19 Jul 1843. Sponsors were Thomas Farrell and Bridget O'Neil. [12]

viii. Denis Farrell, baptized 17 March 1848. Sponsors were John Keegan and Bridget Farrell. [13]

[9] Ancestry.com, Ireland Catholic Parish Registers, 1655-1915, Ardagh and Moydow 1793 - 1842 (image 89/149)

[10] Ancestry.com, Ireland Catholic Parish Registers, 1655-1915, Ardagh and Moydow 1793 - 1842 (image 93/149)

[11] Ancestry.com, Ireland Catholic Parish Registers, 1655-1915, Ardagh and Moydow 1793 - 1842 (image 98/149)

[12] Ancestry.com, Ireland Catholic Parish Registers, 1655-1915, Ardagh and Moydow 1842-1876 (image 5/83)

[13] Ancestry.com, Ireland Catholic Parish Registers, 1655-1915, Ardagh and Moydow 1842-1876 (image 12/83)

These records stir up more questions.

- Are the sponsors Thomas Farrell, Peter Farrell, Michael Farrell, and Bridget Farrell the siblings of John Farrell, the father of these eight children?
- Was John's oldest brother named Thomas, perhaps?
- Are the two Thomas Farrells the same person? Was Thomas Farrell married to Anne or Bridget, or was Bridget his second wife perhaps?
- Are John Kane, Betty Kane, and Ellen Kane all siblings of Mary Kane, the mother of the children mentioned above?
- If Patrick was the first-born-male, was John Farrell's father named Patrick?
- If Mary was the first-born-female, was Mary Kane's mother named Mary?
- What is the relationship among all the Kanes mentioned in Mary Farrell's baptismal record?
- Is Thomas Keenan related to Catherine Farrell's second husband William Keenan?

I leave it to future family historians to answer these questions.

Catherine Farrell and Francis Greene

John and Mary's seventh child in the list above, Catherine Farrell, was born in July 1843. Nothing is known about her early life in Ireland. She emigrated from Ireland to the USA about 1867.

We have three different records that mention her immigration. The 1900 US census says Catherine had been in the USA for 33 years, meaning the year of immigration was 1867.[14] The 1905 census says 1870,[15] and her 1909 death certificate says she had been in the United States for 50 years (1859). She lived in the City of New York for the last 27 years (1882).[16] When dates vary so widely, the earliest record usually holds the greatest weight, so I am guessing Catherine probably arrived in the USA about 1867. Her ship's passenger list has not been found.

Catherine Farrell married Francis Greene probably between 1872 and 1874,[17] judging from the date that their first child Thomas was born, which was 1874 or 1875. Their marriage may have been in Ireland, but more probably in Brooklyn between 1872 and 1874.

Read more about the family of Catherine Farrell and Francis Greene in the next chapter.

Denis Farrell and Ann Ward

Denis Farrell, John and Mary's youngest child, was baptized on 17 Mar 1848. He remained in Ireland much longer than his sister Catherine did.

---

[14] 1900 US census, Kings County, Brooklyn, SD 2, ED 377, Sheet 19 B.
[15] 1905 NY State census, Kings County, Brooklyn, AD 12, ED 28, Page 46.
[16] Death Certificate for Catherine Green Keenan #22971, NYC Dept of Health, 11 Dec 1909.
[17] 1875 NYS Francis and Catherine with their son Thomas, 7 months old. This means Thomas was born about Nov or Dec 1874, and their marriage was probably a year or so before that.

Denis married a woman named Anne Ward in his home parish of Ardagh and Moydow on 23 Nov 1873. Here is their marriage registry. Their witnesses were James Kenny and Mary Ward.[18]

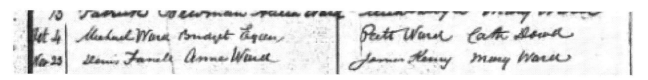

His children were born in Ireland. He was identified as a "farmer" on their Irish civil birth records.

Irish Records of Denis and Ann's Children

Denis and Anne had at least eight children, all baptized in their parish of Ardagh and Moydow.

   i. Mary Farrell, baptized 13 Oct 1874, sponsors Thomas Ward and Margaret Kane[19]

   ii. John Farrell, baptized 9 Jun 1876, sponsors Peter ? and Ellen Ward[20]

   iii. Anne Farrell, baptized 18 Sept 1877, sponsors Patrick Ward and Bridget Hughes[21]

   iv. Bridget Farrell, born 6 Apr 1879 to Denis Farrell (farmer) and Anne Ward in Lissanisky, Longford, [22] baptized 9 Apr 1879, sponsors John Keegan and Catherine--- [23]

---

[18] Ancestry.com, Ireland, Catholic Parish Registers, 1655-1915, parish of Ardagh and Moydow, image 67/83.
[19] Ancestry.com, Ireland, Catholic Parish Registers, 1655-1915, parish of Ardagh and Moydow, image 47/83.
[20] Ancestry.com, Ireland, Catholic Parish Registers, 1655-1915, parish of Ardagh and Moydow, image 49/83.
[21] Ancestry.com, Ireland, Catholic Parish Registers, 1655-1915, parish of Ardagh and Moydow, image 50/83.
[22] https://civilrecords.irishgenealogy.ie/churchrecords/images/birth_returns/births_1879/02917/2068782.pdf
[23] Ancestry.com, Ireland, Catholic Parish Registers, 1655-1915, parish of Ardagh and Moydow, image 53/83.

v. Patrick Farrell, born 30 Sep 1880 in Lisinsky[sic], Longford[24]

vi. Denis Farrell, born 7 Jan 1882 in Lisanisky, Longford.[25]

vii. Joseph Farrell, born 18 Dec 1884 in Lisaniska[sic], Longford (though registered in 1885).[26]

viii.   Ellen (Nellie) Farrell, born 25 Dec 1886.[27]
(No images of actual birth or baptism entries in Irish records have been found for Nellie yet.)
Denis, Anne, and eight children including infant Nellie emigrated from Ireland together. Their ship, the Lord Gaugh, landed in Philadelphia, PA on 23 March 1887.[28] With them is a Richard Farrell and a William Farrell, and it is reasonable to suppose that they are related to Denis somehow.

---

[24] https://civilrecords.irishgenealogy.ie/churchrecords/images/birth_returns/births_1880/02850/2044455.pdf
[25] https://civilrecords.irishgenealogy.ie/churchrecords/images/birth_returns/births_1882/02792/2024844.pdf
[26] https://civilrecords.irishgenealogy.ie/churchrecords/images/birth_returns/births_1885/02656/1979381.pdf
[27] Ancestry.com, California Death Index for 1940-1997 says she was born on 25 Dec 1887. That should say 1886 because we know she arrived in the USA on 23 March 1887 (source is the ships list of the Lord Gaugh.) Nellie is listed as an infant on the ships list.
[28] Ancestry.com, Ship's Passenger List for Lord Gough., arriving in Philadelphia on 23 Mar 1887.

Pennsylvania, Passenger and Crew Lists, 1800-1962 for Dennis Farrell
T840 - Philadelphia, 1883-1945 › 008

Once in the USA, the family migrated westward, and, by 1900, they were settled in California. The 1900 US census was dated June 1 of that year, and it enumerated the whole family at 417 Grove Street in San Francisco, CA. [29] They were renting their residence in a two-family house. It mentions these occupations of the Farrell family: Dennis, day laborer; wife Annie is keeping house; Mary, public-school teacher; John, bartender; Annie, shirt finisher; Bridget, shirt-sleeve maker; Patrick, Dennis and Joseph, dry-goods salesmen; Nellie is at school.

Michael McKenna shared this family lore about his great-grandfather:

> Denis, or Dennis, Farrell was an imposing figure. After a rough trip on the Lord Gough, Denis brought his family directly to California where he worked on the railroad, supposedly as the foreman of a gang of Chinese laborers. Then he took a job helping to build Golden Gate Park under the direction of John McLaren. [30]

---

[29] 1900 US census, California, San Francisco, SD 1, ED 147, Sheet 1B.
[30] Email from Michael McKenna to the author on 27 Jan 2020. Michael and the author shared Farrell research after being connected as DNA matches on AncestryDNA.com

The 1910 US census[31] on Apr 23 enumerated Denis, Annie and their two youngest children Joseph A. and Nellie C. at 963 Hayes Street, a single-family home that they rented. Denis is listed as a laborer in an electric light company, Joseph is working as a machinist in an automobile shop, and Nellie is a clerk in a title insurance company.

The 1910 census mentions that Annie had given birth to nine children. Eight of her nine children are listed on the ship's passenger list. Seven were living in 1910. Patrick died in 1906,[32] so he was one of the two who were deceased. The other seven children who immigrated with Denis and Annie are enumerated in later censuses. There are several excellent family trees on Amazon.com posted by Denis's descendants, so I recommend that readers of this book who want to know names, occupations, residences and more about his descendants refer to those trees.

Michael McKenna sent me this wonderful photo of his great-grandfather Denis Farrell. It was taken in San Francisco in the early 1900s.

1915 San Francisco city directory lists Denis and Annie's address as 238 20th Street. Annie died the next year in San Francisco. She was buried with her son Patrick in Holy Cross Cemetery, San Mateo CA.

1920 US census[33] on Jan 10 enumerates Denis Farrell age 71, widowed, as a lodger living in a boarding house at 1200 9th Ave, San Francisco. It says he was naturalized in 1892, and he is still working as a laborer. He is not living with family members at this time.

Denis died on 29 Oct 1924 at age 76 of a ruptured aorta and arteriosclerosis.[34] His death certificate says he was living at 1523 Funston Ave when he died, which is in the 5th Ward of San Francisco. He was buried with Annie and Patrick. His youngest son Joseph is also buried in this plot.

---

[31] 1910 US census, California, San Francisco, AD 37, ED 161, Sheet 8A.
[32] http://ww.sfgenealogy.com/php/cemetery/cemeteryindex.php? Patrick was buried in Holy Cross Cemetery, San Mateo CA on 24 Mar 1906 in Section B, Row 19, Area 4, Grave 6.
[33] 1920 US census, California, San Francisco, SD 4, Precinct 37, AD 27, ED 342, Sheet 14B.
[34] Death Certificate #6384 for Dennis Farrell, CA State Board of Health, San Francisco, filed 31 Oct 1924.

Outline Descendant Tree for John Farrell and Mary Kane

..... 1 John Farrell b: Abt. 1800 in Ireland, d: Bef. 1900
..... +Mary Kane
.... 2 Patrick Farrell b: Mar 1831 in Ardagh and Moydow, Longford, Ireland
.... 2 Mary Farrell b: Jan 1833 in Ardagh and Moydow, Longford, Ireland
.... 2 Stephen Farrell b: Dec 1834 in Ardagh and Moydow, Longford, Ireland
.... 2 Margaret Farrell b: Jul 1837 in Ardagh and Moydow, Longford, Ireland
.... 2 Thomas Farrell b: Jan 1839 in Ardagh and Moydow, Longford, Ireland
.... 2 Eleanora Farrell b: May 1841 in Ardagh and Moydow, Longford, Ireland
.... 2 Catherine Farrell b: Jul 1843 in Ardagh and Moydow, Longford, Ireland, d: 11 Dec 1909 in Brooklyn, NY
.... +Francis Greene b: Abt. 1845 in Edgeworthstown, Longford, Ireland, d: 24 Oct 1884 in Brooklyn, NY, m: Abt. 1874 in NY
.... 3 Thomas Greene b: Abt. 1875 in Brooklyn, NY, d: Jun 1896 in Brooklyn, NY
.... 3 Mary Greene b: Abt. 1876 in Brooklyn, NY, d: Sep 1883 in Brooklyn, NY
.... 3 Katharine T. Greene b: 26 Oct 1878 in Brooklyn, NY, d: 12 May 1933 in Smithtown, Suffolk, NY
.... +Edward Joseph Doheny b: 25 Aug 1874 in Graigue, Tipperary, Ireland, d: 05 Apr 1953 in New York, NY, m: 28 Sep 1904 in New York, NY
.... 4 Catharine Doheny b: 09 Apr 1905 in NY, d: 10 Apr 1905 in NY
.... 4 Edward Joseph Doheny Jr. b: 10 May 1907 in New York, d: 23 Aug 1972 in Brooklyn, NY
.... +Catherine Idola Talbott b: 10 Jun 1910, d: 16 May 1976 in Brooklyn, NY, m: 01 Jul 1939 in Brooklyn, NY
.... 4 Thomas J. Doheny b: Abt. Aug 1908, d: Oct 1908 in Brooklyn, NY
.... 4 Francis William Doheny b: 07 Nov 1909 in New York, NY, d: 16 Aug 1973 in Northport, Suffolk, NY
.... +Madeline Hendrickson b: 10 Mar 1919 in Bronx, NY, d: 12 Jul 2006 in Northport, Suffolk, NY
.... 4 Gerard J Doheny b: 12 Oct 1910 in Brooklyn, NY, d: 31 Dec 1933 in Tampa, Hillsborough, Florida
.... 4 Lawrence Aloysius Doheny b: 27 Feb 1912 in Brooklyn, NY, d: 24 May 1978 in New York, NY
.... +Catherine A "Bobby" Doonan b: 10 Aug 1928, d: 2017 in NY, m: 1949 in Brooklyn, NY
.... 4 Bernard Greene Doheny b: 11 Oct 1913 in Brooklyn, NY, d: 18 May 1989 in So Venice, Sarasota, FL
.... +Grace Dolores Vogelbach b: 19 Oct 1918 in Brooklyn, NY, d: 05 Nov 2005 in So Venice, Sarasota, FL, m: 21 Aug 1943 in Brooklyn, NY
.... 3 Francis Joseph Greene b: 08 Nov 1880 in Brooklyn, NY, d: Jun 1959 in Blue Point, Suffolk, NY
.... 3 Helen V. Greene b: 05 Dec 1884 in Brooklyn, NY, d: 08 Aug 1968 in Bronx, NY
.... +William Keenan m: 09 Jul 1889 in Brooklyn, NY
.... 2 Denis Farrell b: Mar 1848 in Ardagh and Moydow, Longford, Ireland, d: 29 Oct 1924 in San Francisco, CA
.... +Anne Ward b: 1848 in Ireland, d: 1916 in San Francisco, CA
.... 3 Mary Farrell b: Oct 1874 in Longford, Ireland, d: 13 Jan 1944 in San Francisco, California
.... 3 John Farrell b: Jun 1876 in Longford, Ireland, d: 05 Feb 1930 in San Francisco, CA
.... +Margaret M Clifford b: 1884, d: 1927
.... 4 John C Farrell b: 02 Sep 1905 in CA, d: 10 Feb 1984 in Sonoma, CA
.... 4 Paul Farrell b: 07 May 1907 in California, d: 04 Nov 1972 in El Dorado, CA
.... 4 Joseph Farrell b: 1910, d: Aft. 1970
.... 4 Margaret Mary Farrell b: 04 Apr 1915 in San Francisco, CA, d: 25 Sep 1970 in San Francisco, CA
.... 3 Annie Farrell b: Sep 1877 in Lissanisky, Longford, Ireland, d: 05 Jul 1961 in Berkeley, CA
.... +Michael S. McKenna b: 1879, d: Unknown
.... 4 Norbert McKenna b: 01 Jul 1908 in CA, d: 10 Apr 1942 Lost at Sea
.... 4 Mary A McKenna b: 07 Aug 1909 in Berkeley, CA, d: 01 Nov 2002 in Oakland, CA
.... 4 Clement Joseph McKenna b: 09 Mar 1911 in Oakland, CA, d: 13 Aug 1992 in Marin, CA
.... 4 Adrian A McKenna b: 21 Nov 1912 in CA, d: 19 Feb 1993 in San Joaquim, CA
.... 4 Angela Jeanne McKenna b: 23 Feb 1915 in Alameda, CA, d: 15 Jan 1981 in Sonoma, CA
.... 4 James Francis McKenna b: 17 Jan 1919 in Alameda, CA, d: 19 Apr 2001 in Clayton, CA
.... 3 Bridget Farrell b: 06 Apr 1879 in Lissanisky, Longford, Ireland, d: 02 Sep 1954 in San Mateo, CA
.... +Michael Joseph Costello
.... 4 John Cornelius Costello b: 1894, d: 1974

.... 4 Marie Helen Costello b: 1895, d: 1982
.... 3 Patrick Farrell b: 30 Sep 1880 in Lissanisky, Longford, Ireland, d: 22 Mar 1906 in San Francisco, CA
.... 3 Denis Farrell b: 07 Jan 1882 in Lissanisky, Longford, Ireland, d: 14 Jun 1944 in San Francisco, CA
.... 3 Joseph A Farrell b: 18 Dec 1884 in Lissanisky, Longford, Ireland, d: 08 Sep 1948 in Napa, CA
.... 3 Nellie Farrell b: 25 Dec 1886 in Ireland, d: 05 Dec 1966 in Santa Clara, CA
.... +Elmer John Gallagher b: 05 Sep 1888, d: 07 Jan 1950 in San Francisco, CA
.... 4 Elmer John Gallagher Jr. b: 1914, d: 1991
.... 4 Eleanor R Gallagher b: 1918, d: 2001
.... 4 Rita M Gallagher b: 1920, d: 1995

Chapter Twelve

Thomas Greene (early 1800s)

Margaret Kane (early 1800s)

The records for the Greene family were not as easy to find compared with the records for the Doheny and Farrell families, so this chapter will include some of the strategies I used to research the lives (and loves) of some of our Greene ancestors.

When I started, I relied on the fact that my father's middle name was Greene (spelled with an e), and that it was his mother's maiden name. He had told me that I was named after his mother Catherine, and I knew his mother had siblings named Helen and Francis.

I wanted to find out:
- Was my father's mother born in the US?
- If not, what part of Ireland was she from?
- Where did she live in the United States?
- When was she married? Who were her witnesses?
- Who were her parents?
- When did she die; how did she die?

The most important source of information for family historians like me is a stash of family documents and memorabilia that has been passed down through the generations. Some genealogists are lucky enough to inherit a packet of vital records (old birth, marriage and death certificates), letters, award certificates, military records, wills, deeds, old family bibles, and stories that members of the older generation would be willing and even anxious to share. I had none of these sources for my father's parents. My Aunt Helen Greene had been dead since 1968, so I couldn't ask her about her ancestors. My father, who died in 1989, passed down no Greene family stories to us. I had no older person in the Greene family to interview.

I began my Greene family research with a search for the marriage record for my Doheny grandparents, Edward Doheny and Catherine Greene. I hoped to find Catherine's parents' names that way, the names of their witnesses, and maybe some other leads of any kind.

Searching for their marriage certificate required a trip to the New York City Archives in downtown Manhattan. There were microfilms at the Archives containing marriage indexes, sorted according to the Soundex code, for each of the boroughs of New York City. (I always kept a little "cheat sheet" near me to decipher the Soundex code while I searched such microfilms. See the Appendix.) Having had no luck searching the Brooklyn marriage index, I turned to the Manhattan index and eventually found an Edward J. Doheney married to Catharine T. Greene. It was my first experience dealing with alternate spellings of names in public records. I would find Catherine variously spelled Catharine, Kathrine, Katharine, Katie, and Kate, and Doheny spelled Doheney, Dohony, and Dohoney. (I have kept the alternate spelling when transcribing a document, but otherwise I have usually spelled my father's mother as Katharine and her mother's name as Catherine, and surnames as Doheny and Greene.) The date on the marriage certificate is 28 Sep 1904, and the place is Manhattan. The date made sense, since their child, my Uncle Ed, would have been born in that decade. The place matched, too, since I knew Doheny relatives had lived in Manhattan. I paid the $15 fee for the archives staff to find the actual marriage certificate. When I received the marriage certificate (a copy is in this book's Appendix), I found new, very important information on it:

> Edward J. Doheney, 30 years old, lived at 252 West 20th Street, Manhattan.
> Edward was born in Ireland.
> His parents were William Doheney and Ann Scully.
>
> Catharine T. Greene, 26 years old, lived at 287 Prospect Park West, Brooklyn.
> Catharine was born in Brooklyn.
> Her parents were Francis Green and Catharine Farrell.
>
> Edward and Catharine were married at St. Francis Xavier Parish, West 16th Street, Manhattan on 28 Sept 1904.
> Their witnesses were John Doheny and Helen V. Greene.
>
> The actual signatures of the bride and groom and their witnesses are on the certificate – Edward Doheny and Katharine T. Greene

A minor surprise was that Katharine Greene and Edward Doheny (using the spelling of their signatures) were married in the groom's parish, not the bride's Brooklyn parish; I wondered why. John Doheny was a new name; I hadn't heard of a John Doheny in the family. Maybe John was Edward's brother. I saw that Aunt Helen's middle initial was V, and Katharine said she was born in Brooklyn. All of that information would prove helpful as I continued my journey.

Since I now had the names of all four of my father's grandparents, plus an address for Katharine in 1904, maybe I could find her and other family members at that address in the 1900 census. That would be my next focus.

United States and New York State Censuses

Census records are the second most important source of information for genealogists. They are primary documents for where people lived on "Census Day," and they are also great secondary sources for such information as a person's age, occupation, place of birth, year of immigration and naturalization, place of birth of parents, whether the household had a radio in 1930, whether the family owned or rented their home, how much rent they paid or what their home was worth, what level of schooling each person had, and much, much more. Accuracy of the data depended on the knowledge and/or truthfulness of the person who was interviewed by the census taker and how accurately any census taker transcribed his or her notes onto the official schedules.

The Greene Family in the 1900 Census

In the 1900 census, I wanted to find a family comprised of a father Francis Green(e), wife Catherine, and children Katharine, Helen and Francis.

Available to me was an extraordinarily useful card index to the 1900 US census created by the WPA, the Work Projects Administration, during the 1930s. After the cards were created, they were arranged by state or territory, then by last names of the head of household alphabetized under the Soundex Code. Then the cards were microfilmed and the films stored in various National Archives buildings. The Mormon Church made copies of the microfilms, stored the films out in Salt Lake City, and loaned them to their various Family History Centers, like the one on Beneva Road in Sarasota. Figuring out which census films to order was relatively easy for this particular census, because the WPA actually listed the volume number, the enumeration district, and page and line numbers of the original census schedules right on the index cards.

After ordering the microfilm of the 1900 index for Brooklyn, I waited about two weeks for its delivery. Then I searched and searched for Francis Green(e), but after a great deal of effort, I had to give up. I had found no Francis Green or Greene with a wife Katherine, Katie, Catherine, or any other name variants on those cards.

Persistence is my middle name, so instead of relying just on the index, I decided to order the microfilm of the actual census pages for the part of Brooklyn where 287 Prospect Park West was located. I first had to figure out the Ward number and the Enumeration District from several finding aids that the government had produced. The Mormon Church on Beneva had copies of the finding aids. I eventually ordered the appropriate microfilm and then went page by page through the handwritten population schedules for that part of Brooklyn. It took a few mornings, working about two hours at a time, but I found our Greene family living at 287 9th Ave, Brooklyn. (I also looked at a modern-day map and discovered that Prospect Park West was an alternate name for 9th Ave, Brooklyn, so the census address was a match with the address on Edward and Catharine's marriage certificate.). Here is what I found in the 1900 census:

1900 US census, New York, Kings County, Brooklyn, SD 2, ED 377, Sheet 19B, June 1.
- Kate Green, head of household, born Apr 1850, age 50, widow, mother of 6 children, 3 now living, born in Ireland as were both parents, year of immigration 1867, 33 years in the US, no occupation, can read, write and speak English, owned her home with a mortgage.
- Frank Green, son, born Nov 1880, age 19, single, born in NY, both parents born in Ireland, worked as a farm laborer, can read, write and speak English.
- Helen Green, daughter, born Dec 1884, age 15, single, born in NY, both parents born in Ireland, was attending school, can read, write and speak English.

My grandmother Katharine is not living at home at the time of the census in 1900. In the years since finding the above 1900 census entry, I have tried in vain to find her in this census. There are scores of Catherine Greens and Greenes in this census in New York and Brooklyn, name spelled many ways, of the right age, and born in New York or Brooklyn. She would have been about 22 in 1900. I suspect she was a houseworker/servant somewhere, as that was her occupation on other documents. She may not have been enumerated in the census. A certain small percentage of people in every census are not enumerated.

However, there was plenty in the 1900 census to investigate further. For example, how did Kate get the money to buy a home, and how did she pay her mortgage? What did the home look like? The 1900 census said Kate Green was a widow, so her husband Francis Green died sometime before the 1900 "Census Day," 1 Jun 1900. I looked for him in the Brooklyn death index on microfilm at the Mormon Church, but couldn't be sure I was finding him among the many Francis Green(e)s who died before 1900. I decided to search for his obituary in old newspapers. In the early 2000s some generous Brooklyn genealogists were posting important reference material on their website for free. *The Brooklyn Daily Eagle* was on their site, so I searched for my g-grandfather's obituary there, and I found it in the 25 Oct 1884 edition on page 5!

> GREEN—On Friday, October 24, FRANCIS GREEN, Town of Edgeward, County of Longford, Ireland.
> Relatives and friends are respectfully invited to attend the funeral from his late residence, Eighteenth st. and Tenth av, on Sunday at 2 P. M.

Wow! I read that the Greene line of my family was from a town named Edgeward in County Longford, that Francis died on 24 Oct 1884, and that his last residence was 18th Street and 10th Ave, Brooklyn.

The first thing I did was look up Edgeward, County Longford, on the internet. The preferable spelling turned out to be Edgeworthstown. In 1935, the name was officially changed to Mostrim which sounded close to its traditional Irish name. In 1974, the name was changed back to Edgeworthstown. Wikipedia says both names are in use today.

I sent away for Francis Green's death certificate from the New York City Department of Records and Information Services (DORIS) and received it a few weeks later. It told me:

- Francis was 45 years old when he died, making his birthday approximately 1839.
- Francis was born in Ireland, immigrated 17 years before his death, lived in Brooklyn 17 years. That would make his immigration year about 1867.
- Francis lived on the 2nd floor of a three-family house at 18th Street and 10th Ave., he suffered for 9 days because of pneumonia and asthenia (meaning an abnormal weakness and lack of energy from a chronic respiratory disease) before he died.
- Francis's death certificate was delivered to Henry Green, not his wife (maybe she was too distraught) at 8am on the 25 Oct 1884 by James McManus, MD, of 187 13th Street. Maybe Henry was a brother of Francis.
- Francis was buried in Holy Cross Cemetery, Brooklyn, on 26 Oct 1884.

What his death certificate did not tell me were the names of his parents. If I had that information, it would have made searching Irish records much easier.

Realizing that graves often contain several burials, my next step was to call Holy Cross Cemetery[1] to see who was buried with Francis, and I was rewarded with the names, dates of burial, and ages at death of these family members.

Holy Cross Cemetery, Section Vernon, Range D, Plot 411, purchased 1883 by Francis Green

Name	Burial Date	Age at death
Mary Green	14 Sep 1883	7 yrs
Francis Green	26 Oct 1884	45 yrs
Thomas Green	14 Jun 1896	21 yrs
Catherine Greene Keenan	14 Dec 1909	66 yrs
Francis J. Greene	12 Jun 1959	79 yrs
Helen V. Greene	12 Aug 1968	84 yrs

Hmmmm. It looked like Greene could be spelled with or without the "e". It looked like Francis and Catherine had two children I hadn't heard of, Mary and Thomas; and who was Catherine Greene Keenan? Perhaps Catherine Farrell Greene married a second time? But the 1900 census recorded her with the last name Green. Maybe she married Mr. Keenan between 1900 and her death in 1909. What was Mr. Keenan's first name? Who was he?

Who Was Mr. Keenan?

I put the following items on my "To Do List":
1. a search for a Catholic parish marriage record of Catherine Green(e) and a Mr. Keenan
2. a search for a civil marriage record of Catherine Green(e) or Farrell and a Mr. Keenan.
3. a search of the 1905 census to see if a Mr. Keenan is enumerated with Catherine.

1. I sent a donation to Holy Name of Jesus Church on Prospect Park West, because that would have been the nearest Catholic Church, for a search through their records for the marriage of a Keenan and a Farrell or Green(e) between 1884 (when Francis died) and 1909 (when Catherine died). They found two records.

The most promising of the two records was for a William Keenan and a Catherine Farrell married on 9 Jul 1889. The witnesses were George Creighton and Catherine Greene. Could Catherine Greene be my grandmother, the bride's 10-year-old daughter? A line for remarks has the cryptic abbreviation, "Disp." It might mean "dispensation." I wondered if Catherine Farrell might have married a first cousin, which would need a church dispensation, or needed a dispensation to have a 10-year-old as a witness, and I would later find Keenans in Catherine's natal village in Ireland.

2. For the civil marriage record of Catherine Farrell and William Keenan, I sent my $15 fee to DORIS, but got the reply that they could not find a record for this marriage, and, of course, the fee was non-refundable. Perhaps DORIS could find a civil record, though, for Catherine Farrell's first marriage, her marriage to Francis Green(e), in the period of 1873-1874. I picked that time period

---

[1] Holy Cross Cemetery, 3620 Tilden Ave., Brooklyn (718-284-4520). The plot had been purchased by Francis Green in 1883, probably to bury his daughter Mary. He would be buried there the following year.

based on 1875 being the birth year of their first child Thomas, but again a letter came back from DORIS saying that this marriage record was not found.

3. A search of the 1905 NY State census came next. It did not have an index back in 2000 when I did my search. (Since then it has been indexed and the index is digitized.) Back then I had to go directly to the handwritten schedules. I located 287 Prospect Park West which had three families in residence: a young couple, another couple plus that wife's three siblings, and our Greene family:

1905 New York State census, Kings, Brooklyn, AD12, ED28, Page 46, 287 Prospect Park West

- Catherine Green, head of household, age 50, born in Ireland, immigrated 35 years ago, citizen, occupation was housework.
- Frank J. Green, son, age 24, born in US, citizen, day laborer, wage earner.
- Helen V. Green, daughter, age 20, citizen, in high school (What did that mean? She is too old to be a high school student.)

There was no Mr. Keenan. Did they marry between 1905 and her death in 1909? Not in Katherine's parish, anyway, as far as the parish secretary could tell.

Chapter Eleven mentions Keenans from the Farrell's home parish, Ardagh and Moydow. A Keenan was Catherine's sister Margaret's baptismal sponsor. There is a chance that her new husband was someone she knew from Ireland. In any case, Catherine's second marriage seems to have been brief; she died in 1909 and is buried with her first husband and her children Thomas, Mary, Francis and Helen.

1892 NY State Census

The 1890 US census was mostly destroyed by fire. The fragments that do survive do not include Brooklyn. New York State took a census in 1892, and I wondered if it might have something to tell us about Mr. Keenan. After entering a variety of names and combinations in the search fields, a William Keenan, age 50, did surface, living in Brooklyn with family members Kate age 40, Thomas age 14, Katie age 12, Frank age 10, and Ellen age 7! It looks like the parish secretary did indeed find Catherine's marriage to Mr. Keenan, and it does seem that young Katharine, only 10 years old, was one of the witnesses! Their 1892 residence was "between Windsor Place and Prospect Ave." (The 1892 NY State census seldom listed specific addresses. But, 287 Prospect Park West, where the Greene family lived in 1900, is in this vicinity.) There is no occupation listed for William on this census record, unfortunately, and Brooklyn Directories of the time list no William Keenan in the area. There are six William Keenans who died between 1892 and 1900 and are buried in Holy Cross Cemetery. Their burials dates are 24 Jan 1892, 2 Dec 1892, 2 Jan 1896, 14 Sept 1898, 22 Jan 1899, and 16 Mar 1899.

The Greene Family in the 1880 Census

A search of the 1880 census came next; it has an excellent searchable index, and searches are free on many websites. I found the family quite easily living at 684 Sixth Ave, Brooklyn. It was the home of three working-class families, the Greens being one of them. Though censuses are only truly reliable for where people resided, the 1880 census did suggest some new information.

Along with their parents Francis and Katherine, were my own grandmother Katherine and her older siblings Thomas and Mary, all names found in the Holy Cross Cemetery record. The 1900 census said Francis and Catherine had 6 children. With the help of the 1880 census, we now had the names of five of them: Thomas, Mary, Katharine, Francis and Helen.

1880 US census, New York, Kings County, Brooklyn, SD 2, ED 63, page 50B, 684 Sixth Ave.
- Francis Green, 41, head of household, laborer, born in Ireland as were both of his parents. He could read but not write.
- Katharine Green, 35, wife, keeping house, born in Ireland as were her parents. Could read, write.
- Thomas Green, age 5, son, at school, born in New York, both of his parents were born in Ireland.
- Mary Green, age 3, daughter, born in New York, both of her parents were born in Ireland.
- Katharine Green, age 1, daughter, born in New York, both of her parents were born in Ireland.

Since the 1880 census said that 5-year old Thomas had been born in New York, maybe I could find Francis, Catherine, and Thomas in the 1875 NY State census.

The Greene Family in the 1875 Census

The 1875 NY State census was not indexed when I searched it, though it is now. Again, to search this census required going to the Family History Library at the Mormon Church on Beneva Road, Sarasota. First, I had to find the film number of the Brooklyn Ward and Enumeration District that I thought they might live in. I examined ward maps of Brooklyn from the late 19th century and picked likely wards. That allowed me to order a few films that seemed promising. In a couple of weeks, the films were delivered to the Family History Library in Sarasota, and they called me to say the films had arrived. Next, I spent many mornings using their antique microfilm readers, going page by page through those wards.

I was rewarded by this entry. At 792 Dean Street, Brooklyn was Francis, Catherine, and seven-month-old Thomas. A man named Henry Green, boarder, is also living with them. It was another indication that Francis had a brother or close relative named Henry.

Following is a transcription.

<u>1875 New York State census, Kings County, Brooklyn, 9th Ward, ED 5, page 4.</u>

792 Dean Street is a frame house, worth $800, the home of three working-class households - the Greens and two couples with no children. Our family consisted of:

- Francis Green, 30, born in Ireland, a general laborer, not naturalized, can read.
- Catherine Green, 28, wife, born in Ireland, keeping house, can read.
- Thomas Green, 7 months, child, born in Brooklyn.
- Henry Green, 23, boarder, born in Ireland, single, general laborer, not naturalized, can read.

All we would ever know about the occupation of Francis Greene was that he was among the thousands of Irish laborers in Brooklyn. This census says he was born about 1845.

Continuing my census research, I was curious to see who lived at 287 Prospect Park West, or 287 Ninth Ave., Brooklyn in 1910.

The Greene Family in the 1910 Census

Here is an image of the census record for residents of 287 Prospect Park West, followed by a transcription. Now, my grandparents Edward J Doheny and Katharine T. Greene are living there with two children and Katharine's siblings Francis and Helen.

<u>1910 US census, New York, Kings County, Brooklyn, Ward 22, SD2, ED 575, Sheet 11A, Apr 15.</u>

- Edward J. Doheny, Head, age 35, 1st marriage, married 5 years, born in Ireland as were both of his parents, immigrated in 1895, naturalized, speaks English, earns wages as a bookkeeper in an insurance office, can read and write, rents their residence
- Katharine T. Doheny, Wife, age 31, 1st marriage, married 5 yrs, birthed 3 children, 2 now living, born in New York, both parents born Ireland, speaks English, can read and write, unemployed
- Edward J. Doheny, Jr, Son, age 2 11/12, born in NY, father born in Ireland, mother born in NY
- Francis W. Doheny, Son, age 5/12, born in NY, father born in Ireland, mother born in NY
- Francis J. Green, Lodger, age 29, single, born in NY, both parents born in Ireland, speaks English, employed for wages as a trimmer in a City Park, out of work for 16 weeks during 1909, can read and write
- Helen V. Green, Lodger, age 25, single, born in NY, both parents born in Ireland, spoke English, employed for wages as a Public School teacher, can read and write

The new information in the 1910 census was Aunt Helen's and Uncle Frank Green's employment, and that Uncle Frank was out of work for about four months in 1909. Edward was now the head of household, renting the apartment. Had the family sold the building after Catherine Greene Farrell Keenan died and just remained living there? The 1900 census had said she owned the building. The reason for the discrepancy in the two censuses remains unknown.

The Greene Family in the 1915 Census

The 1915 NY State census was not indexed when I searched it. (It is now digitized and searchable.) It was one of those that had to be examined page by page at the Mormon Church's Family History Center on Beneva Road. It was worth it; I found the family living at 647 19th Street.

1915 New York State census, Kings county, Brooklyn, AD 16, ED 60, page 15, June 1, 647 19th St.
- Kathrine Doheney, head, age 36, born in the US, a citizen, doing housework
- Edward J. Doheney, son, age 8, born in the US, a citizen, at school
- Francis W. Doheney, son, age 5, born in the US, a citizen, at school
- Gerard Doheney, son, age 4, born in the US, a citizen
- Lawrence Doheney, son, age 3, born in the US, a citizen
- Bernard Doheney, son, age 1, born in the US, a citizen
- Francis J. Greene, brother, age 34, born in the US, a citizen, wage laborer in the Parks Dept.
- Helen V. Greene, sister, age 30, born in the US, a citizen, earned wages as a public school teacher

Uh, oh. Katharine is the head of household in 1915. Her husband is not living at home with them. This was an indication that Edward and Katharine's marriage was in trouble by the time my father was only a year old. Katharine's occupation was housework – all the wives, as well as the two female heads of households on this page, are listed as doing housework.

The Greene Family in the 1920 Census

In the 1920 census, Aunt Helen is still living with her sister Katharine. Katherine is again the head of the household. Uncle Frank Greene is not with them in the 1920 census.

1920 US census, Kings County, Brooklyn, SD 3, ED 710, Sheet 18A, Jan 1, 220 Greenwood Ave.
- Katharine Doheny, head, rented their single family home, age 41, divorced, able to read, write, and speak English, born NY, both parents born in Ireland and their native tongue was English, she is a housewife
- Edward, son, age 12, attended school, able to read, write, and speak English, born NY, father born in Ireland and spoke English, mother born in NY
- Francis, son, age 10, attended school, able to read, write, and speak English, born NY, father born in Ireland and spoke English, mother born in NY
- Gerard, son, age 9, attended school, born NY, father born in Ireland and spoke English, mother born in NY
- Lawrence, son, age 7, born NY, father born in Ireland and spoke English, mother born in NY

- Bernard, son, age 6, born NY, father born in Ireland and spoke English, mother born in NY
- Helen V. Greene, sister, age 30, single, able to read, write, and speak English, born NY, both parents born in Ireland and their native tongue was English, earned wages as a public school teacher

The notation that Katharine Greene Doheny was divorced was new information. We knew she and Edward were separated at some point, but telling the census taker that she was divorced gave new insight into their relationship.

Mysteries in the 1925 and 1930 Censuses

The 1925 census also held some surprising news for me. Katharine is not enumerated with her boys; Edward is living with his four youngest sons, and they have moved to the same building as Edward's sister Annie and her husband Jim Farrell in Manhattan.[2] Where was my grandmother Katharine living? Maybe the 1930 census would solve this mystery.

The 1930 census was released in 2002. (There is a US law that says population schedules have to wait 72 years to be released.) It was released with a searchable index, to the joy of genealogists. I found Aunt Helen, but not Uncle Frank Greene, and not my grandmother Katharine.

Helen B. [sic] Greene is living alone in 1830 in a large apartment building called Warwick Hall at 526 Second Street in Brooklyn. She has a radio, and is paying $85 in rent. She has one of the most expensive apartments in the building. She is single, 36, can read and write, born in NY, both parents were born in Ireland, and she is working as a public-school teacher. Almost all of the occupants of Warwick Hall were either professionals or skilled workers.[3]

I decided to cast a wider net for Katharine Greene Doheny's 1930 census record and searched the entire New York State index. One likely "hit" was for a Katherine Doheny out in Smithtown, Long Island. When I located the actual census page,[4] this time the news was startling! My grandmother was in Kings Park State Hospital, an institution for people suffering from mental illness. Here is a transcription of the census record:

Katherine Doheny, Inmate, age 52, married, can read, write and speak English, born in the US, birthplace of parents was Unknown, no occupation. Notice the marital status doesn't say divorced. It is possible that the 1920 census taker was told "divorced," though Katharine's actual marital status was "separated."

The Search for Katharine Greene Doheny's Kings Park Hospital Records

Perhaps I could obtain my grandmother's Kings Park Hospital medical records. I sent an email to NYS Records Management and got a prompt reply. The staff person suggested writing or phoning

---

[2] 1925 NY State census, New York County, ED 14, Page 25, June 1, 101 9th Ave, Manhattan.
[3] 1930 US census, NY, Kings County, Brooklyn, SD 30, AD 12, ED 24-602, Sheet 19B.
[4] 1930 US census, NY, Suffolk County, Township of Smithtown, Village of Kings Park, Institution – Kings Park State Hospital, SD 36, ED 52-109, Sheet 35A, April 1.

Kings Park Psychiatric Center, Kings Park NY 11754, 516-544-2957. The email said "Certain summary patient records of the various facilities operated by the Office of Mental Health were recently transferred to the State Archives. I am therefore also referring your inquiry to the References Services unit of the State Archives for their response. Their phone number is 518-474-8955."

My letter to Kings Park was returned as "Undeliverable, forwarding address expired;" the facility had closed in 1996. Next, I phoned the State Archives and received instructions about how to request records, which I promptly did. A week later, I received a form letter with the box checked off that said, "Archives staff have *not* located any information relevant to your request."

I found a phone number for Suffolk County Mental Health, called them and was connected to Forensics. A very helpful staff member said that the Registrar of Kings Park, Smithtown Township, is the place to request death certificates for people who died at Kings Park Hospital. The death certificate might have the information I was seeking. I phoned the Smithtown Town Clerk's office and asked if they had the records from Kings Park. That person said Pilgrim Psychiatric Center maintains the old Kings Park Hospital death registry. She gave me the phone number of the Records Department and the address I needed. I called Pilgrim Psychiatric Center and the staff person said they would search the archives and make a copy of a Registry of Death. The charge was $4.00. She promised that she would also forward my letter to another department that might be able to tell me her diagnosis and how long she was a patient at Kings Park Hospital.

That very day, I sent my request, and less than two weeks later received a "Verified Transcript of the documentation recorded in our Register of Death." The cover letter stated that my request for medical records had been forwarded to the Medical Records Department.

Name of Deceased:	Katherine G. Doheny
Died:	12 May 1933
Age:	54 yrs, 6 mos, 16 days
Marital status:	Separated
Occupation:	Houseworker
How long a Resident of Kings Park Hospital:	7 yrs, 5 mos, 15 days
Father's Name:	Francis Green
Mother's Name:	Catherine Farrell
Place of Death:	Kings Park State Hospital
Place of Burial:	Calvary Cemetery, Brooklyn NY

When I eventually heard from the Medical Records Department, I was disappointed to read that, after a thorough search, they said no medical records were found.

When I learned that Katharine had died in Kings Park State Hospital in Suffolk County, I felt very sad. I so wanted to tell my father about this. He died ten years before I uncovered this death record. My father told me his mother had died when he was a child, but now I knew that he was actually 20 when his mother died. I surmised that the family had just told him she had died, not that she had mental problems and had been sent to a hospital far out on Long Island.

I still had the question about where Katharine was in 1925. Maybe she was in Kings Park at the time of that census, too. After another search of the 1925 census, I found that, Yes, Katharine was enumerated at Kings Park Hospital in 1925, and the record said she had been there since 1923.

<u>1925 NY State census, Suffolk County, Smithtown, Kings Park State Hospital, AD2, ED3, page 7.</u>
Katherine G. Doheny, permanent residence 423 4th Street, Brooklyn, age 45, born in US, a citizen, an Inmate since 1923.

When I told my sisters about our grandmother being sent to Kings Park when our father was 10, and eventually dying there, we all reflected on her hard life. Her life is described in greater detail in Chapter Five, but for our purposes here, let me recount that she had lost two children as infants; she had five surviving boys, very active, very close in age; she was dealing with an absentee husband who had an alcohol problem; and she shared her living quarters with her brother Frank and her sister Helen, the school teacher. I remember Helen as a very strict and demanding person.

I phoned Calvary Cemetery next to learn Katharine's grave number and who she was buried with. I sent the $28 fee, and here is the information the staff person sent me. Katharine was buried with four of her children. When the family buried Uncle Ed in 1972, one of "the boys" must have paid the fee at that time for perpetual care.

Section 32, Range 6, Plot T, Grave 6, New Calvary, purchased by Edward Doheny, 10 Apr 1905 (Perpetual care for this burial site was paid in 1972.)

Name	Burial date	Age at death	Year born
Catharine Doheny	10 Apr 1905	1 day	1905 in NY
Thomas J. Doheney	23 Oct 1908	2 months	1908 in NY
Katharine T. Doheny	15 May 1933	54	1878 in NY
Gerard Doheney	5 Jan 1934	22	1911 in NY
Edward J. Doheny II	28 Aug 1972	65	1907 in NY

We don't know what Katharine's personality was like. We just have a few photos from around 1913 and 1914 that we can use to try to "meet her."

Katharine and Bernard   Katharine with Ed, Francis, Larry, Gerard   Katharine with Frank, Gerard, Larry, Ed

Helen V. Greene, Daughter of Francis Greene and Catharine Farrell

Helen was born on 5 Dec 1884 in Brooklyn. She was 11 when her brother Thomas died.

Aunt Helen was the first person in the Greene family to have an extended education. She told us she had attended Normal School. I looked up "NY City Normal School" and found information about The New York City Normal College, which would one day become Hunter College of the City University of New York. The Normal College "was founded in 1870 by Irish immigrant and social reformer Thomas Hunter as a teacher-training school for young women. Created by the New York State Legislature, Hunter was deemed the only approved institution for those seeking to teach in New York City during this time. The school incorporated an elementary and high school for gifted children, where students practiced teaching."[5] Earlier in this chapter, in the notes about the 1905 Census, there was an indication that Helen was age 20 in high school. Now, I think this meant that she attended normal school and practiced teaching.

My first memories of Aunt Helen date from the early 1950s when we visited her at her apartment on Lenox Road, Brooklyn. It was filled with beautiful furniture and luxurious oriental rugs, so wonderful to touch and sit on. Once, we stayed overnight, and Anne and I slept right on the living room rug. For baby Betty, I think they put a bureau drawer on the floor and lined it with a soft blanket for her to sleep in. I remember Aunt Helen's bathroom floor was made of tiny black and white hexagonal tiles that fascinated me with their pattern. The apartment was small but very clean and very neat. My mother warned us not to touch anything, and I was afraid that Aunt Helen would get angry at me if I did.

Aunt Helen loved her nephews very much; her apartment drew them together. Many celebrations were held there. This photo was taken in Oct 1944 a few days before my father was inducted into the Army for WWII.

In this photo, I think you can see Helen's pride and pleasure of being with her family. She is 57. Pictured are her brother Frank Greene, Bernard Doheny, Helen, Francis Doheny, and Edward Doheny III in the arms of Edward II.

My father listed Aunt Helen's address as his mailing address when he was inducted into the Army. I wanted to search the 1940 census to see if Aunt Helen was living on Lenox Rd in 1940. I had to wait until 2012 to search it, as population schedules are released 72 years after their date.

As soon as the schedules were released, I found her!
1940 US census, NY, Kings County, Brooklyn, SD6, ED 24-2477, Sheet 8A, April 1, 130 Lenox Rd. Helen Greene, Head, age 35 (really 55), single, living alone, rent was $55/month, had two years of college, born in New York, worked a 35-hour week as a public-school teacher, earned $3,800 and had no other source of income.

[5] https://etc.usf.edu/clipart/54500/54575/54575_college-nyc.htm

In June 1958, I was asked to give the valedictorian speech at the end of my sixth grade. Our class was "moving up" to junior high school. Aunt Helen helped me write my speech. What a disaster! I practiced it aloud over and over again to try to memorize it, and all the while Aunt Helen was correcting my diction. The words didn't sound like me at all. Maybe she wanted me to sound like her, but her diction was very old-fashioned. I was so nervous when the day came, that I did a terrible job. With all good intentions on Aunt Helen's part, an event that could have been a highlight of my elementary school career was a very bad experience.

Aunt Helen came to live with our family about 1960 because her nephews noticed she was developing some dementia. She had helped take care of my father and his brothers when they were young, and now we would take care of her when she was old. Aunt Helen sometimes hogged our only bathroom, which was hard on a family that consisted of my mother and father, the four of us girls, and usually Uncle Larry on the weekends. We kept a covered enamel pot outside the bathroom door for "emergencies."

When Aunt Helen's dementia became severe, she would sometimes run out of the house without telling anyone, and we'd have to search the neighborhood for her. Once she ran out of the house half-naked. She also fell down the basement stairs at least once. When she got so infirm that my parents were afraid for her well-being, there was a big discussion among "the boys," and it was agreed that she should move to a nursing home. The first home she lived in put her in a straight-jacket and heavily sedated her. When my parents saw Aunt Helen in that state, they moved her to a NYC owned nursing home in the Bronx near the Saw Mill River Parkway, which was a more pleasant place. She died in the Bronx State Hospital on 8 Aug 1968.

My sister Anne has a small oriental throw rug and a glass front bookcase that was once owned by Aunt Helen.

Francis Joseph Greene, Aunt Helen's Brother

Francis J. Greene was born in Brooklyn in Nov 1880. He worked as a farm hand when he was very young, and later he was a caretaker in a New York City park. He lived with his sister Katharine's family and sometimes with his sister Helen. His WWII draft card from 1942 shows his residence was 142 Winthrop St, Brooklyn, but his mailing address was his sister Helen's apartment, 130 Lenox Rd. He was not employed at the time he registered for the draft, but since he was 61 already, he was not called into active service. Francis died on 12 Jun 1959 at age 78 in Blue Point, Suffolk County, NY.[6]

After finding Francis Greene Sr.'s obituary, many years passed before another big breakthrough in my Greene Family Research. In the interim, I published two books about my mother's ancestors –

---

[6] Ancestry.com, NY State Death Index, Death Certificate #45069. The date of death in this death index matches the cemetery burial record. I don't know when or why he moved to Blue Point before he died.

the Vogelbach and Beyers Families. In 2011, I had a kidney removed because of cancer. From 2012 to 2017, I was heavily involved in gardening; I helped to found the largest county community garden in Florida, here in Sarasota FL. In 2017, my husband and I moved to a lovely retirement community, I gave up my plot and many responsibilities in the community garden, and again had the time to concentrate on writing a book about my father's ancestors.

Finding More Relatives in Brooklyn

In 2017, I proceeded to build on two small pieces of information. (1) an obituary *(see page 112)* for my great-grandfather Francis Greene (my father's maternal grandfather) said he was born in Edgeward, County Longford Ireland. (2) Census reports and his death certificate placed Francis Greene's birth between 1839 and 1845.

Online, I couldn't locate an Irish town called Edgeward, but there was an Edgeworthstown, County Longford. Irish websites informed me that Mostrim was an alternate name of the town and its parish. Referring to a map, I found that Edgeworthstown is scarcely two miles from Lissanisky where our Farrell family lived, and I thought Francis Greene and Catherine Farrell MAY even have known each other in Ireland, and they MAY have immigrated the same year. Francis's death certificate says he had been in the USA for 17 years and was a resident of Brooklyn for the same amount of time. That would make his immigration year about 1867. As discussed in Chapter Eleven, it is likely that Catherine Farrell also immigrated in 1867. However, immigration and/or naturalization records for them have not yet been found, so we don't know if they emigrated together or separately.

I aimed to find a baptismal record for Francis Green(e) in Edgeworthstown, or Mostrim, County Longford, and perhaps learn Francis's parent's names, then find a Henry Green(e) born in the same town, maybe to the same parents, and then try to find other siblings for Francis. This would need many different strategies.

I happened to be looking through *The Brooklyn Daily Eagle* online for obituaries for various family members when the name Henry Green turned up, not in an obituary for him, but in a Surrogate Court Notice in 1888 for the family of a Mary Green.[7] To my great delight, the names of my g-grandmother and all of her living children were mentioned in the notice:

"Thomas Green, Katie Green, Ellen [sic] Green and Frankie Green, infants under the age of fourteen years, residing with their mother, Kate Green, at Brooklyn."

The notice also revealed:

SURROGATE'S NOTICES.

THE PEOPLE OF THE STATE OF NEW YORK—To Henry Green, residing at Brooklyn; Catharine Green and Ann Green, residing at Edgeworthstown, County Longford, Ireland; Thomas Green, Katie Green, Ellen Green and Frankie Green, infants under the age of fourteen years, residing with their mother, Kate Green, at Brooklyn; Thomas Green, an infant of twenty years of age, residing at Brooklyn; John Green, Maggie Green, Bridget Green and Mary Green, infants over the age of fourteen years, residing at Edgeworthstown, County Longford, Ireland—Whereas, Patrick Hughes, of the City of Brooklyn, has lately petitioned to our Surrogate's Court of the County of Kings to have a certain instrument in writing bearing date the 25th of June, 1888, relating to real and personal estate, duly proved as the last will and testament of MARY GREEN, late of the City of Brooklyn, deceased. Wherefore, You and each of you are hereby cited and required to appear before our said Surrogate, at the Surrogate's Court to be held in the City of Brooklyn, in said county, on the 15th day of October, 1888, at ten o'clock in the forenoon, and attend the probate of the said last will and testament. And the above named infants are hereby notified to then and there show cause why a special guardian should not be appointed to appear for them on said probate, on the application of the petitioner.

In testimony whereof we have caused the seal of the Surrogate's Court of Kings County to be hereunto affixed. Witness, Hon. Abraham Lott, [L. S.] Surrogate of our said county, at the City of Brooklyn, the tenth day of August, in the year of our Lord one thousand eight hundred and eighty-eight.   WILLIAM MURRAY,
                Clerk of Surrogate's Court.
M. L. TOWNS, Attorney, 16 Court st, Brooklyn, N. Y.
au18 6wS

---

[7] *The Brooklyn Daily Eagle*, 1888-09-01, page 4, available on newspapers.com

- Mary had a brother named Henry.
- The term "their mother Kate" implies that Kate's deceased husband, Francis, was Mary's brother.
- A Catherine and Ann Green were adults living in Edgeworthstown.
- There was another relative, Thomas Green, who was 20 years old living in Brooklyn.
- Relatives John Green, Maggie Green, Bridget Green, and Mary Green, ages between 14 and 21, were living in Edgeworthstown
- Mary's will was dated 25 Jun 1888; she had been a resident of Brooklyn, but was now deceased.
- On 10 Aug a court date had been set for probating her will on 15 Oct 1888 at 10 am at the Surrogate Court of Kings County, 16 Court St, Brooklyn.

GREENE—At 765 Bergen st, MARY GREENE, after a ... of her soul. Interment at Holy Cross Cemetery.

Maybe there was an obituary for Mary Green in *The Brooklyn Daily Eagle*. I searched backwards starting in August for a Green obituary, and found it in June 1888.[8] After all that effort, the entry was in a fold of the page, unfortunately, so it was digitized poorly. The obituary might be missing two lines of text and might say, "At 765 Bergen St, Mary Greene, after a brief illness, died peacefully at home. A solemn mass of burial will be held at 9 A.M. for the repose of her soul. Interment at Holy Cross Cemetery." Having Mary's home address would prove useful later, as would knowing she was buried in Holy Cross.

For my next task, I decided to try to prove that certain people mentioned in the Surrogate Court Notice were siblings: Mary, Henry, Catherine, Ann, and my g-grandfather Francis.

A search of Surrogate Court Records on FamilySearch.org turned up Mary's actual will, submitted for probate on 29 Jun 1888, with family names and relationships further explained in it.[9]

"All the heirs and all the next-of-kin of said deceased are as follows, to wit: no father, mother, husband, children, brothers or sisters, or the descendants of any of them except as follows:
- Henry Green, a brother of full age residing in Brooklyn.
- Catharine Green, a sister residing at Edgeworthstown, County Longford Ireland, of full age.
- Ann Green, a sister of full age residing at Edgeworthstown, County Longford Ireland, of full age.
- Thomas Green, Katie Green, Ellen Green and Frankie Green infants under the age of fourteen residing with their mother Kate Green of Brooklyn, children of a deceased brother Frank Green.
- Thomas Green an infant of twenty years of age, child of a deceased brother James Green, residing at Brooklyn.

---

[8] *The Brooklyn Daily Eagle*, 1888-06-26, page 5, available on newspapers.com
[9] "New York, Kings County Estate Files, 1866-1923," database with 16 images, FamilySearch.org (https://familysearch.org/ark:/61903/1:1:N7LK-LWR : 9 March 2018), Mary Green, 1888; Surrogate Court, Brooklyn; FHL microfilm 4190838.

- John Green, Maggie Green, Bridget Green, and Mary Green, infants over the age of fourteen, children of a deceased brother James Green, residing at Edgeworthstown, County Longford Ireland.

This was a list of all the members of my Greene Family who were alive in 1888, both in Brooklyn and in Ireland. What a find!

On page eight of Mary's probate documents, there is an address for Henry Green living with his nephew Thomas Green on "Bergen St. near Grand," in Prospect Heights, Brooklyn, and an address for Kate (Farrell) Green and her children, "Third Ave near 12th Street," Park Slope, Brooklyn.

Having Mary's obituary, I guessed she probably died in June 1888, so I sent away for Mary's death certificate.[10] When I received it, I noticed that her date of death was the same as the date on her will. Apparently, her deathbed wishes were in her will, which was marked just by an X and sworn to by her witnesses.[11] Here is a transcription of her will.

In the name of God. Amen.

I, Mary Green, of the City of Brooklyn, County of Kings and State of New York being of sound mind and memory do hereby make, publish and declare this to be my last Will and Testament.

First, I direct that all my just debts and funeral and testamentary expenses be paid by my Executor.

Second, I give and bequeath to my sister Catharine Green of Edgeworthstown, County Longford, Ireland, One hundred Dollars.

Third, I give and bequeath to my niece Maggie Green, of Edgeworthstown, County Longford, Ireland, the sum of Two hundred Dollars.

Fourth, I give and bequeath to Thomas Green, son of my brother Frank, the sum of Two hundred Dollars.

Fifth, I give and bequeath to my nephew and niece Frankie and Katie Green, children of my brother Frank the sum of One hundred Dollars each.

Sixth, I give, devise, and bequeath all the rest, residue, and remainder of my estate of whatever value or kind to my nephew Thomas Green, son of my brother James, to him, his heirs, and assigns forever.

---

[10] Certificate of Death for Mary Green, died 25 Jun 1888, Dept of Health, City of Brooklyn, #8435.
[11] Liber 134, page 203, and Letter Testamentary is in Oct 8, 1888, liber 39, p226.
https://www.familysearch.org/ark:/61903/3:1:3QS7-L99B-JH?i=613&cc=1920234&cat=317954

> *Seventh*, I hereby nominate, constitute, and appoint my friend *Patrick Hughes* of 819 Bergen St., Brooklyn, the Executor of this my Last Will and Testament, hereby revoking all former Wills by me made.
>
> *In Witness Whereof* I have hereunto set my hand and seal this 25th day of June in the Year 1888.
>
> In presence of Jno. J. Hughes, 819 Bergen St   Mary (x her mark) Green (L.S)
> And Mary McCue, 765 Bergen St.

My grandmother Katharine and two of her siblings, Thomas and Francis, but not Helen, inherited a total of $400. I wonder how they spent their inheritance from Aunt Mary. Did their mother appropriate the money, perhaps, to buy the building at 287 Prospect Park West, or was the indication on the 1900 census that said she owned that building a mistake and a false lead? I re-read Katherine Farrell Green's 1909 Surrogate Court documents and found that it said she indeed owned real estate at the time of her death, and it was worth $5,500. Her son Frank, her executor, inherited it. It is unknown when Frank sold it, and for how much.

I found the record of the sale of Mary Green's property by searching the indexes for Grantor in 1888 and 1889 on the Mormon website, FamilySearch.org. Unfortunately, the images of actual Brooklyn deeds available on the Mormon site stop in 1885.[12]

There are many more questions that could be asked about Mary's life. Did she leave Ireland before her brothers Francis and Henry? What was her life like in Brooklyn? How often did the Greene Family get together? Was she active in her parish, in the community? Did she have hobbies? I have so many questions about our ancestors, but most details about their lives are lost forever.

---

[12] The deed, though, is in the Kings County Court records, 1889, Liber 1854, Page 407, according to the index. The Grantor is the Estate of Mary Green, and the Grantee is Michael Teehan. The conveyance is dated 10 Jan 1889.

Henry Green, sibling of Francis, Mary, James, Catherine, and Ann

Perhaps determining Henry Green's date of death and then sending for his death certificate might reveal the names of his parents? Maybe his will was also online, along with the associated Surrogate Court records. In one week, I located all these documents, and I did the Genealogy Happy Dance.

Holy Cross Cemetery burials are searchable online, and I thought one of the Henry Greens buried there was likely to be Francis's brother. One of the Henrys was buried on 6 Sep 1912, and an obituary in *The Brooklyn Daily Eagle*[13] seemed to be associated with this person. He and his wife Margaret, and a child named Marguerite, are all buried in the same grave: St. Stephen Section, Row P, plot 24. Here are obituaries for Henry in 1912, Margaret in 1911, and their daughter Marguerite in 1898.[14] [15]

GREEN—On Monday, September 3, 1912, HENRY, beloved husband of the late Margaret Green. Relatives and friends are requested to attend the funeral from his late residence, 1027 Pacific st, on Friday, September 6, 1912, at 9:30 a.m.; thence to St. Joseph's Church, Pacific st, near Vanderbilt av. Interment in Holy Cross Cemetery.

MARGARET GREEN,

On Wednesday Margaret Green died suddenly at her home, 1207 Pacific street. She was the wife of Henry Green. Funeral services will be held at her late home to-morrow morning at 9:30 o'clock, thence to the R. C. Church of St. Joseph, Pacific street, near Vanderbilt avenue, where a solemn requiem mass will be celebrated. Interment will be made in Holy Cross Cemetery under direction of Undertaken F. H. McGuire, of 589A Washington avenue.

GREEN—On Monday, December 19, MARGUERITE, only daughter of Harry and Margaret Green, aged 10 years. Relatives and friends are requested to attend the funeral, from her late residence, 1,027 Pacific st, on Thursday, December 22, at 2 P. M.; thence to St. Joseph's Church, Pacific st, near Vanderbilt av. 20-2

Since I found Mary Green's siblings and heirs by searching Brooklyn Wills and Surrogate Court records, maybe I would be able to determine if I had found the "right" Henry Green(e) by comparing the names in his will with those mentioned in Mary's will.

Lo and behold, there was a will for Henry Green of Brooklyn dated 26 Aug 1912 with associated Surrogate Court records dated 20 Nov 1912. [16] The names mentioned in Henry's documents were the same as the names in Mary Green's, plus a few more. It looked like some people had died between 1888 (year of Mary's probate records) and 1912 (Henry's probate records), some Irish relatives had immigrated to the US, and some had moved to Dublin in that period.

A search of the 1892 New York State census revealed that Henry and family lived at 1027 Pacific St., North Side.[17] His occupation is "Liquors."

Next, I sent for Henry's 1912 death certificate in the hope that Henry's parents' names were on it. Yes! His parents were Thomas Green and Margaret Kane. Could Margaret Kane be related to Mary Kane, the wife of our other ancestor John Farrell? Further research may prove or disprove this.

---

[13] *The Brooklyn Daily Eagle*, 4 Sep 1912, obituary for Henry Green, page 18, available on newspapers.com

[14] *The Standard Union*, Brooklyn, 7 Jul 1911, obituary for Margaret Green, page 4, available on newspapers.com

[15] *The Brooklyn Daily Eagle,*, 21 Sep 1898, obituary for Marguerite Green, page 5, available on newspapers.com

[16] "New York, Kings County Estate Files, 1866-1923," Surrogate Court, Brooklyn, database with images, FamilySearch (https://familysearch.org/ark:/61903/3:1:939N-PM97-MV?cc=1466356&wc=MP7K-9LC%3A44954901%2C107006801%2C107650801 : 21 May 2014), Green, Henry (1912), image 1 of 17

[17] 1892 NY State census, Kings County, Ward 9, ED 11, page 7. It says Henry is 33 [sic].

It would be necessary to find Irish records to properly document that Thomas Green(e) and Margaret Kane were also the parents of my g-grandfather Francis Green and his siblings Mary, James, Catherine and Ann from Edgeworthstown, County Longford, Ireland.

Here are some details found on Henry's Surrogate Court Records that would prove helpful:

- Henry's will was dated 26 Aug 1912, and signed by his witnesses George R. Holahan Jr. (of 389 Sterling Place) and John H. Barry (of 198 Monroe St.). Henry died on 3 Sep 1912.
- Henry intended to leave money to the following people:
  - Thomas should receive $900 to pay any of his outstanding bills and for such things as erecting a monument on Henry's grave.
  - Holy Cross Cemetery should receive $500 for perpetual care of his plot.
  - His niece Delia (Bridget) Green should receive $1,500.
  - His niece Margaret Green should receive $1,500.
  - His nephew Thomas Green, his executor, should receive the remainder of Henry's estate.
  - If Henry's personal assets were not sufficient to cover the bequests, Thomas was directed to sell his real estate assets. (Henry owned a liquor store, according to the 1900 census.)
- The probate notice appeared in *The Brooklyn Daily Eagle* once a week for six weeks beginning on 1 Oct 1921.
- Henry's will was admitted to probate on 20 Nov 1912. Petitioner was Thomas Green, his executor.
- The probate records state that Henry's estate consisted of real property valued at $1,000 and personal property of about $100. (If he owned a liquor store, these numbers can't be right. His heirs certainly wouldn't get the amount of money that was mentioned in his will!)
- His heirs were
  - nephew Thomas Green of 448 17th St. Brooklyn (1910 census says he lives at 488 17th St.)
  - niece Bridget (Delia) Green of 20 Remsen St., Brooklyn
  - niece Margaret Green of 20 Remsen St., Brooklyn
- His wife had predeceased him, as had all of his siblings. Henry also had no living children.
- His surviving next-of-kin, all of full age and sound mind, were

  the five living children of a pre-deceased brother James
  - Thomas Green, nephew, the petitioner, resident of Brooklyn
  - Bridget (Delia) Green, niece, resident of Brooklyn
  - Margaret (Maggie) Green, niece, resident of Brooklyn
  - John Green, nephew, resident of Fair View, Edgeworthstown, Longford, Ireland
  - Mary Ann Green, niece, resident of Fair View, Edgeworthstown, Longford, Ireland

  the three living children of a pre-deceased brother Francis
  - Catherine Green, niece, resident of 651 19th St., Brooklyn
  - Helen Green, niece, resident of 651 19th St., Brooklyn
  - Frank Green, niece, resident of 651 19th St., Brooklyn

  the four living children of a pre-deceased brother (The brother is unnamed, but I think the document should have said "a pre-deceased sister Ann")
  - Michael, nephew, resident of Fair View, Edgeworthstown, Longford, Ireland

- John, nephew, resident of Fair View, Edgeworthstown, Longford, Ireland
- Catherine, niece, resident of Avondale, Black Rock, County Dublin, Ireland
- Margaret, niece, resident of Avondale, Black Rock, County Dublin, Ireland

I thought I now had enough clues to do research on some Irish websites and find all these families in Edgeworthstown Parish registers, just as I had done when searching the Dohenys in and Farrells in their parish records. It turned out that the Edgeworthstown (or Mostrim) parish registers were not as easily researched as the others were. In many cases the handwriting was illegible and the indexes seemed incomplete. As a result, I only have guestimates for most baptismal dates. We do have a marriage record and baptismal records for one complete family, that of James Green and Ann Macken.[18]

James Green, a sibling of Francis, Mary Green, Henry, Catherine, and Ann

James Green and Ann Macken Marriage certificate, Mostrim, Edgeworthstown, County Longford. Their witnesses were Dennis Gallagher and Margaret Gill.

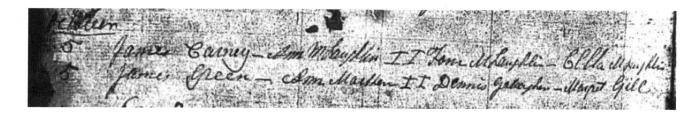

His children's baptismal records are these:

Thomas Green, baptized 10 Jan 1869. His sponsors' names are illegible to me.

John Green, baptized 7 Jun 1870. His sponsors are John Macken and -?- Reilly.

Margaret Green, baptized 4 May 1872. Her sponsors were Michael Reilly and Biddy Macken.

[18] All of these records are found in the Mostrim Parish Registers on Microfilm 04233/06 available on the website of the National Library of Ireland, https://registers.nli.ie/

Mary Ann Green, baptized 30 Sep 1875. Her sponsors were Peter Connor and Margaret -?-

Bridget Green, baptized 17 Mar 1877. Her sponsors were Pat and Mary Green.

James died before 1888, according to his sister Mary Green's Brooklyn Surrogate Court records, and apparently did not emigrate to the US. His oldest son Thomas did emigrate, however, and was named as the trusted executor for his Uncle Henry's estate. James's daughters Margaret and Bridget would follow Thomas to the US a few years later, because Henry's will mentions that they lived at 20 Remsen St., Brooklyn, in 1912.

Thomas Greene, the Immigrant Son of James, and Executor of Henry's Will

Mary and Henry both left the bulk of their assets to their nephew Thomas. He must have been important in their lives. I decided to trace Thomas in public documents to see if there was any information on him that I could add to this narrative. The most interesting thing I found was that Thomas's family lived on the same block as my father's family when he was born. Read on…

On 9 Jan 1869, as noted above, Thomas was baptized. His parents were James Green and Ann Machen.

In 1882, Thomas Green emigrated to the US according to the 1910 US census.

In 1888, Thomas Green, age 20, estimated birth year was 1868, was living with his Uncle Henry Green on "Bergen St. near Grand Av, Brooklyn" according to Mary Green's probate papers, page 8.

In 1891, at about age 22, he married Elizabeth Curley of Brooklyn, according to the 1910 census.

The 1892 NY State census[19] places the couple in the 9th Ward, no street address, and Thomas's occupation is "gasfitter."

---

[19] 1892 NY State census, Kings, Brooklyn, Ward 9, ED 8, Page 5.

The 1900 census[20] records them at 942 Pacific St., Brooklyn.[21] Thomas Green, born Feb 1870 (which doesn't match his baptismal record), age 30, married 9 years, immigrated from Ireland in 1882, 18 years ago. He was naturalized and worked as a plumber. He rented his home. Elizabeth, his wife, born Jul 1872, gave birth to 7 children, 5 now living. His children are Ella, Thomas, Mary, Harry, and Walter.

The 1905 NY State census[22] records them at 865 Myrtle Ave. Thomas is working as a plumber.

The 1910 US census[23] records Thomas Green renting their home at 488 17th St., Brooklyn. His family consisted of his wife Elizabeth and children Eleanor 17, Thomas Jr. 15, Mary 13, Henry J 12, Walter F 11, and George 8. Thomas and Elizabeth were married for 19 years. She had given birth to 8 children, 6 now living. Thomas Sr. worked as a gasfitter in a plumbing shop. His daughter Eleanor did housework for a private family. Thomas Jr. was a stock boy in a leather factory.

In 1912, Thomas Green is living at 488 17th St., Brooklyn, according to Henry Green's probate record, p 2.

The 1915 NY State census[24] records Thomas Greene's family at 488 17th St., Brooklyn.

The 1920 US census[25] records Thomas J Greene, his wife Elizabeth, and his children Thomas and George at 536 6th Ave, Brooklyn. That is just a few doors down and on the other side of the street from the address on my father's 1913 birth certificate: 523 6th Ave., Brooklyn. Thomas Sr., age 50, is working in a plumbing shop. Thomas Jr is a clerical worker in the Brooklyn Navy Yard. George is working with his father in a plumbing shop. Thomas J Greene and my grandmother Katharine Greene Doheny were first cousins, and I imagine their families interacted often. They lived only a few blocks from each other.

1925 NY State census[26] records Thomas Green 56, with wife Elizabeth 53, and son Joe (George) 23 at 536 6th Ave, Brooklyn. Thomas is working for wages as a plumber, as is his son Joe. Thomas is a citizen, naturalized on "26 Oct 1894 in a court of Brooklyn."

The 1930 census[27] records Thomas Green 59, Elizabeth 57, and son George 29, living at 648 60th St., Brooklyn. Thomas is no longer working, but his son George is working as a plumber in Brooklyn. They were renting an apartment in a 3-family house for $40/month. And they owned a radio. Henry said he was 20 and Elizabeth said she was 18 when they were married.

---

[20] 1900 US census, Kings, Brooklyn, Ward 9, ED 127, Page 13 B.
[21] 1900 US census, New York, Kings, Brooklyn, Ward 9, ED 127, Sheet 13 B.
[22] 1905 NY State census, Kings, Brooklyn, AD 6, ED 13, page 13-25 (image 14/21 on Ancestry.com)
[23] 1910 US census, New York, Kings, Brooklyn, Ward 22, ED 575, Sheet 3 A.
[24] 1915 NY State census, Kings, Brooklyn, AD 7, ED 13, Page 33.
[25] 1920 US census, Kings, Brooklyn, AD 12, ED 691, Sheet 2A.
[26] 1925 NY State census, Kings, Brooklyn, AD 12, ED 10, Page 3.
[27] 1930 US census, Kings, Brooklyn, AD 9, ED 24-1166, Sheet 20 B.

They moved again, because Thomas's obituary says his family lived at 835 59th St., Brooklyn. It seems only three of their children are still living, because only Thomas, Harry and George are mentioned.

I found two 1934 obituaries for Thomas Greene, each with some details about the family in 1934.[28] The Knights of Galena, I learned, was a benevolent society for Brooklyn plumbers and pipe fitters.

GREENE—THOMAS J., on Oct. 11, at his home, 835 59th st; born in Edgeworth Town, County Longford, Ireland, beloved husband of Elizabeth Curley Greene and father of Thomas, Harry and George Greene. Funeral Monday, at 9:30 A. M., with a solemn requiem mass at Our Lady of Perpetual Help R. C. Church at 9:30 A. M. Interment Holy Cross Cemetery.

THOMAS J. GREENE, former delegate-treasurer of the Plumbers' Union, Local 1, died Thursday in his home, 835 59th St. He was born in Ireland and lived in Brooklyn for the past 50 years. Mr. Greene, a member of the Knights of Galena, is survived by his wife, the former Elizabeth Curley; three sons, Thomas, Harry and George; two sisters, Margaret and Delia, and a brother, John, in Ireland. The funeral was held Monday at 9:30 a.m. from the home, with a solemn requiem mass in Our Lady of Perpetual Help R. C. Church, at 9:30 a.m. Burial was in Holy Cross Cemetery.

He is buried in Holy Cross Cemetery in a plot adjoining his Uncle Henry's. [29]

- Henry Green is buried in St Stephen, Row P, Plot 23. (son of Margaret Kane)
- Thomas Green is buried in St. Stephen, Row P, Plot 24. (nephew of Henry, Mary and Francis))
- Mary Green is buried in Vernon Range D, Plot 412 (daughter of Margaret Kane)
- Francis Green, his wife Catherine Farrell, and four children Mary, Thomas, Francis and Helen are buried in Vernon Range D, Plot 411

He must have been well loved and respected by his family and the community. His obituaries reveal his status in the Plumbers Union and his membership in the Knights of Galena. The Knights were incorporated on 2 Oct 1934, and Thomas may have helped to make that happen. I searched for the Knights of Galena in The Brooklyn Daily Eagle, and found a list of the attendees at a fancy Ninth Anniversary Ball in Jan of 1914. Among the many guests were Thomas and his wife "Bessie, with their sons Thomas and Harry Green. Also attending the ball was my 29-year-old Aunt Helen Green![30]

---

[28] *Brooklyn Times Union*, 14 Oct 1934 and *The Brooklyn Daily Eagle*, 17 Oct 1934, at newspapers.com
[29] Brooklyn Catholic Cemeteries, https://www.ccbklyn.org/information-news/locate-a-loved-one/
[30] *The Brooklyn Daily Eagle*, 11 Feb 1914, page 26, available on Newspapers.com.

In Conclusion

In 1019 and 2020, I became almost obsessed with writing this book, spending two or three hours most days writing the narratives and solving the final research problems. Back in 1996, all I knew was that my father's ancestors were Irish. I had no idea where in Ireland they were from. Where should I start? So, I joined a genealogical society in Sarasota and read books about immigration, naturalization and ships passenger lists, about how to do census research, and about how to document my research.

Over the years it seemed that every answer to every small question exploded into more and more problems to solve, leading to other great information about my ancestors. Though the research will never end, I feel I have achieved what I set out to do in this book. I wanted to trace my father's ancestors back to their natal villages and then make them somehow become real to my readers. For families like mine who have no letters or diaries from ancestors, it falls to a family historian to paint a picture of their lives and honor them. This labor of love took patience and extraordinary persistence, and that tells our descendants something about me.

And as my father used to say, "Sláinte!"

Outline Descendant Tree for the Greene Family

… 1 Thomas Greene, b. Abt. 1820 in Ireland
… +Margaret Kane, b. Abt. 1823 in Ireland
.... 2 Mary Greene b: Abt. 1843 in Edgeworthstown, Longford, Ireland, d: 25 Jun 1888 in Brooklyn, NY
.... 2 Francis Greene b: Abt. 1845 in Edgeworthstown, Longford, Ireland, d: 24 Oct 1884 in Brooklyn, NY
.... +Catherine Farrell b: Jul 1843 in Ardagh and Moydow, Longford, Ireland, m: Abt. 1874 in USA, d: 11 Dec 1909
              in Brooklyn, NY
.... 3 Thomas Greene b: Abt. 1875 in Brooklyn, NY, d: Jun 1896 in Brooklyn, NY
.... 3 Mary Greene b: Abt. 1876 in Brooklyn, NY, d: Sep 1883 in Brooklyn, NY
.... 3 Katharine T. Greene b: 26 Oct 1878 in Brooklyn, NY, d: 12 May 1933 in Smithtown, Suffolk, NY
.... +Edward Joseph Doheny b: 25 Aug 1874 in Graigue, Tipperary, Ireland, d: 05 Apr 1953 in New York, NY,
              m: 28 Sep 1904 in Manhattan, NY
.... 4 Catherine Doheny b: 9 Apr 1905 in Brooklyn, NY, d: 10 Apr 1905 in Brooklyn, NY
.... 4 Edward Joseph Doheny II b: 10 May 1907 in Brooklyn, NY, d: 23 Aug 1972 in Brooklyn, NY
.... 4 Thomas Doheny b: Aug 1908 in Brooklyn, NY, d: Oct 1908 in Brooklyn, NY
.... 4 Francis William Doheny b: 7 Nov 1909 in Brooklyn, NY, d: 16 Aug 1973 in Northport, Suffolk, NY
.... 4 Gerard J. Doheny b: 12 Oct 1910 in Brooklyn, NY, d: 31 Dec 1933 in Tampa, Hillsborough, FL
.... 4 Lawrence Aloysius Doheny b: 27 Feb 1912 in Brooklyn, NY, d. 24 May 1978 in Manhattan, NY
.... 4 Bernard Greene Doheny b. 11 Oct 1913 in Brooklyn, NY, d: 18 May 1989 in So.Venice, Sarasota FL
.... 3 Francis Joseph Greene b: 08 Nov 1880 in Brooklyn, NY, d: Jun 1959 in Blue Point, Suffolk, NY
.... 3 Helen V. Greene b: 05 Dec 1884 in Brooklyn, NY, d: 08 Aug 1968 in Bronx, NY
.... 2 James Greene b: Abt. 1847 in Edgeworthstown, Longford, Ireland, d: Bef. 1888 in Edgeworthstown, Longford,
              Ireland
.... + Ann Macken m: 5 Oct 1868 in Edgeworthstown, Longford, Ireland
.... 3 Thomas Greene b: Jan 1869 in Edgeworthstown, Longford, Ireland, d: 11 Oct 1934 in Brooklyn, NY
.... +Elizabeth Curley b: July 1872 in Brooklyn, NY, d: 15 Oct 1944 in Brooklyn, NY
.... 4 Eleanora Greene b: Mar 1892 in Brooklyn, NY, d: Unknown
.... 4 Thomas James Greene Jr. b: 8 Mar 1894 in Brooklyn, NY, d: 14 Dec 1955 in Brooklyn, NY
.... 4 Mary E. Greene b: Jul 1895 in Brooklyn, NY, d: Unknown
.... 4 Henry Joseph Greene b. 4 Nov 1896 in Brooklyn, NY, d: Oct 1974 in Glens Falls, Warren, NY
.... 4 Walter F. Greene b. 15 Aug 1897 in Brooklyn, NY, d: Jan 1978 in Brooklyn, NY
.... 4 George William Greene b. 3 Feb 1901 in Brooklyn, NY, d: Jan 1975 in Brooklyn, NY
.... 3 John Greene b: 7 Jun 1870 in Edgeworthstown, County Longford, Ireland, d: Aft. 1912 in Ireland
.... 3 Margaret "Maggie" Greene b: May 1872 in Edgeworthstown, County Longford, Ireland, d: Aft. 1912
              probably in Brooklyn, NY
.... 3 Mary Ann Greene b: Sep 1875 in Edgeworthstown, County Longford, Ireland, d: Aft. 1912 in Ireland.
.... 3 Bridget Greene b: Mar 1877 in Edgeworthstown, County Longford, Ireland, d: d: Aft. 1912 probably in
              Brooklyn, NY
.... 2 Catharine Greene b: Abt. 1848 in Edgeworthstown, Longford, Ireland, d: Bef. 1912 in Ireland
.... 2 Ann Greene b: May 1849 in Edgeworthstown, Longford, Ireland, d: Bef. 1912 in Ireland
.... 3 Michael b: probably in Edgeworthstown, County Longford, Ireland, d: probably in Longford, Ireland
.... 3 John b: probably in Edgeworthstown, County Longford, Ireland, d: probably in Longford, Ireland
.... 3 Catherine b: probably in Edgeworthstown, County Longford, Ireland, d: probably in Dublin, Ireland
.... 3 Margaret b: probably in Edgeworthstown, County Longford, Ireland, d: probably in Dublin, Ireland
.... 2 Henry Greene b: Abt. 1850 in Edgeworthstown, Longford, Ireland, d: 3 Sep 1912 in Brooklyn, NY
.... + Margaret Mary b: About 1852 in Ireland, d: 5 Jul 1911 in Brooklyn, NY
.... 3 Marguerite Greene b. 1888 in Brooklyn, NY, d: 19 Dec 1898 in Brooklyn, NY

Section II

Doheny
Genealogical
Summary

Doheny Family Genealogical Summary

Numbers are assigned to people in a genealogy. The numbering system employed here is a Modified Register System. It is based on the numbering system devised by the *New England Historic and Genealogical Register Quarterly* (NGQ) and later refined by the *National Genealogical Society Quarterly* (NGSQ). In this numbering system, everyone in a direct line from a progenitor on down gets a unique bold Arabic number to the left of their name. Notice the italicized numbers after the first names. These numbers indicate the generation. Only the line for the eldest child contains the generation numbers. The plus sign (+) in front of Timothy's name, for example, indicates that Timothy has children, and they will appear farther down the chart.

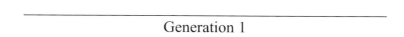

Generation 1

1. **WILLIAM**[1] **DOHENY** was born about 1837 in Graigue, County Tipperary, Ireland. He married Anne Scully from Tipperary or Kilkenny on 11 Feb 1858 in their local parish of Gortnahoe.[1] They had at least 10 children. William died on 20 May 1877,[2] and Anne died on 8 Sep 1893.[3] Both died in Graigue. They did not emigrate to the USA.

The known children of William Doheny and Anne Scully:

+ 2. i. **TIMOTHY A.**[2] **DOHENY** (*William*[1]) was born in Dec 1858 in Graigue.[4] He emigrated to the USA before 1890.[5] He married Bridget Maher, also an immigrant, about 1893,[6] and they had two children. Timothy died on 26 Dec 1899 in Bridgeport, CT.[7] Bridget probably died between 1905 and 1910.[8]

   3. ii. **JOHN JOSEPH DOHENY** was born in Sep 1860 in Graigue.[9] He emigrated in 1893.[10] John never married. He died on 24 May 1911 in Manhattan, NY.[11]

---

[1] Catholic Parish Registers, the National Library of Ireland, Microfilm No. 02493/05, available on Ancestry.com.

[2] Kilkenny South Eastern Health Board recorded William's place and date of death and approximate year of birth: William Dohony died 20 May 1877, tailor, age 40, married to Anne. Cause: paralysis 1 month. Certified (means a doctor was present).

[3] Kilkenny South Eastern Health Board: Anne Dahoney died 8 Sep 1983 at Graigue, age 55, widow tailor. Ill 8 mos. Son Richard present at death.

[4] Catholic Parish Registers, the National Library of Ireland, Microfilm No. 02493/04, available on Ancestry.com. Timothy was baptized on 14 Dec 1858, so was probably born in Dec.

[5] Timothy appears in the Bridgeport CT City Directory in 1890.

[6] 1900 US census, CT, Fairfield County, Bridgeport, ED 10, Sheet 4A. Timothy's daughter Margaret was born in CT in Oct 1894, so Timothy was probably married in 1893 or 1894 in CT. Bridget was born in Ireland; immigrated in 1891.

[7] CT Wills and Probate Records, CT State Library, Hartford, CT, available on Ancestry.com.

[8] 1910 US census, NY, Manhattan, ED 1121, Sheet 20B. By 1910, her orphaned children are living with Timothy's sister Maria and brother John.

[9] Catholic Parish Registers, the National Library of Ireland, Microfilm No. 02493/04, available on Ancestry.com. John was baptized on 22 Sep 1860, so he was probably born in Sep.

[10] 1900 US census, NY, Manhattan, ED 579, Sheet 4A. John immigrated in 1893, had lived in the US for 7 yrs.

[11] Dept of Health, City of New York, Certif 7316. John died on 24 May 1911 at 1:45 am in Presbyterian Hospital.

4. iii. **JAMES DOHENY** was born in June or July 1862 in Graigue.[12] Nothing more is known for sure about him at this time.

5. iv. **MARIA DOHENY** was born in Sep 1863 in Graigue.[13] She emigrated between 1890 and 1893.[14][15] She married James Barry in Sep 1922;[16] the couple had no children. Maria died on 10 Mar 1945 in Bronx, NY.[17] James Barry died on 15 Apr 1939 in Bronx, NY.[18]

+ 6. v. **PATRICK DOHENY** was born in Jan 1865 in Graigue.[19] He emigrated to NY about 1891.[20] He married Bridget Corcoran, also an Irish immigrant,[21] on 24 Sep 1899 in Manhattan, NY.[22] They had one child. Patrick died in Feb 1906 in NY.[23] Bridget died before 1920.[24]

+ 7. vi. **RICHARD DOHENY** was born on 16 Jul 1866 in Graigue.[25][26] He arrived in New York via Philadelphia on 14 April 1895.[27] Richard married Catherine Kelly, born Nov 1864 in Longfordpass, County Tipperary,[28] on 3 Oct 1899 in Manhattan, NY.[29] They had one child. Richard died on 8 Aug 1920 in Manhattan.[30] Catherine died in Oct 1944.[31]

---

[12] Catholic Parish Registers, the National Library of Ireland, Microfilm No. 02493/04, available on Ancestry.com. James was baptized on 5 July 1862, so he was probably born in June or July.

[13] Catholic Parish Registers, the National Library of Ireland, Microfilm No. 02493/04, available on Ancestry.com. Maria was baptized on 29 Sep 1863, so she was probably born in Sep.

[14] 1905 NYS Census, Manhattan, ED 1, AD 5, page 2. Maria had been in the US for 15 years.

[15] New York Passenger Lists, 5 Oct 1893, SS Majestic, Maria Doheney, age 25, seamstress, could be our Maria. This arrival date is one month after Anne Scully died.

[16] NYC Municipal Archives, Borough Manhattan, Vol 11, license #26166, dated 6 Sep 1922. Maria and James were probably married that month.

[17] Bureau of Records, Dept of Health, Borough of Bronx, Death Certif #2703. Maria died 12 Mar 1945 at 2:16 pm.

[18] New York, NY, Death Index 1862-1948 available on Ancestry.com.

[19] Catholic Parish Registers, the National Library of Ireland, Microfilm No. 02493/04, available on Ancestry.com. Patrick was baptized on 14 Jan 1865, so he was probably born in Jan 1865.

[20] NY Passenger Lists, 1820-1957, available on Amazon.com. Patrick arrived aboard the SS Chester on 28 Mar 1891.

[21] 1900 US census, NY, Manhattan ED 579, Sheet 4A. Bridget arrived in the US from Ireland in 1895.

[22] New York, NY, Marriage Index 1866-1937, available on Amazon.com.

[23] Calvary Cemetery Records, Patrick was buried on 18 Feb 1906 in Sect 19, Range 14, Grave 17, New Calvary.

[24] 1920 US census, NY, Manhattan, AD 12, ED 909, Sheet 7B. Patrick and Bridget's daughter Elizabeth is living with Uncle Richard in 1920, so it is likely that her mother died before 1920.

[25] Catholic Parish Registers, the National Library of Ireland, Microfilm No. 02493/04, available on Ancestry.com. Richard Shinney [sic] was baptized on 19 Jul 1866.

[26] Office of the Superintendent Registrar of Births, Deaths and Marriages, Urlingford, Ireland, certified copy dated 27 May 1918. Richard was born on 16 July 1866 in Graigue.

[27] Pennsylvania, Passenger and Crew Lists 1800-1962, available on Ancestry.com.

[28] Catholic Parish Registers, the National Library of Ireland, Microfilm No. 02493/04, available on Ancestry.com.

[29] New York, NY, Marriage Index 1866-1937, available on Amazon.com.

[30] New York, NY, Death Index 1862-1948 available on Ancestry.com.

[31] Calvary Cemetery Records, Catherine was buried on 12 Oct 1944 in Sect 23, Range 14, Plot D, Grave 19.

8. vii.   **WILLIAM DOHENY** was born on 22 Oct 1867 in Graigue.[32] He died there about three months later on 5 Feb 1868.[33]

9. viii.   **MICHAEL DOHENY** was born in 17 Jan 1871 in Graigue.[34] He died there ten days later on 27 Jan 1871.[35]

+10. ix.   **EDWARD JOSEPH DOHENY** was born in Aug 1874 in Graigue.[36] He immigrated to NY on 16 Mar 1895.[37] Edward married Katharine T. Greene on 28 Sep 1904 in Manhattan.[38] They had at least seven children. Edward died 5 Apr 1953 in Manhattan.[39] Katharine died 12 May 1933 in Kings Park, NY.[40]

11. x.   **ANNE DOHENY** was born in Sep 1977 in Graigue.[41] She arrived in New York via Philadelphia on 14 April 1895.[42] Anne married James F. Farrell in Sep 1922.[43] The couple had no children. Anne died 30 Jun 1952 in Manhattan.[44] James died on 22 Mar 1964 in Bronx.[45]

Generation 2

---

2. **TIMOTHY A.** [2] **DOHENY** (*William¹*) was born in Dec 1858 in Graigue. He emigrated to the USA before 1890. He married Bridget Maher, also an immigrant, about 1893, and they had two children. Timothy died on 26 Dec 1899 in Bridgeport, CT. Bridget probably died between 1905 and 1910.

The known children of Timothy Doheny and Bridget Maher:

12. i.   **ANNA MARGARET**[3] **DOHENY** (*Timothy², William¹*) was born on 4 Oct 1894 in Bridgeport, CT.[46] She married Pearce Shepherd, born in IL, on 25 Nov 1929.[47] They

---

[32] Ireland, Select Births and Baptisms, 1620-1911, available on Ancestry.com. William's birth was recorded in the civil records at Urlingford, County Kilkenny.

[33] Rootsireland.ie Civil Death Record, copyright Rothe House Trust Ltd, Kilkenny.

[34] Catholic Parish Registers, the National Library of Ireland, Microfilm No. 02493/04, available on Ancestry.com.

[35] Rootsireland.ie Civil Death Record, copyright Rothe House Trust Ltd, Kilkenny.

[36] Catholic Parish Registers, the National Library of Ireland, Microfilm No. 02493/04, available on Ancestry.com.

[37] New York Passenger Lists, 1820-1957, available on Ancestry.com.

[38] Bureau of Records, Borough of Manhattan, Certificate of Marriage #2134.

[39] NY Dept of Health and Vital Records, Certificate of Death #107975

[40] Register of Deaths at Kings Park State Hosp, Kings Park, NY, held at Pilgrim Psychiatric Center, W Brentwood, NY.

[41] Catholic Parish Registers, the National Library of Ireland, Microfilm No. 02493/04, available on Ancestry.com.

[42] Pennsylvania, Passenger and Crew Lists 1800-1962, available on Ancestry.com.

[43] New York, NY, Marriage Index 1866-1937, available on Amazon.com. Certif #22766.

[44] NY Bureau of Records, Dept of Health, Borough of Manhattan, Certificate of Death #14665

[45] New York, NY, Death Index, 1949-1965, Certif #3491.

[46] Application for Social Security Card, dated 1941, birth is 4 Oct 1900, but 1900 US census, CT, Bridgeport, ED 10, Sheet 4A says birth was in Oct 1894. I thing Margaret lied about her year of birth.

[47] New York, NY, Marriage Index 1866-1937, available on Ancestry.com. Certif #30445

had no children. Anna Margaret died in July 1982 in Rumson, NJ.[48] Pearce was born 3 Dec 1901 in Chicago, IL, and died in Sep 1969 in Montclair, NJ.[49]

+13. ii. **WILLIAM E. DOHENY** was born on 13 Dec 1898 in Bridgeport, CT.[50] He married Irene S. Eeck in 1925 in Philadelphia, PA.[51] They had two children. William died on 28 Jan 1960 in NJ.[52]

6. **PATRICK² DOHENY** (*William¹*) was born in Jan 1865 in Graigue. He emigrated to NY about 1891. He married Bridget Corcoran, also an Irish immigrant, on 24 Sep 1899 in Manhattan, NY. They had one child. Patrick died in Feb 1906 in NY. Bridget died before 1920.

The known child of Patrick Doheny and Bridget Corcoran:

14. i. **ANNA ELIZABETH³ DOHENY** (*Patrick², William¹*) was born in 14 Sep 1904 in Yonkers, NY. She died on 21 Nov 1922 in Manhattan. [53]

8. **RICHARD² DOHENY** (*William¹*) was born in Jul 1866 in Graigue. He emigrated in 1895. Richard married Catherine Kelly from Longfordpass, County Tipperary, 3 Oct 1899 in Manhattan, NY. They had one child. Richard died in Aug 1920 in Manhattan. Catherine died in Oct 1944.

The known child of Richard Doheny and Catherine Kelly:

15. i. **ANNA JOSEPHINE³ DOHENY** (*Richard², William¹*) was born on 30 Mar 1901 in Manhattan.[54] She married James Murphy on 29 Jun 1932 in Flushing NY. James was born on 19 May 1902 in Milcove, County Cork, Ireland.[55] They had two children. Anna died on 19 Oct 1971 in Hyde Park, NY.[56] James died on 29 Sep 1981.[57]

10. **EDWARD JOSEPH² DOHENY** (*William¹*) was born in Aug 1874 in Graigue. He emigrated to NY in 1895. Edward married Katharine T. Greene on 28 Sep 1904 in Manhattan. They had at least seven children. Edward died 5 Apr 1953 in Manhattan. Katharine died 12 May 1933 in Kings Park, NY.

[48] Social Security Death Index.
[49] Social Security Death Index. It also gives the date of birth. SSN 135-01-9288
[50] 1900 US census, CT, Bridgeport, ED 10, Sheet 4A. William was born in Dec 1898. US, Find a Grave Index, available on Ancestry.com gives the day of birth.
[51] Pennsylvania Marriages, 1852-1968, available on Ancestry.com.
[52] U.S., Find a Grave Index, available on Ancestry.com. William was buried in Beverly, Burlington County, NJ.
[53] Yonkers City Directory, available on Ancestry.com, situates the family in Yonkers NY in1903. Dept of Records, City of New York Health Dept, Annie Elizabeth's Death Certificate, #8329, provides the date of birth.
[54] New York, NY, Birth Index, 1891-1902, available on Ancestry.com. Certif.# is 14398.
[55] Letter from Anne Murphy Heidel dated 1 Feb 1999 to the author provided marriage information and James Murphy's birth details.
[56] US Social Security Death Index. Anna died while residing with her daughter Anne Murphy Heidel's family.
[57] Letter from Anne Murphy Heidel dated 2 Mar 1999 to the author provided Anna's date and place of death and James' date of death.

The known children of Edward Doheny and Katharine Greene:

16. i. **CATHARINE[3] DOHENY** (*Edward[2], William[1]*) was born on 9 Apr 1905 in NY. She lived only one day.[58]

+17. ii. **EDWARD JOSEPH DOHENY II** was born on 10 May 1907 in Manhattan.[59] He married Catherine Idola Talbott on 1 Jul 1939 in Brooklyn, NY.[60] They had two children. Edward died on 23 Aug 1972 in Brooklyn.[61] Idola died on 16 May 1976 in Brooklyn.[62]

18. iii. **THOMAS DOHENY** was born in Aug 1908 in Manhattan and died there in Oct 1908.[63]

19. iv. **FRANCIS WILLIAM DOHENY** was born on 7 Nov 1909 in Manhattan.[64] He died on 16 August, 1973 in Northport, NY.[65]

20. v. **GERARD DOHENY** was born 12 Oct 1910 in Brooklyn, NY, and died 31 Dec 1933 in Tampa, FL.[66]

21. vi. **LAWRENCE ALOYSIUS DOHENY** was born on 27 Feb 1912 in Brooklyn, NY.[67] He married Kathleen A. Doonan about 1949 in Manhattan.[68] They had two children who are still living. Lawrence died 24 May 1978 in Manhattan.[69] Kathleen was born on 10 Aug 1928 in Manhattan and died 25 Jan 2017 in Rockaway Beach, NY.[70]

22. vii. **BERNARD GREENE DOHENY** was born 11 Oct 1933 in Brooklyn.[71] He married Grace Vogelbach on 21 Aug 1943.[72] They had four children who are still living. Bernard died on 18 May 1979 in South Venice, FL.[73] Grace was born on 19 Oct 1918 and died on 5 Nov 2005 in South Venice, FL.[74]

---

[58] Calvary Cemetery Records, Catharine was buried on 10 Apr 1905 in Sect 32, Range 6, Plot T, Grave 6, New Calvary.

[59] US Social Security Death Index provided the date of birth. The family was living in Manhattan betw. 1904 and 1910.

[60] A dated photo taken on their wedding day. Brooklyn marriage license #9490 was issued on 9 Jun 1939.

[61] A dated memorial card from Walter B. Cook, Inc., Funeral Service, for Edward J. Doheny, d. 23 Aug 1972.

[62] A dated memorial card from Walter B. Cook, Inc., Funeral Service, for Catherine I. Doheny, d. 16 May 1976.

[63] Calvary Cemetery Records, Thomas, 2 months old, was buried on 23 Oct 1908 in Sect 32, Range 6, Plot T, Grave 6.

[64] City of New York, Dept of Health, Certificate of Birth #57529. Copy owned by the author.

[65] A dated memorial card from Taylor Funeral Home, 81 Scudder Ave, Northport NY, Frank W. Doheny d.16 Aug 1973

[66] Florida State Board of Health, Bureau of Vital Statistics, Hillsborough County, District #19-01. Certificate #19229 provided birth and death dates and places. Copy owned by the author.

[67] City of New York, Dept of Health, Brooklyn birth certificate # 7805. Copy owned by the author.

[68] Manhattan, NY Marriage License #34691, issued 29 Dec 1949.

[69] US Social Security Death Index, SSN 051-09-2689. Lawrence's death benefit was claimed in Levittown, NY 11756.

[70] Doonan Family Tree on Ancestry.com, managed by TraceyDoonan.and Mikell Family Tree managed by Kalen Mikell.

[71] City of New York, Dept of Health, Brooklyn Certificate of Birth, certificate #36593. Copy owned by the author.

[72] Certificate of Marriage, Our Lady of Refuge, Brooklyn NY, copy owned by the author.

[73] State of Florida, Office of Vital Statistics, Certified Death Certificate owned by the author.

[74] State of Florida, Office of Vital Statistics, Certified Death Certificate owned by the author. Grace had no birth certificate issued at the time of her birth. There was confusion at the time of the 1918 flu epidemic.

Generation 3

13. **WILLIAM E.**[3] **DOHENY I** (*Timothy*[2]*, William*[1]) was born on 13 Dec 1898 in Bridgeport, CT. He married Irene S. Eeck in 1925 in Philadelphia, PA. They had two children. William died on 28 Jan 1960 in NJ.

The known children of William Doheny and Irene Eeck are:

23. i. **WILLIAM E.**[4] **DOHENY II** (*William*[3]*,Timothy*[2]*, William*[1]) was born on 17 Dec 1925 in New Jersey.[75] He married Patricia Vanduyne in Oct 1954 in Crawford, NJ.[76] They had five children. William died on 10 Feb 2013 in Salisbury, NC.[77]

24. ii. **Donald G. Doheny** was born on 14 Dec 1932 in New Jersey. [78] Donald married Pauline E. Bierylo in Apr 1954 in Elizabeth, NJ.[79] He married Joan Strauss in Dec 1971 in Long Branch, NJ.[80] Donald died on 5 Jun 2013 in Seaford, Sussex County, Delaware. [81]

17. **EDWARD JOSEPH**[3] **DOHENY II** (*Edward*[2]*, William*[1]) was born on 10 May 1907 in Manhattan. He married Catherine Idola Talbott on 1 Jul 1939 in Brooklyn, NY. They had two children. Edward died on 23 Aug 1972 in Brooklyn. Idola died on 16 May 1976 in Brooklyn.

The known children of Edward Doheny II and Catherine Idola Talbott are:

25. i. **EDWARD JOSEPH**[4] **DOHENY III** (*Edward*[3]*, Edward*[2]*, William*[1]) was born on 16 Jan 1942 in Brooklyn, NY. He married Living Steil. They had two children. Edward III died on 21 April 2016 in Vancouver, Washington.[82]

26. ii. **RICHARD J. DOHENY** was born on 24 Mar 1945 in Brooklyn, NY. Richard fathered a child before his first marriage. He married Living Munson.[83] They had three children. Richard married Living Gross about 2011. He and his second wife had one child together. He died on 19 Apr 2013 in Ardsley, Westchester County, NY.[84]

[75] Ancestry.com, US Public Records Index, 1950-1933, Vol 1, record for William E. Doheny Jr of Titusville, FL.
[76] Ancestry.com, New Jersey Marriage Index 1901-1966, Certificate #33802, Crawford, Union county, NJ
[77] Legacy.com, The Star-Ledger, published 15 Feb 2013, obituary for William E. "Bill" Doheny.
[78] http://www.tributes.com/obituary/show/Donald-G.-Doheny-96011531
[79] Ancestry.com, New Jersey Marriage Index 1901-1966, Certificate #10149, Elizabeth, Union County, NJ.
[80] Ancestry.com, New Jersey Marriage Index 1901-2016, Certificate #54957
[81] Ancestry.com, U.S. Find a Grave Index, 1600s-Current, provides birth and death dates, cemetery, and spouse name.
[82] Obituary for Edward J Doheny III, https://www.hamiltonmylan.com/obituary/3678752
[83] Ancestry.com, New York, New York Marriage License Indexes, 1907-1955, License #12182
[84] http://www.tributes.com/obituary/show/Richard-J.-Doheny-95733113

Section III

Appendix

A. Soundex Code

Soundex is the name given to a system for coding and indexing family names based on the phonetic spelling of the name. The code consists of the first letter of the family name, followed by 3 digits representing the first three phonetic sounds found in the name. Similar sounding family names have similar Soundex codes. Zeroes are added to the end of short codes. Double letters are treated as though they are single letters.

Soundex Codes	
Code	Letters
ignore	A, E, H, I, O, U, W, Y
1	B, F, P, V
2	C, G, J, K, Q, S, X, Z
3	D, T
4	L
5	M, N
6	R

Doheny is D500
Scully is S240
Farrell is F640
Greene is G650
Kane is K500

B. Doheny, Greene Cemetery Records

Calvary Cemetery, 4902 Laurel Hill Blvd., Woodside NY 11377 (718-786-8000)
(Sections 17 to 36 are called "New Calvary.")
Section 32, Range 6, Plot T, Grave 6, New Calvary, purchased by Edward Doheny, 10 Apr 1905
(Perpetual care for this burial site was paid in 1972.)

Name	Burial date	Age at death	Year born
Catharine Doheny	10 Apr 1905	1 day	1905 in NY
Thomas J. Doheney	23 Oct 1908	2 months	1908 in NY
Katharine T. Doheny	15 May 1933	54	1878 in NY
Gerard Doheney	5 Jan 1934	22	1911 in NY
Edward J. Doheny II	28 Aug 1972	65	1907 in NY

Section 19, Range 14, Plot Y, Grave 17, New Calvary, purchased by Bridget Doheny, 19 Feb 1906

Patrick Dohoney	18 Feb 1906	41	1865 in Ireland
Annie E. Doheny	23 Nov 1922	18	1904 in NY
Annie Doheny Farrell	3 Jul 1952	74	1877 in Ireland
James Farrell	25 Mar 1964	90	ca.1874 in NY

Section 23, Range 14, Plot D, Grave 20, purchased by Maria Doheny, May 26, 1911

John Doheny	26 May 1911	50	1860 in Ireland
Maria Barry	13 Mar 1945	82	1863 in Ireland
Edward Doheny I	8 Apr 1953	78	1874 in Ireland

Section 23, Range 14, Plot D, Grave 19, purchased by Richard Doheny, 26 May 1911

Richard Doheny	11 Aug 1920	54	1866 in Ireland
Catherine Kelly Doheny	12 Oct 1944	80	1864 in Ireland
Nora Kelly	10 Feb 1950	77	ca.1873 in Ireland

Holy Cross Cemetery, 3620 Tilden Ave., Brooklyn NY 11203 (718-284-4520)
Section Vernon, Range D, Plot 411, purchased by Francis Greene

Mary Green	14 Sep 1883	7	ca.1876 in NY
Francis Green	26 Oct 1884	45	ca.1839 in Ireland
Thomas Green	14 Jun 1896	21	ca.1875 in NY
Catherine Greene Keenan	14 Dec 1909	66	1843 in Ireland
Francis J. Greene	12 Jun 1959	79	1880 in NY
Helen V. Greene	12 Aug 1968	84	1884 in NY

Section Vernon, Range D, Plot 412, purchased by Mary Green in 1884

Mary Green	27 Jun 1888	50	ca. 1838 in Ireland

Section St. Stephen, Row P, Plot 23

Marguerite Green	23 Dec 1898	10	1888 in NY
Mary Margaret Green	8 Jul 1911	ca. 46	1911 in Ireland
Henry Green	6 Sep 1912	ca. 60	ca. 1852 in Ireland

Section St. Stephen, Row P, Plot 24

Thomas J. Greene	15 Oct 1934	65	1869 in Ireland
Elizabeth Curley Greene	19 Oct 1944	68	1872 in NY
Thomas J. Greene Jr	17 Dec 1955	61	1894 in NY
George William Greene	13 Jan 1975	74	1901 in NY
Walter Green	15 Aug 1978	79	1898 in NY
Edith Greene	29 Jan 1980	unknown	unknown

Francis W. Doheny (63) born 1909, buried LI Nat Cemetery, Farmingdale NY, Sect 24, Grave 5919.
Lawrence A. Doheny (66) born 1912, buried LI Nat Cemetery, Farmingdale NY, Sect 2T, Grave 1623-A
Bernard G. Doheny (75) born 1913, buried Calverton Nat Cemetery, Calverton NY, Sect 8, Grave 2955.

C. Edward Doheny's Declaration of Intention, 11 July 1895

United States of America.

STATE OF NEW YORK,
CITY AND COUNTY OF NEW YORK, } ss.

Be it Remembered, That on the ____11th____ day of ____July____ in the year of our Lord, one thousand eight hundred and ninety-five, personally appeared ____Edward Doheny____ in the **Court of Common Pleas** for the City and County of New York (*said Court being a Court of Record, having common law jurisdiction, a Clerk and a Seal*), and made his Declaration of Intention to become a Citizen of the United States of America, in the words following, to wit :

"I, ____Edward Doheny____ do declare on oath, that it is *bona fide* my **Intention** to become a **Citizen of the United States of America**, and to renounce forever all allegiance and fidelity to any foreign Prince, Potentate, State or Sovereignty whatever, and particularly to the QUEEN OF THE UNITED KINGDOM OF GREAT BRITAIN AND IRELAND, of whom I am a subject, (and that I arrived in the United States on the ____16____ day of ____March____ 18 95)."

Sworn, this ____11th____ day of ____July____ 189 5

ALFRED WAGSTAFF,
Clerk.

Edward Doheny
Residence, 158 Clinton St.
City

In Attestation Whereof, and that the foregoing is a true copy of the original Declaration of Intention remaining of record in my office, I, ALFRED WAGSTAFF, Clerk of the said Court, have hereunto subscribed my name and affixed the seal of the said Court, this ____11th____ day of ____July____ 189 5

Alfred Wagstaff
Clerk.

Transcription of Edward Doheny's Declaration of Intention, 11 July 1895

United States of America
State of New York, City and County of New York

Be it remembered, That on the 11th day of July in the year of our Lord one thousand eight hundred and ninety-five, personally appeared Edward Doheny in the Court of Common Pleas for the City and County of New York (said court being a Court of Record, having common law jurisdiction, a Clerk and a Seal), and made his Declaration of Intention to become a Citizen of the United States of America, in the words following, to wit:

"I, Edward Doheny do declare on oath, that it is bona fide my intention to become a Citizen of the United States of America, and to renounce forever all allegiance and fidelity to any foreign Prince, Potentate, State or Sovereignty whatever, and particularly to the Queen of the United Kingdom of Great Britain and Ireland, of whom I am a subject, (and that I arrived in the United States on the 16th day of March 1895)."

Sworn this 11th day of July 1895, Edward Doheny. Residence 158 Clinton St, City.
Signed Alfred Wagstaff, Clerk.

In Attestation Whereof, and that the foregoing is a true copy of the original Declaration of Intention remaining of record in my office, I, Alfred Wagstaff, Clerk of the said Court, have hereunto subscribed my name and affixed the seal of the said Court, this 11th day of July 1895.
Signed Alfred Wagstaff, Clerk.

D. Edward Doheny's Citizenship Certificate, 26 Jun 1900

598

District Court of the United States
FOR THE SOUTHERN DISTRICT OF NEW YORK.

IN THE MATTER OF THE APPLICATION OF

Edward Doheny

By occupation *Porter*

PETITION.

TO BE ADMITTED A CITIZEN OF THE UNITED STATES OF AMERICA.

The above-named applicant, being over twenty-one years of age, hereby petitions to be admitted to become a Citizen of the United States of America, and avers that two years or more have elapsed since he declared his intention to become such Citizen, and that a certified copy of said declaration is hereunto annexed.

Subscribed and sworn to before me this ___ day of June 190_

APPLICANT.

United States District Court, Southern District of New York.

IN THE MATTER
of the application of the above-named applicant to be admitted a Citizen of the United States.

REPORT.

To the Honorable the Judge of the District Court of the United States for the Southern District of N. Y.

IN PURSUANCE of a rule of this Court adopted January 18th, 1896, I, the undersigned special Commissioner, do respectfully report:

That I have been attended on such reference by the applicant and his witness, who have been by me orally examined, and have taken the proofs offered by him, which are hereto annexed.

And I find and report thereon that the said applicant has complied with the requirements requisite to become a Citizen. I further find that said applicant can ___, read ___ the English language intelligibly.

Dated June ___

COMMISSIONER.

IN THE MATTER
of the application of the above-named applicant to be admitted a Citizen of the United States.

TESTIMONY ON REFERENCE.

... being duly sworn, deposes and says, that he resides ... City of New York ... and by occupation a ... personally acquainted with the above-named applicant for admission ... and has known him for the past ___ years; that his occupation ... and that he resides at No. ___ Street, Borough of ___ City of New York; that ... personally knows that ... has resided continuously within the limits and under the jurisdiction of the United States ... and continuously within the State of New York ... ; that during all time of his residence within the United States and within the State, he has behaved as a man of good moral character, attached to the principles of the Constitution of the United States, and well disposed to the good order and happiness of the same.

Sworn to before me this 26 ___

John Powers

WITNESS.

Edward Doheny

... being duly sworn, deposes and says, that ... admitted as a Citizen of the United States ... that he was born ... and emigrated to the United States landing at the port of ___ ... in the year A. D. 18__ ... and resided at No. ___ Street, in the City of New York ... that he is over the age of twenty-one years; that he has resided continuously within the United States ... and continuously within the State of New York since ___ A.D. 18__.

Sworn to before me this ___

Edward Doheny

APPLICANT.

COMMISSIONER.

UNITED STATES OF AMERICA, Southern District of New York, ss: I, Edward Doheny, the above-named applicant, do solemnly swear that I will support the Constitution of the United States; and that I do absolutely and entirely renounce and abjure all allegiance and fidelity to every foreign Prince, Potentate, State or Sovereignty whatever, and particularly to the ___ of whom I have heretofore been a subject. So help me God.

Sworn in open Court, this 26th day of June

Edward Doheny

APPLICANT.

CLERK.

At a Stated Term of the District Court of the United States of America, held for the Southern District of New York, at the U. S. Court House and P. O. Building in the City of New York, on the 26th day of June one thousand nine hundred ___.

PRESENT—The Honorable ADDISON BROWN.

IN THE MATTER
of the application of the above-named applicant to be admitted a Citizen of the United States of America.

The said applicant appearing personally in Court, producing the evidence required by the acts of Congress, and having made such declaration and renunciation, and having taken such oaths as are by the said acts required, IT IS ORDERED by the said Court that the said applicant be admitted to be a Citizen of the United States of America.

CLERK.

Transcription of Edward Doheny's Citizenship Certificate, 26 Jun 1900

District Court of the United States
for the Southern District of New York

In the matter of the application of Edward Doheny, by occupation Porter, to be admitted a citizen of the United States of America.

The above-named applicant, being over twenty-one years of age, hereby petitions to be admitted to become a citizen of the United States of America, and avers that two years or more have elapsed since he declared his intention to become such Citizen, and that a certified copy of said declaration is hereunto annexed.

Subscribed and sworn to before me Edward Doheny this 26 day of June 1900.

Commissioner Paul H Lyman, United States District Court, Southern District of New York.

REPORT to the Honorable the Judge of the District Court of the United States for the southern District of N.Y. - In the matter of the application of the above-named applicant to be admitted a citizen of the United States. In pursuance of a rule of this court adopted January 18, 1896, I, the undersigned special commissioner, do respectfully report:

That I have been attended on such reference by the applicant and his witness, who have been by me orally examined, and have taken the proofs offered by him, which are hereto annexed.

And I find and report thereon that the said applicant has complied with the requirements of statute in regard to admission to become a Citizen. I further find that said applicant can speak, read, and write the English language intelligibly.

Dated June 26, 1900. Signed P.H.Lyman, Commissioner.

TESTIMONY ON REFERENCE in the matter of the application of the above-named applicant to be admitted a Citizen of the United States.

John Powers, being duly sworn, deposes and says, that he resides at 53 Floyd, W. Brooklyn, and is by occupation a porter, that he is a citizen of the United States, and has known him for the past 5 years; that his occupation is that of porter, and that he resides at 109 W 60th Street, Borough of Manhattan, City of New York, NY, that he personally knows that the applicant has resided continuously within the limits and under the jurisdiction of the United States and within the State, he has behaved as a good and moral character, attached to the principles of the Constitution of the United States, and well-disposed to the good order and happiness of the same.

Sworn to me, this 26th day of June 1900. John Powers, Witness, and P.H.Lyman, Commissioner

Edward Doheny being duly sworn, deposes and says, that he is the above named applicant for admission as a Citizen of the United States of America, that he was born on the 13th day of August in the year one thousand eight hundred and 75 and emigrated to the United States, landing in the Port of New York in the State of NY on or about the 16th day of March A.D. 1895, and that he now resides at No. 109 W 60th Street, in the City of new York; that he has arrived at the age of twenty-one years; that he has resided continuously within the United States since March 16, 1895 and continuously within the state of New York since March 16, 1895.

Sworn to me this 26 day of June 1900. Signed Edward Doheny, Applicant and P.H.Lyman, Commissioner.

ATTACHMENT: I, Edward Doheny, the above-named applicant, do solemnly swear that I will support the Constitution of the United States; and that I do absolutely and entirely renounce all allegiance and fidelity to every foreign Prince, Potentate, State or Sovereignty whatever, and particularly to the Queen of Great Britain and Ireland of whom I have been heretofore subject. So help me God.

Sworn in open court this 26th day of June 1900, Edward Doheny, Applicant, and Paul H Lyman, Clerk.

At a Stated Term of the District Court of the United States of America, held in and for the Southern District of New York, at the U.S. Court House and P.O. Building in the City of New York, on the 26th day of June one thousand nine hundred. **PRESENT** – The Honorable Addison Brown. IN THE MATTER of the application of the above -named applicant to be admitted a Citizen of the United States of America. The said applicant appearing personally in Court, producing the evidence required by the acts of Congress, and having made such declaration and renunciation, and having taken such oaths as are by the said acts required, IT IS ORDERED by the said court that the said applicant be admitted to be a Citizen of the United States of America. Signed Paul H. Lyman, Clerk.

E. Edward Doheny and Katharine Greene's Marriage Certificate

F. Edward Doheny's 1918 World War I Draft Registration Card

Serial Number 234, Order Number A3366
Edward Joseph Doheny

Permanent Home: 243 East 39th St, N.Y.C.
Age 44, Date of Birth August 23 - 1874
Race: White   Naturalized Citizen

Occupation: Insurance. Employer: Metropolitan Life Co., 1 Madison Ave, Manhattan
Nearest Relative: Mrs. E. J. Doheny, 243 East 39th St., Manhattan

Registrar's Report 31-9-123-C
Physical Description: Medium height and build, blue eyes, gray hair
No physical disqualifications.
Registrar's Signature: Mary E. Dawson, 12 Sept 1918
Local Draft Board No 123
St. Gabriel's Public Library
East 36th St., New York City, N.Y.

G. Edward Doheny's
Certificate of Death

H. Death Registry for Katharine Greene Doheny

A VERIFIED TRANSCRIPT
FROM THE REGISTER OF DEATHS

Date of Death_____May 12, 1933_____Registered No_____95____

Name of Deceased____Katherine G. Doheny____

Age:__54____Years__6__Months__16__Days

Single, Married, Widowed or Divorced____Separated____

Race or color, if other than white_____

Social Security No._____

Occupation_____Houseworker_____

Birthplace____Brooklyn, New York____

How Long } Here_____7 years, 5 months, 15 days____
a }
Resident } In U.S. if foreign_____

Father's Name_____Francis Green____

Mother's Name_____Catherine Farrell____

Place of Death:____Kings Park State Hospital____

- -

Medical Attendant or other Attestant____Joseph J. Catalano, M.D.____

Place of Burial____Calvary Cemetery, Brooklyn, New York____

Undertaker____J.J. Craiels, Kings Park, New York____

I hereby Solemnly Attest   That this is a true transcript from the Public Register of Deaths as kept in the

_____Pilgrim Psychiatric Center_____

County of_____SUFFOLK_____State of New York

Dated at_____West Brentwood_____N.Y.

the__17th__day__December__19__99

(Signed) _Margaux Simai_

(Official Title)   Registrar

Obituary
In *The Brooklyn Daily Eagle*
14 May 1944, page 13

DOHENY—KATHARINE T. DOHENY (nee Greene), on May 12, 1933. Funeral from home of her sister, Miss Helen V. Greene, 530 2d St., Brooklyn, Monday, May 15; mass of requiem 10 a.m. at St. Francis Xavier Church. Interment Calvary Cemetery.

I. Maria Doheny Barry's
Death Certificate

J. John Doheny's Death Certificate

14 H—1907

THE CITY OF NEW YORK.   STATE OF NEW YORK.   No. of Certificate,
DEPARTMENT OF HEALTH.

CERTIFICATE AND RECORD OF DEATH ᴋ7316

OF

John Doheny

Sex	*Male*	Place of Death	*Presbyterian*
Age	*46* Yrs. Mos. Days	Character of premises, whether tenement, private, etc. If hotel, hospital or other institution, state full title	*Hospital*
Single, Married, Widowed or Divorced	*Single*		
Occupation	*Elevator runner*	Father's Name	*William Doheny*
Birthplace	*Ireland*	Father's Birthplace	*Ireland*
How long in U.S. (if of foreign birth)	*19 yrs*	Mother's Maiden Name	*Anna Dunlby*
How long resident in City of New York		Mother's Birthplace	*Ireland*

MARGIN RESERVED FOR BINDING — *NO MUTILATED CERTIFICATE WILL BE RECEIVED*

I hereby certify that I attended deceased from *May 7* 1901, to *May 24* 1901, that I last saw *him* alive on the *24th* day of *May* 1901, that *he* died on the *24th* day of *May* 1901, about *1.50* o'clock A. M., or P. M., and that, to the best of my knowledge and belief, the cause of *his* death was as follows:

Aneurysm of left common carotid artery

SPECIAL INFORMATION

required in deaths in hospitals and institutions and in deaths of non-residents and recent residents.

Former or usual residence } *590 3 Ave*

How long resident at place of death } *17 Days*

Witness my hand this *24th* day of *May* 1901

(Signature) *E. R. Evans* M. D.

(Residence) *Presbyterian Hospital*

K. Annie Doheny Farrell's
Death Certificate

Certificate of Death

Certificate No. _156-52-114665_

OF RECORDS
ENT OF HEALTH
OF MANHATTAN

1952 AM 9:05 JUN 30

1. NAME OF DECEASED _Annie_ _Farrell_
(Print or Typewrite)   First Name   Middle Name   Last Name

PERSONAL PARTICULARS
(To be filled in by Funeral Director)

2 USUAL RESIDENCE: (a) State _New York_

(b) Co. _New York_ (c) Post Office and Zone _N 434_

(d) No. _603 Isham Ave St._
(If in rural area, give location)

(e) Length of residence or stay in City of New York immediately prior to death _60 yrs._

3 SINGLE, MARRIED, WIDOWED, OR DIVORCED (write the word) _Married_

4 DATE OF BIRTH OF DECEDENT (Month) _Sep._ (Day) _19,_ (Year) _1877_

5 AGE _74 yrs._ If under 1 year _mos._ _days_ If less than 1 day, _hrs. or_ _min._

6 Occupation
a. Usual Occupation (Kind of work done during most of working life, even if retired) _Housewife_

b. Kind of Business or Industry in which this work was done _Own Home_

7 SOCIAL SECURITY NO. _None_

8 BIRTHPLACE (State or Foreign Country) _Ireland_

9 OF WHAT COUNTRY WAS DECEASED A CITIZEN AT TIME OF DEATH? _U.S._

10a. WAS DECEASED EVER IN UNITED STATES ARMED FORCES? _no_   10b. IF YES, Give war or dates of service

11 NAME OF FATHER OF DECEDENT _John Doheny_

12 MAIDEN NAME OF MOTHER OF DECEDENT _Nancy Scully_

13 NAME OF INFORMANT _James Farrell_ RELATIONSHIP TO DECEASED _Husband_ ADDRESS _603 Isham St._

14a. Name of Cemetery or Crematory _Calvary Cemetery_ 14b. Location (City, Town or County and State) _Long Island, N.Y._ 14c. Date of Burial or Cremation _July 3, 1952_

21 FUNERAL DIRECTOR _Conner Funeral Home_ ADDRESS _4955 B'way_ PERMIT NUMBER _116_

MEDICAL CERTIFICATE OF DEATH
(To be filled in by the Physician)

15 PLACE OF DEATH:

(a) NEW YORK CITY: (b) Borough _Manhattan_

(c) Name of Hospital or Institution _Francis Delafield_
(If not in hospital or institution, give street and number.)

(d) If in hospital, give Ward No. _4 West_

16 DATE AND HOUR OF DEATH (Month) _June_ (Day) _29,_ (Year) _1952_ (Hour) _4:25P_

17 SEX _Female_   COLOR OR RACE _White_   19 Approximate Age _74_

20 I HEREBY CERTIFY that (I attended the deceased) (a staff physician of this institution attended the deceased)

from _June 21,_ 19_52_ to _June 29,_ 19_52_

and last saw her alive at _4:25P_ M on _June 29,_ 19_52_

I further certify that death † _was not_ caused, directly or indirectly by accident, homicide, suicide, acute or chronic poisoning, or in any suspicious or unusual manner, and that it was due to NATURAL CAUSES more fully described in the confidential medical report filed with the Department of Health.

* Cross out words that do not apply.
† See first instruction on reverse of certificate.

Witness my hand this _9_ day of _July_ 19_52_

Signature _Cadman Owen Gaffney_ M. D.

Address _Francis Delafield Hospital_

BUREAU OF RECORDS AND STATISTICS   DEPARTMENT OF HEALTH   CITY OF NEW YORK

L. Lawrence Doheny's Birth Certificate and WWII Draft Registration

M. Lawrence Doheny's Death Certificate

THE CITY OF NEW YORK
VITAL RECORDS CERTIFICATE

VITAL RECORDS
DEPARTMENT OF HEALTH
BOROUGH OF MANHATTAN

CERTIFICATE OF DEATH | 156-78-108715 #33

Certificate No. _____

DATE FILED 78 MAY 26 P 2

1. NAME OF DECEASED (Type or Print): Lawrence | Doheny
   First Name | Middle Name | Last Name

MEDICAL CERTIFICATE OF DEATH *(To be filled in by the Physician)*

2. PLACE OF DEATH — a. BOROUGH: MANHATTAN (NEW YORK CITY)
b. Name of hospital or institution, if not hospital, street address: 530 WEST 55th STREET
c. If in hospital (Check): 1☐ DOA 2☐ Emerg. Rm. 3☐ Outpatient 4☐ Inpatient
d. If inpatient, date of current admission: Month | Day | Year

3a. DATE AND HOUR OF DEATH: 5 | 24 | 78 (Month | Day | Year)
3b. HOUR: unknown AM/PM
4. SEX: Male
5. APPROXIMATE AGE: 65 yrs.

6. I HEREBY CERTIFY that, in accordance with the provisions of law, I took charge of the dead body at OFFICE OF CHIEF MEDICAL EXAMINER 520 FIRST AVENUE, N.Y. 16, N.Y. on the 25 day of MAY 19 78
I further certify from the investigation and post mortem examination ☐ with ☒ without autopsy that in my opinion death occurred on the date X and at the hour stated above and resulted from ☐ Natural Causes ☐ Accident ☐ Suicide ☐ Homicide ☐ Undetermined Circumstances ☐ Pending Further Investigation

and that the causes of death were:

PART 1
a. Immediate cause: Acute and chronic alcoholism. Fatty liver.
b. Due to or as a consequence of
c. Due to or as a consequence of

PART 2 Contributory causes

M.E. Case No. 3524   Signed: *Michael Baden*
Michael Baden (Chief) (Medical Examiner) M.D.

PERSONAL PARTICULARS *(To be filled in by Funeral Director)*

7. USUAL RESIDENCE — a. STATE: New York 530 West 55th St.
b. COUNTY: New York
c. CITY, TOWN OR LOCATION: New York
d. STREET AND HOUSE NUMBER: 530 West 55th Street
e. INSIDE CITY LIMITS OF 7c: ☒YES ☐NO

8. MARITAL STATUS (Check one): 1☐ Never Married 2☐ Married or Separated 3☐ Widowed 4☒ Divorced
9. CITIZEN OF WHAT COUNTRY: United States
10. NAME OF SURVIVING SPOUSE (if wife, give maiden name):

11. DATE OF BIRTH OF DECEDENT: 2 | 27 | 1912 (Month | Day | Year)
12. AGE AT LAST BIRTHDAY: 65
If UNDER 1 Year: mos. | days
If LESS than 1 Day: hrs. | min.

13. USUAL OCCUPATION (Kind of work done during most of working lifetime; do not enter retired.): Elevator Operator
b. KIND OF BUSINESS: Office Building
14. SOCIAL SECURITY NO.: 051-09-2689

15. BIRTHPLACE (State or Foreign Country): NEW YORK
16. OTHER NAME(S) BY WHICH DECEDENT WAS KNOWN: LAWRENCE A. DOHENY

17. NAME OF FATHER OF DECEDENT: EDWARD DOHENY
18. MAIDEN NAME OF MOTHER OF DECEDENT: KATHERINE GREENE

19a. NAME OF INFORMANT: Bernard Doheny
b. RELATIONSHIP TO DECEASED: Brother
c. ADDRESS: 462 Morton Blvd. (City) Plainview (State) N.Y.

20a. NAME OF CEMETERY OR CREMATORY: Long Island National Cemetery
b. LOCATION (City, Town, State and Country): Pinelawn New York
c. DATE OF BURIAL OR CREMATION: 5/31/78

21a. FUNERAL DIRECTOR: Thomas F. Dalton Funeral Home, Inc. ___ km Ave Hicksville N.Y.

Gretchen Van Wye, Ph.D. City Registrar

This is to certify that the foregoing is a true copy of a record on file in the Department of Health and Mental Hygiene. The Department of Health and Mental Hygiene does not certify to the truth of the statements made thereon, as no inquiry as to the facts has been provided by law.

Steven P. Schwartz, Ph.D., City Registrar

Do not accept this transcript unless it bears the security features listed on the back. Reproduction or alteration of this transcript is prohibited by §3.19(b) of the New York City Health Code if the purpose is the evasion or violation of any provision of the Health Code or any other law.

R04273296

November 19, 2019

The City of New York

ANY ALTERATION OR ERASURE VOIDS THIS CERTIFICATE

N. Bernard Doheny's Birth and Baptismal Certificates

2 H—1913

THE CITY OF NEW YORK.
DEPARTMENT OF HEALTH.

STATE OF NEW YORK.

CERTIFICATE AND RECORD OF BIRTH

No. of Certificate, 36698

Name of Child: Bernard Green Doheny

Sex	Male	Father's Occupation	Clerk
Color	White	Mother's Name	Katherine Doheny
Date of Birth	Oct. 11/13	Mother's Name before Marriage	" Green
Place of Birth, Street and No.	523 - 6 ave.	Mother's Residence	523 - 6 ave.
Father's Name	Edward Doheny	Mother's Birthplace	U. S.
Father's Residence	523 - 6 ave.	Mother's Age	34 yrs.
Father's Birthplace	Ire	Number of previous Children	6
Father's Age	39 yrs.	How many now living (in all)	5

I, the undersigned, hereby certify that I attended professionally at the above birth and I am personally cognizant thereof; and that all the facts stated in said certificate and report of birth are true to the best of my knowledge, information and belief.

Signature, M. Edwin Clafford M.D.

DATE OF REPORT, Oct. 20 1913 Residence, 256 - 9 ave.

...Certificate of Baptism...

This is to Certify, that Bernard Clifford

Child of Edward J. Doheny and Catherine Greene

was born on the 11th day of Oct 1913

and baptized according to the rite of the Roman Catholic Church

on the 26th day of Oct. 1913, in the

Church of the Holy Family, Thirteenth Street, Brooklyn, N. Y.

by Rev. A. J. Reichert D. D.

Sponsors: Francis Greene
Helen Greene

The above is a true copy from the Register of Baptisms of Holy Family Church.

Attest: F. X. Debold Asst. Pastor.

O. Bernard Doheny and Grace Vogelbach's Marriage Certificate

Certificate of Marriage

Church of

Our Lady of Refuge
Brooklyn, N.Y.

This is to Certify

That *Bernard Greene Doheny*

and *Grace Dolores Vogelbach*

were lawfully **Married**

on the *21st* day of *August* 1943

According to the Rite of the Roman Catholic Church

and in conformity with the laws of the State of

New York, Rev. *James F. Kelly*

officiating, in the presence of *Francis H. Doheny*

and *Jean Vogelbach* Witnesses, as appears

from the Marriage Register of this Church.

Dated *August 21, 1943.*

Rev. James F. Kelly, As't Pastor.

NO. 212 © D. P. MURPHY CO., NEW YORK

P. Bernard Doheny's Death Certificate

STATE OF FLORIDA

OFFICE of VITAL STATISTICS

CERTIFIED COPY

CERTIFICATE OF DEATH
FLORIDA

LOCAL FILE NO.

1. DECEDENT'S NAME (First, Middle, Last)	BERNARD G. DOHENY
2. SEX	Male
3. DATE OF DEATH (Month, Day, Year)	May 18, 1989
4. SOCIAL SECURITY NUMBER	057-07-0158
5a. AGE-Last Birthday (Years)	75
6. DATE OF BIRTH (Month, Day, Year)	October 11, 1913
7. BIRTHPLACE (City and State or Foreign Country)	Brooklyn, New York
8. WAS DECEDENT EVER IN US ARMED FORCES?	Yes
9a. PLACE OF DEATH	(OTHER: Nursing Home XX Residence)
9b. INSIDE CITY LIMITS?	No
9c. FACILITY NAME	526 Carmel Road
9d. CITY, TOWN, OR LOCATION OF DEATH	Venice
9e. COUNTY OF DEATH	Sarasota
10a. DECEDENT'S USUAL OCCUPATION	Accounting Clerk
10b. KIND OF BUSINESS/INDUSTRY	Investment Banking
11. MARITAL STATUS	Married
12. SURVIVING SPOUSE (If wife, give maiden name)	Grace D. Vogelbach
13a. RESIDENCE — STATE	Florida
13b. COUNTY	Sarasota
13c. CITY, TOWN, OR LOCATION	Venice
13d. STREET AND NUMBER	526 Carmel Road
13e. INSIDE CITY LIMITS?	No
13f. ZIP CODE	34293
14. WAS DECEDENT OF HISPANIC OR HAITIAN ORIGIN?	XX No
15. RACE	White
16. DECEDENT'S EDUCATION	12
17. FATHER'S NAME (First, Middle, Last)	Edward J. Doheny
18. MOTHER'S NAME (First, Middle, Maiden Surname)	Catherine Greene
19a. INFORMANT'S NAME (Type/Print)	Grace D. Doheny
19b. MAILING ADDRESS	526 Carmel Road, Venice, 34293
20a. METHOD OF DISPOSITION	XX Removal from State
20b. PLACE OF DISPOSITION	Calverton National Cemetery
20c. LOCATION — City or Town, State	Calverton, New York
21a. SIGNATURE OF FUNERAL SERVICE LICENSEE	(signature)
21b. LICENSE NUMBER	1878
21c. NAME AND ADDRESS OF FACILITY	Lemon Bay Funeral Home, 1935 S. Tamiami Tr., Venice, FL 34293

CERTIFIER

22a. To the best of my knowledge, death occurred at the time, date and place and due to the cause(s) as stated. (Signature and Title) — (signature)

22b. DATE SIGNED (Mo, Day, Yr)	5/18/89
22c. HOUR OF DEATH	9:45 A.M.
24. NAME AND ADDRESS OF CERTIFIER	Stephen V. Orman, M.D., 901 S. Tamiami Trail, Venice, FL 34285
25b. LOCAL REGISTRAR — SIGNATURE	(signature)
DATE REGISTERED	May 1989

CAUSE OF DEATH BY CERTIFIER

26. PART I. Enter the diseases, injuries, or complications that caused the death. Do not enter the mode of dying, such as cardiac or respiratory arrest, shock, or heart failure. List only one cause on each line.

IMMEDIATE CAUSE (Final disease or condition resulting in death)
a. Sideroblastic Anemia
DUE TO (OR AS A CONSEQUENCE OF):
b. Atherosclerotic Heart Disease

27a. WAS AN AUTOPSY PERFORMED?	No
28. CASE REPORTED TO MEDICAL EXAMINER?	No

29. IF FEMALE, WAS THERE A PREGNANCY IN THE PAST 3 MONTHS? — NO

31. PROBABLE MANNER OF DEATH

HRS Form 612, Jan. 86 (Obsoletes Previous Editions)

Q. Francis Green's Death certificate

DEPARTMENT OF HEALTH OF THE CITY OF BROOKLYN   11534

Certificate of Death.

1.–Full Name.* *Francis Green*

2.–Age. *45* years, ... months, ... days.

3.–Sex. Male Female.*   4.–White, Colored.*

DEPARTMENT OF HEALTH,
OFFICE OF REGISTER,
OCT. 25 1884

5.–Single, Married, Widow, Widower.*

6.–Birthplace, *Ireland.*   7.–Occupation, *Laborer*

8.–If of foreign birth, how long in the U.S. *17* years.   9.–How long resident in City, *17* years.

10.–Father's Birthplace,* *Ireland*   11.–Mother's Birthplace,* *Ireland.*

12.–Place of Death,* No. *N. E. Cor 18th St. & 10th Av.*   Brooklyn. Ward. *8th*

13.–Number of Families in House, *3*   14.–On what Floor, *2nd*

15.–I HEREBY CERTIFY that I attended the deceased from *Oct. 19th* 188 *4* to *Oct. 24* 188 *4*

that I last saw him alive on the *24th* day of *October* 188 *4*; that he died on the *24* day of *October* 188 *4* about *2* o'clock A.M. or P.M. and that the following was the

16.–Cause of Death.*

I.   *Pneumonia*   Time from attack till death. *9 days.*

II.   *Asthenia*

This Certificate delivered to *Henry Green* at *8 a* M., *Oct* *25th* 188 *4*

Signed by *James McManus* M.D., No. *187* *19th* Street

Medical Attendant.

See other side for explanations and directions.

11534

17.–Place of Burial, *Holy Cross* Cemetery.

18.–Date of Burial, *Oct 26 1884*   In case of contagious diseases ...... A. M. or P. M.

19.–Undertaker, *Thos Newman*   Place of Business, *Court St*

*   Write FAMILY NAME plainly and exactly. If the deceased was a child *not named*, state the names of both parents.

3, 4, 5, 15.–Draw a line through the *words not required* on these lines.

6. 10, 11.–Insert name of State or Country.

12.–If in a *Public Institution*, please state its name, and erase line 12.

16.–I. Name the *Organic*, Principal, or most influential Disease or Injury. If an autopsy was made, please so state.

II. Name any complication, remote cause, important event (as Operation, in Surgical Cases,) or the Manner of Dying (as Asphyxia, Asthenia, Syncope, etc.), or prominent symptom (as Convulsions, Dropsy, Jaundice, Paralysis, etc.) If the disease was Puerperal in origin, this should be stated.

18.–Small Pox, Scarlet Fever, Diphtheria, Measles.

Note to Undertakers.–Physicians are responsible for the correctness of all facts inserted upon the face of this certificate; therefore no changes or additions made by undertakers or others can be accepted.

The law requires that the remains of those dying from a contagious disease shall be immediately disinfected, placed in a tightly sealed coffin, and that the interment shall take place within 24 hours after death and be strictly private; and that the remains be conveyed in a hearse—the use of carriages or wagons for this purpose not being permitted. Undertakers and all other persons having charge of the remains of deceased persons, are responsible for any violation of these rules.

Office for Burial Permits, Municipal Department Building.

Hours from 9 to 4. Sundays and Holidays, 9 to 12.

R. Mary Green's Death Certificate

S.   Last Will of Henry Green

107

IN THE NAME OF GOD, AMEN,

I, HENRY GREEN of the Borough of Brooklyn, City and State of New York, being of sound and disposing mind and memory, and considering the uncertainty of this life, do make, publish and declare, this to be my last Will and Testament as follows:

FIRST: After my lawful debts are paid, I give devise and bequeath to my Executor hereinafter named, the sum of Nine hundred ($900.) Dollars and direct that he apply such sum toward the erection of a suitable monument upon my burial plot in Holy Cross Cemetery, Brooklyn, New York and toward the improvement and embellishment of said plot.

SECOND: I give, devise and bequeath to the Holy Cross Cemetery of Brooklyn, New York the sum of Five hundred ($500.) Dollars in trust to apply the income thereof to the perpetual care, maintenance, improvement and embellishment of my said burial plot in the said Holy Cross Cemetery.

THIRD: I give, devise and bequeath unto my niece Delia Green, daughter of James Green, the sum of Fifteen hundred ($1500.) Dollars.

FOURTH: I give, devise and bequeath unto my niece Margaret Green, daughter of James Green, the sum of Fifteen hundred ($1500.) Dollars.

FIFTH: All the rest, remainder and residue of my estate of which I may die seized or possessed or to which I may be entitled, whether real, personal or mixed and wheresoever the same may be situate, I give, devise and bequeath unto my nephew Thomas Green, son of James Green, his heirs and assigns forever.

SIXTH: In the event that the personal property of which I may die possessed be insufficient to pay and satisfy the bequests made herein in paragraphs First, Second, Third and Fourth, then and in that event, I direct that the said bequests be charged upon the real property of which I may die seized, and I hereby direct and empower my Executor hereinafter named to sell at public auction or private sale, as soon after my death as may be expedient, so much of my said real property as may be necessary to satisfy and pay the said bequests, and I hereby give my said Executor full power and authority to make, execute and deliver all necessary and proper deeds or other instruments to convey title to the real property so sold, and I hereby direct that in the event of such sale or sales the proceeds thereof or so much thereof as may be necessary be applied to the payment of the said bequests.

SEVENTH: I hereby revoke all former wills and codicils by me at whatsoever time made.

EIGHTH: I hereby appoint my nephew Thomas Green, son of James Green, to be Executor of this my last Will and Testament.

IN WITNESS WHEREOF, I have hereunto subscribed my name, and affixed my seal, this twenty sixth day of August in the year of our Lord, one thousand nine hundred and twelve.

WITNESSES
            Henry Green (Seal)

George R. Holahan Jr
John H. Barry

Subscribed by HENRY GREEN, the Testator named in the foregoing Will, in the presence of each of us, and at the time of making such subscription the above instrument was declared by the said Testator to be his last Will and Testament, and each of us, at the request of said Testator and in his presence and in the presence of each other, sign our names as witnesses thereto, at the end of the Will.

T.   Henry Green's Death Certificate

14 fi—1912

1 PLACE OF DEATH

BOROUGH OF *Brooklyn.*

No. *St. Mary's General Hosp.* St.

Character of premises, whether tenement, private, hotel, hospital or other place. *Hospital*

2 FULL NAME *Henry Green*

STATE OF NEW YORK

Department of Health of The City of New York
BUREAU OF RECORDS
STANDARD CERTIFICATE OF DEATH

Registered No. *16757*

3 SEX	4 COLOR OR RACE	5 SINGLE, MARRIED, WIDOWED OR DIVORCED (Write the word)
Male	*White*	*Married*

6 DATE OF BIRTH
_____, 1____
(Month)   (Day)   (Year)

7 AGE *54* yrs. ____ mos. ____ ds.   If LESS than 1 day, ____ hrs. or ____ min.?

8 OCCUPATION
(a) Trade, profession, or particular kind of work. *None.*
(b) General nature of industry, business or establishment in which employed (or employer)____

9 BIRTHPLACE (State or country) *Ireland.*

(9 A) How long in U.S. (if of foreign birth) *4 yrs.*   (9 B) How long resident in City of New York *4 yrs.*

PARENTS OF DECEASED

10 NAME OF FATHER *Thomas Green*

11 BIRTHPLACE OF FATHER (State or country) *Ireland*

12 MAIDEN NAME OF MOTHER *Margaret Kane.*

13 BIRTHPLACE OF MOTHER (State or country) *Ireland.*

14 Special INFORMATION required in deaths in hospitals and institutions and in deaths of non-residents and recent residents.

Former or usual residence } *1027 Pacific St.*

Where was disease contracted, if not at place of death? *1027 Pacific St.*

FILED

15 DATE OF DEATH *September 3rd*, 1912.
(Month) (Day) (Year)

16 *I hereby certify that the foregoing particulars (Nos. 1 to 14 inclusive) are correct as near as the same can be ascertained, and I further certify that I attended the deceased from Aug. 27 1912 to Sept. 3 1912; that I last saw him alive on the 3rd day of Sept. 1912, that death occurred on the date stated above at 3 A.M., and that the cause of death was as follows:*

Cardiac Asthenia following operation for gastric carcinoma

_____ duration ____ yrs. ____ mos. ____ ds.

Contributory _____
(Secondary)

_____ duration ____ yrs. ____ mos. ____ ds.

Witness my hand this *3* day of *Sept* 1912

Signature *S. Shumway* M.D.

Address *St. Mary's Hosp.*

17 PLACE OF BURIAL *Holy Cross Cem.*   **DATE OF BURIAL** *Sept. 6*, 1912

18 UNDERTAKER *Est. of F. H. McGuire*   **ADDRESS** *589 Washington Ave*

U.   Catherine Farrell Green Keenan's Death Certificate

V.   Denis Farrell's Death Certificate

Denis is the brother of Catherine Farrell Green Keenan and uncle of Katharine T. Greene Doheny.

W.   Helen Greene's Death Certificate

DIVISION OF RECORDS
DEPT. OF HEALTH
BOROUGH OF BRONX

Helen Greene (50)

CERTIFICATE OF DEATH

Certificate No. 156-68-308922

DATE FILED

'68 AUG 10 AM 11: 32

1. NAME OF DECEASED *(Type or Print)*	HELEN		GREENE
	First Name	Middle Name	Last Name

MEDICAL CERTIFICATE OF DEATH *(To be filled in by the Physician)*

2. PLACE OF DEATH	a. New York City	c. Name of Hospital or Institution. If not in hospital, street address
	b. Borough Bronx	Bronx State Hospital

3a. DATE AND HOUR OF DEATH	(Month)	(Day)	(Year)	3b. Hour	AM	4. SEX	5. APPROXIMATE AGE
	August	8	1968		PM	Female	83 yrs.

6. I HEREBY CERTIFY in OFFICE OF CHIEF MEDICAL EXAMINER provisions of law, I took charge of the dead body at 520 FIRST AVENUE, N. Y. 16, N. Y. on 9 day of Aug. 19 68
I further certify from the investigation and post mortem examination XXXX (without) autopsy that in my opinion, death occurred on the date and at the hour stated above and resulted from (natural causes) XXXXXXXXXXXXXXXXXXXXXXXXXXXXXXXXXXXXXXXXXXXXXXXXXXXX and that the causes of death were:

PART 1	a. Immediate cause	GENERALIZED ARTERIOSCLEROSIS.
	b. Due to or as a consequence of	
	c. Due to or a consequence of	

PART 2	Contributory causes

M.E. Case No.	2911	Signed John F. Devlin
		Associate XXXXXXXXXXXXXXXXXX (Medical Examiner) M.D.

PERSONAL PARTICULARS *(To be filled in by Funeral Director)*

7. USUAL RESIDENCE	a. State NEW YORK	b. County KINGS	c. City or Town BROOKLYN	d. Inside city limits (specify Yes or No) yes
	e. Street and house number 130 Lenox Rd		f. Length of residence or stay in City of New York immediately prior to death. Life	

8. SINGLE, MARRIED, WIDOWED or DIVORCED (Write in word) Single	9. NAME OF SURVIVING SPOUSE (If wife, give maiden name)

10. DATE OF BIRTH OF DECEDENT	(Month)	(Day)	(Year)	11. AGE at last birthday 83 Yrs	If under year		If LESS than 1 day	
	Dec. 5, 1884				mos.	days	hrs or	min.

12a. USUAL OCCUPATION (Kind of work done during most of working life, even if retired.) Ret'd Teacher	b. KIND of BUSINESS or INDUSTRY Bd Of Ed, NYC	13. SOCIAL SECURITY NO. 063-38-1872

14. BIRTHPLACE (State or Foreign Country) N.Y.	15. OF WHAT COUNTRY WAS DECEASED A CITIZEN AT TIME OF DEATH. U.S.

16. ANY OTHER NAME(s) BY WHICH DECEDENT WAS KNOWN

17. NAME OF FATHER OF DECEDENT Frank Greene	18. MAIDEN NAME OF MOTHER OF DECEDENT Catherine Farrell

19a. NAME OF INFORMANT Edward J. Doheny	b. RELATIONSHIP TO DECEASED Nephew	c. ADDRESS 73 St.Paul's Pl, Bklyn

20a. NAME OF CEMETERY OR CREMATORY Holy Cross Cemetery	b. LOCATION (City, Town or County and State) Brooklyn, N.Y.	c. DATE of Burial or Cremation 8/12/68

21a. FUNERAL DIRECTOR John T. Gallagher Funeral Home Inc	b. ADDRESS 2549 Church Ave., Bklyn, NY

BUREAU OF RECORDS AND STATISTICS — DEPARTMENT OF HEALTH — THE CITY OF NEW YORK

Bibliography

Websites:

Ancestry ....Ancestry.com
Ask about Ireland..askaboutireland.ie
Brooklyn Public Library...BklynLibrary.org
Dr. Marion McGarry's Blog ....drmarionmcgarry.weebly.com
Family Search ....FamilySearch.org
Family Tree DNA ....familytreedna.com
Find My Past..findmypast.com
Grenham's Irish Surnames ....JohnGrenham.com/surnames
Internet Archive ....Archive.org
The IreAtlas Townland Database ....thecore.com/seanruad/
Irish Genealogy...IrishGenealogy.ie/en/
Irish Genealogy Toolkit..irish-genealogy-toolkit.com
Ireland Reaching Out ....irelandxo.com
The National Archives of Ireland.......................................NationalArchives.ie
National Library of Ireland – Catholic Parish Registers.....registers.nli.ie
Roots Ireland..RootsIreland.ie
Shane Wilson Irish Family History Databases..................swilson.info
Stephen P. Morse Census Finding Aids............................stevemorse.org
Tipperary Studies, County Library Service ....tipperarystudies.ie/historical-society/

Books

Colletta, John P. *They Came in Ships: A Guide to Finding Your Immigrant Ancestor's Arrival Record.* Revised 3rd Edition. Orem, UT: Ancestry Publishing, an imprint of MyFamily.com, Inc., 2002

DeBartolo-Carmack, Sharon. *A Genealogist's Guide to Discovering Your Immigrant and Ethnic Ancestors.* Cincinnati OH: Betterway Books, an imprint of F&W Publications, 2000.

_____. *Organizing Your Family History Search.* Cincinnati OH: Betterway Books, an imprint of F&W Publications, 1999.

_____. *You Can Write Your Family History.* Salt Lake City UT: Ancestry Inc., 2003.

Galton, F.W., Ed. *Select Documents: Illustrating the History of Trade Unionism: I. the Tailoring Trade.* London, New York, and Bombay: Longmans, Green, and Co., 1896

Hatcher, Patricia Law. *Producing a Quality Family History.* Salt Lake City UT: Ancestry Inc., 1996.

Kempthorne, Charley. *For All Time: A Complete Guide to Writing Your Family History.* Portsmouth NH: Boynton/Cook Publishers (Heinemann), a subsidiary of Reed Elsevier, Inc., 1996.

McCutcheon, Marc. *Everyday Life in the 1800's: a Guide for Writers.* Cincinnati OH: Writer's Digest Books, 2001.

Mills, Elizabeth Shown. *Evidence! Citation and Analysis for the Family Historian.* Balt. MD: Genealogical Pub. Co., Inc., 1997

Szucs, Loretto Dennis. *They Became Americans: Finding Naturalization Records and Ethnic Origins.* Salt Lake City UT: Ancestry Inc., 1998.

Databases consulted and Records Repositories visited:

1840-1910 Brooklyn Directories. On microfilms at the 42nd Street Library, Manhattan, NY.

1848-1925 Trow's New York City Directories. FHL films # 1000722 ff and # 1377171 ff, Manhattan Directory databases online at Ancestry.com, and Manhattan Directories available on microfilm at the 42nd Street Library, Manhattan, NY.

1905 New York State Censuses, Kings County, Brooklyn. Microfilm of records at Kings County Clerk, Brooklyn, NY. (1855: FHL film # 1930198), (1865: FHL film # 1930204), (1875: FHL film # 1930215), (1892: FHL film # 1930230), (1905: FHL film # 1930253).

1900, 1910, 1920, and 1930 United States Federal Censuses [databases at Ancestry.com]. Original data: United States of America, Bureau of the Census. Washington, D.C.: National Archives and Records Administration. (1900: T623, 1854 rolls), (1910: T624, 1,178 rolls), (1920: T625, 2,076 rolls), (1930: T626, 2,667 rolls), (1940:T627, 4,643 rolls).

1915 New York State Census, Queens County, AD 4, Microfilm of original at the New York State Library. (FHL film # 523332).

Brooklyn Daily Eagle Online 1841-1902. < http://eagle.brooklynpubliclibrary.org. Brooklyn Public Library, Grand Army Plaza, Brooklyn NY 11238-5619

Brooklyn Deeds, Liber 735 (p. 322-end) to 737 (p. 1-495), 1866-1867. FHL film# 1413536 Original data: *Conveyances, 1724- ; Indexes, 1683-1950, Kings County (New York)*, 832 rolls.

The New York Times Archive 1851-1980. Online access through New York Times electronic subscription.

New York Passenger Lists, 1820-1957 [database on-line at Ancestry.com]. Provo, UT, USA: The Generations Network, Inc., 2006. Original data: *Passenger Lists of Vessels Arriving at New York, New York, 1820-1897*; (National Archives Microfilm Publication M237, 675 rolls); Records of the U.S. Customs Service, Record Group 36; National Archives, Washington, D.C. and *Passenger and Crew Lists of Vessels Arriving at New York, New York, 1897-1957*; (National Archives Microfilm Publication T715, 8892 rolls); Records of the Immigration and Naturalization Service; National Archives, Washington, D.C.

Passenger and Immigration Lists Index, 1500s-1900s, Gale Research. [database on-line at Ancestry.com]. Provo, UT, USA: The Generations Network, Inc., 2006. Original data: Filby, P. William, ed.. *Passenger and Immigration Lists Index, 1500s-1900s.* Farmington Hills, MI, USA: Gale Research, 2006.

Social Security Death Index [database on-line at Ancestry.com], Provo, UT, USA: The Generations Network, Inc., 2007. Original data drawn from Social Security Administration, *Social Security Death Index*, Master File.

World War I Draft Registration Cards, 1917-1918 [database on-line at Ancestry.com]. Provo, UT, USA: The Generations Network, Inc., 2005. Original data: United States, Selective Service System. *World War I Selective Service System Draft Registration Cards, 1917-1918.* Washington, D.C.: National Archives and Records Administration. M1509, 4,582 rolls.

U.S. World War II Army Enlistment Records, 1938-1946 [database on-line at Ancestry.com]. Provo, UT, USA: The Generations Network, Inc., 2005. Original data: *Electronic Army Serial Number Merged File, 1938-1946* [Archival Database]; World War II Army Enlistment Records; Records of the National Archives and Records Administration, Record Group 64; National Archives at College Park, College Park, MD.

U.S. World War II Draft Registration Cards, 1942 [database on-line at Ancestry.com]. Provo, UT, USA: The Generations Network, Inc., 2007. Original data: United States, Selective Service System. *Selective Service Registration Cards, World War II: Fourth Registration.* National Archives and Records Administration Branch locations: National Archives and Records Administration Region Branches.

Miscellaneous

E-Mails, letters, and telephone conversations with relatives and in-laws.

Memorial Cards for various ancestors and relatives.

Index

This index lists all the people and places mentioned in the book. Variant spellings for names have been conflated (merged) into single entries for the reader's convenience. Page numbers in **bold** refer to the primary page(s) for an individual.

Women are listed under their maiden name and married names. Individuals with unknown surnames are at the beginning of the index.

Women's married names are in [ ]; their maiden names are in ( ).

Major categories include Addresses, Causes of Death, Churches, Illnesses and Conditions, Hobbies, Occupations, Schools, and Surnames.

If there are several identical given names under one surname, an attempt has been made to identify unique individuals by parent's name or by some other identifier within ( ).

Abbreviations: NYC (Manhattan, NY), and US Post Office two-letter codes for states in the USA.

Made in the USA
Columbia, SC
01 July 2020